320-5/7

The Research Report Series of the Institute for Social Research is composed of significant reports published at the completion of a research project. These reports are generally prepared by the principal research investigators and are directed to selected users of this information. Research Reports are intended as technical documents which provide rapid dissemination of new knowledge resulting from ISR research.

RESEARCH REPORT SERIES, INSTITUTE FOR SOCIAL RESEARCH

An Evaluation of FREESTYLE

A Television Series to Reduce Sex-Role Stereotypes

Jerome Johnston
James Ettema
Terrence Davidson

Center for Research on Utilization of Scientific Knowledge
Institute for Social Research
The University of Michigan

1980

ISR Code No. 9008

This publication was prepared with funding from The National Institute of Education, U. S. Department of Health, Education, and Welfare under Contract No. NIE-400-76-0096.

The opinions expressed in this publication do not necessarily reflect the positions or policies of NIE or HEW.

Library of Congress Catalog Card Number 80-81676
ISBN 0-87944-256-5

© 1980 by The University of Michigan, All Rights Reserved

Published in 1980 by:

Institute for Social Research
The University of Michigan, Ann Arbor, Michigan

6 5 4 3 2 1

Manufactured in the United States of America

TABLE OF CONTENTS

CHAPTER

1 AN INTRODUCTION TO FREESTYLE AND ITS EVALUATION. 1

2 THE DEVELOPMENT OF THE FREESTYLE MATERIALS 7

3 DESIGNING AND IMPLEMENTING A "PRODUCT VALIDATION" OF FREESTYLE. 19

4 TEACHERS RATE FREESTYLE FOR CLASSROOM USE. 55

5 STATION CARRIAGE AND MARKET RATINGS OF FREESTYLE 73

6 MEASUREMENT OF FREESTYLE OUTCOMES. 81

7 THE IMPACT OF VIEWING PLUS DISCUSSION. 91

8 THE IMPACT OF MERE VIEWING 143

9 SUMMARY AND CONCLUSIONS. 159

10 THE PERSISTENCE OF EFFECTS: AN EPILOGUE 175

Appendix A Glossary 197

Appendix B FREESTYLE Television Shows: Synopsis and Themes 213

Appendix C Goals and Objectives in the FREESTYLE Curriculum Plan. . . . 221

Appendix D Reliability of Student Outcome Measures. 229

Appendix E Descriptions of the Seven Test Sites in the FREESTYLE
Evaluation 241

Appendix F A Community Outreach Experiment to Increase Non-School
Viewing. 253

Appendix G FREESTYLE Teacher Training 261

Appendix H Teacher Post Series Questionnaire. 265

Appendix I Student Questionnaire. 279

Appendix J Raw Data on Persistence. 291

BIBLIOGRAPHY 295

PREFACE

In the Fall of 1975 the National Institute of Education conceived a bold experiment in educational television. They envisioned a TV series which would be capable of changing children's views of appropriate behavior for boys and girls. They wanted an audience of 9-12 year olds to discover that it was all right if girls were mechanically inclined or wished to participate in boys' sports, for such behaviors would be important for the later occupational success of girls. In their own words, they wanted to reduce the "limiting effects of sex role stereotypes" in our society.

There were a number of innovative aspects of the TV Career Awareness Project. Among them was a major commitment to evaluation. While evaluation of new educational products is not uncommon, this particular assessment was unique: the entire project, from the process that developed the materials to the impact of the final product on viewers, was to come under the scrutiny of a third party. It was complained by evaluators in the mid seventies that all too often evaluation was an afterthought which suffered from the twin constraints -- time and money. This meant that it was necessary to perform all the evaluator's tasks -- design the study, collect the information, and interpret the data -- much too quickly to yield worthwhile information; and that the evaluation was frequently underfunded out of leftover funds from the product development phase.

In this project the NIE project officers sought to remedy the problems of time and money by initiating the summative evaluation simultaneous with the beginning of product development; and they funded it at a level sufficient to meet a wide variety of information needs. This report and its companion volume on the product development process are the first fruits of that decision. Others will judge whether the additional resources have made a marked difference in the kind and quality of the information. Meanwhile, the authors are pleased to pay tribute to the vision of the NIE project officers, Bob Wise and Mary Lou Randour, which has made the assessment possible.

ACKNOWLEDGMENTS

Many people contributed to the design and implementation of this evaluation over the last three years, and we would like to recognize them for this contribution.

The blueprint for the evaluation profited from the inputs of Sam Ball, Keith Mielke, Saul Rockman, Jerry Bachman and Patrick O'Malley. The development of the children's measures was influenced by extensive feedback from Aletha Huston and Joe Pleck. Occupational interest measurement was influenced by ideas generated by Frank Womer, Juliet Miller and Marjorie Mastie.

Securing sites in which to test FREESTYLE was a difficult task. A special thanks for their efforts on our behalf go to David Crippens of KCET, Ginny Fox at KET, Bob Suchy in Milwaukee, Joanne Linowes of Massachusetts Educational Television, Kathy Hopkins and Dick Bedard in Worcester, Dian Molton at KCPT, Lorraine Olson at KLRN, Pat Seeley and Ben Holzman in Long Beach.

Six local coordinators maintained the integrity of the experiment at every site. These were designated by their local school districts because they were held in high regard by local teachers and administrators. Without them the experiment could not have succeeded -- especially the data collection. They include Ed Bazinet in Worcester, Jean Grey in Saginaw, Joe Diliberti in Milwaukee, Sharon Mann in North Kansas City, Marilyn Montgomery in Long Beach and Torrance, and Jean Anderton in Covina. The entire field effort was coordinated Chris Lux in Ann Arbor.

Chris made a number of other contributions including designing the newsletters for teachers, writing up descriptions of each of the sites, and doing the ground work for Chapter Five on station carriage and Nielsen data. She was helped in this last effort by Ken Wirt in the Research Department of PBS who not only supplied the information but patiently answered endless questions about the real meaning of an audience "share."

At ISR Linda Shepard coordinated the processing of the many separate questionnaires and the construction of eleven different computer files. Greg

Herr did much of the computer work and is responsible for the study of measurement reliability that appears in the Appendix. Valeria Lovelace reviewed the pertinent scholarly literature which helped us maintain focus on the issues in relevant fields of interest, from communications to sex-role development. Ruth Gladstone edited the text to make it eminently more readable. The analyses profited from the existence of two very sophisticated computer software packages which handled the massive amounts of data with ease. We acknowledge a debt to the developers of the OSIRIS and MIDAS software packages.

Thanks are traditionally extended to typists. But a special commendation goes to Jean Holther. This report is one of the first at ISR to be processed entirely by computer. To accomplish this, Jean had to master the intricacies of a complex software system and tame it to the needs of authors who wanted to take advantage of the machine's capability to do extensive revisions. In the process she identified a number of technical aspects which the system's designers had overlooked and this resulted in refinements to the system itself.

JJ, JE, TND

Chapter One

AN INTRODUCTION TO FREESTYLE AND ITS EVALUATION

The FREESTYLE television series is the major product of the Television Career Awareness Project (TV CAP). Two fundamental ideas guided the development of the shows and supporting materials. The first was that television is a potentially useful tool for the achievement of worthwhile social and educational goals. Specifically, the project set out to produce a series of television shows that could counter sex-role stereotypes and expand career awareness among 9-to-12 year olds either when used by teachers in the classroom or when viewed by the children at home. The messages thus had to be comprehensible, persuasive and entertaining. The second fundamental concept was that top television professionals as well as educators and formative researchers would all work together to develop the project. The success of TV CAP in combining these diverse disciplines and talents is analyzed in a companion volume: Working Together: A Study of Cooperation Among Producers, Educators, and Researchers to Create Educational Television. The project's success in achieving its educational goals of countering sex-role stereotypes and expanding career awareness is the focus of this report.

Goals of the Project

The goal of the project as originally formulated by the National Institute of Education, the project's funder, was to "expand career awareness of 4th to 6th graders by making ethnicity and sex less significant predictors of pre-occupational (or occupational) knowledge, interests and preferences." This goal statement was based upon the recognition of a social problem and a theory about its causes. Most simply stated, the problem is the over-representation of women and minorities in a narrow range of low status occupations. The theory advanced by the National Institute of Education (NIE) as to the cause of this narrow occupational range held that while discrimination and other institutional factors are important causes, so too is limited career <u>awareness</u> which, in turn, may be traced to the ethnic/racial and sex-role stereotypes current in the society.

The "career awareness" construct as formulated by NIE is composed of four elements: knowledge (e.g., knowledge of skills and education required for a particular career), interests/preferences (e.g., liking of activities involved in a particular career), values (e.g., valuation of various attributes of careers such as status or working conditions) and self-concepts (e.g., beliefs about one's own ability to perform the activities of a particular career). Attempts to increase career awareness may usefully focus on this "preoccupational" knowledge and on the interests, values and self-concepts which form prior to the awareness or selection of any particular career, but which ultimately shape and guide career exploration and choice (Wise, Charner and Randour, 1976).

The effects of racial/ethnic and sex-role stereotypes are limiting to career awareness for females and minorities -- particularly during the period of germinating preoccupational knowledge and interests of girls and minority children. This is exemplified by the finding that boys in the early elementary years express interest in three times as many occupations as girls of the same age (Prediger, Roth and Noeth, 1973), and findings that, in the case of Blacks, while aspirations may equal that of Whites (Gump and Rivers, 1975), knowledge about the rules of the social system and strategies for extracting rewards from the system may be limited (Tomlinson and Ten Houten, 1973). It is argued, then, that stereotyped preoccupational and occupational knowledge and attitudes acquired from parents, teachers and other sources inhibit later career awareness and thereby restrict career choice in adulthood.

The aim of the project, in brief, was to intervene in this stereotypic causal system so that at the conclusion of the program "children should know more about, prefer or be interested in more non-traditional occupations than they were previously -- and hold less ethnic or sex stereotyped views of -- adult and occupational roles (Funder's Request for Proposal, 1975)."

In the course of work on the project this original goal was developed, refined and also altered somewhat. The most important development was a broadening of the attack on sex-role stereotypes beyond the provision of non-stereotyped knowledge and the promotion of non-stereotyped preferences and interests. Another important concern came to be the promotion of a number of "behavioral skills" which traditionally have been stereotyped much like interests. These include leadership, independence, initiative and self-direction (all especially important for girls to develop), helping skills, emotional expressiveness and empathy (all especially important for boys to develop) as well as cooperation, assertiveness and reasonable risk-taking for both sexes. The significance of these behavioral skills emerged early in the curriculum planning for the project and later became a cornerstone in the content of the television shows.

Another refinement occurred in the area of adult occupations. Instead of focussing on jobs alone, the concept was expanded to include both work and family roles. More specifically, the topics to be covered included the growing economic need for women to work, the nonmaterial rewards of expanded occupational roles for women and family roles for men as well as non-traditional jobs. A further refinement of the original theme was the delineation of several categories of pre-occupational activities to be promoted for boys and girls. For girls these categories were mechanical activities and spatial relationships (e.g. electronics, use of tools and plans), athletics, mathematics, science, and traditionally masculine household jobs. For boys they were artistic activities, writing and word skills, social service activities, child care and traditionally feminine household tasks. A number of specific interests and activities were enumerated in each of these categories. Not all the potential subdivisions or categories could of course be covered in the FREESTYLE series, but they provided the basis of content selection for the series. As these themes came under development, the focus on ethnic stereotyping was reduced. This change in emphasis evolved from long, often harsh, controversy, but it was finally agreed that ethnicity would be addressed only as it "interacts" with or "affects" sex-role stereotyping. The relationship between ethnicity and sex-role stereotyping was never clearly specified in the curriculum plans, or explicitly dealt with in the series, though several of the shows in the series highlighted the ethnic heritage and context of some of the characters.

In the overview, the goal of TV CAP encompassed three major themes: 1) behavioral skills, 2) nontraditional pre-occupational interests and activities, and 3) adult work and family roles. These three themes were embodied in and interlaced in the six subgoals and 84 learner outcome objectives which constituted the formal curriculum plan for the project. The subgoals and objectives are shown in Appendix C.

Goals of the Evaluation

What purposes can be served by a summative evaluation of this effort? There are several. One is accountability -- to provide evidence that federal monies have been spent to create a product with the type of characteristics and impact called for in the sponsor's specifications. Another is consumer information -- to provide potential users with the necessary product information to assist in decisions of adoption and implementation. A third purpose is policy guidance; a number of policy arenas ranging from career education to telecommunications can be informed by understanding the impact of an intervention as large in scope as FREESTYLE. Finally, an evaluation can provide psychologists with more information on the nature of sex-role stereotypes and the demonstration of possibilities for intervention in their development. This evaluation hopes to serve all of these purposes to at least some extent.

Early in the process of planning the evaluation contact was made with various constituencies or stakeholders who have some interest in the outcome of the FREESTYLE effort.[1] At the federal level these included the project sponsors at NIE and a number of others both in NIE and in other governmental agencies. In the educational television arena were representatives from the Public Broadcasting Service, the Corporation for Public Broadcasting, and ITV

---

[1]This process is discussed in greater detail in a separate paper: Jerome Johnston and Robert Wise, "Using Evaluation Results in Planning: Alternative Views of the Decision-Maker and the Researcher." Toronto: Annual meeting of the American Educational Research Association, March, 1978.

directors from a number of state ITV networks. At the local level were school district administrators and teachers, and last but not least the show's producers. From these contacts nine questions were identified which covered the issues of greatest interest to these diverse groups.

1) During its first two seasons, how often is the show viewed in homes? --in schools?

2) Do children, parents and teachers like the program?

3) How is FREESTYLE used in the classroom and how well does it fit into the grade 4-6 curriculum?

4) At home, do parents watch the show with their children? Do they discuss its content?

5) When FREESTYLE is used under optimal conditions what is the impact of the series on children aged 9-12? Are children this age different in their "career awareness orientation" as a result of experiencing the several components of the series over a four-month period? Is the impact uniform across all types of children (age, sex, racial/ethnic identification)?

6) Is the impact different when FREESTYLE is used in homes as compared to schools?

7) How much do the non-broadcast activities increase the impact of the show? Could the children learn as much from viewing alone as they do from viewing supplemented by mediation of parents and teachers?

8) Do children understand the messages of the show?

9) What cost-benefits can be attributed to the various components of the series?

The questions can be divided into several categories Questions 1-4 concern the "gatekeepers" -- those who influence whether FREESTYLE reaches the children. In a children's TV series the term refers to TV station personnel, teachers, and parents. But it can also be thought of as meaning the children themselves (Question 2) in the sense that their liking of the program is essential in relation to their availability and receptiveness to the messages of the series. These gatekeeper questions are addressed through several different studies. One of these is through surveys of a selected group of teachers and students who used the series; another is station carriage data from the 265 PBS affiliates; the third is Nielsen data from the major TV markets. The findings are described in Chapters Four and Five.

Questions 5-8 ask about the impact of FREESTYLE on the target audience of 9-12 year olds. Are the children different after exposure to FREESTYLE? Does the impact vary according to the type of exposure? These questions are addressed through a study of FREESTYLE's effects when it is used intensively by children. The study design is the substance of Chapter Three; the findings are described in Chapters Seven and Eight.

The final question on cost-benefit was not addressed in the current research. It was decided that such a study was appropriate only if the answers to the first eight questions indicated that FREESTYLE is a sufficiently successful product to warrant the additional time and expense.

Chapter Two

THE DEVELOPMENT OF THE FREESTYLE MATERIALS

The TV Career Awareness Project (TV CAP) was conducted by a consortium of organizations chosen by the National Institute of Education from among the several groups that submitted proposals for the project. Six organizations formed the Consortium which was headquartered in Los Angeles. These were: KCET Community Television of Southern California, Office of the Los Angeles County Superintendent of Schools, Science Research Associates, Annenberg School of Communication at the University of Southern California, East Los Angeles College Foundation and the Institute for Social Research at the University of Michigan.

KCET-TV, a public television station in Los Angeles was responsible for the production of the television series itself. This responsibility was delegated to an executive producer who was hired specifically for the task. The executive producer had a small permanent production staff including his personal assistant who in the course of the project was promoted to associate producer, a unit or business manager and her assistant and a production secretary. Creative personnel such as script writers, directors and musicians were drawn from the Hollywood talent pool on a short-term, as-needed basis. Technicians and other production personnel were drawn from the permanent staff of the station.

The Office of the Los Angeles County Superintendent of Schools, a large educational agency with many consultants and planners on its staff, was responsible for the development of the curriculum plan which was to guide all work on the project other than television production. Responsibility for the plan was delegated to the small (three-to-four person) ad hoc Curriculum Planning Team of which one member served as team leader for planning activities and another as Curriculum Coordinator handling administrative tasks for the team. The Curriculum Planning Team employed several outside consultants for short periods. It was also able to draw upon the resources of a large curriculum advisory committee within the agency which was commissioned to review and critique the team's work. Besides curriculum planning, agency personnel were responsible for developing teacher training materials for the series and assisting with the development of the non-broadcast supporting materials.

Science Research Associates, an educational publisher in Chicago, was responsible for developing the non-broadcast materials which included a teachers' guide for the series, a parents' guide and a student activity magazine. The task of development of these materials was delegated to a project manager who operated from Los Angeles for much of the project. She drew upon freelance artists and writers from Los Angeles, New York and Chicago for much of the content of the materials which were published in Chicago.

The Annenberg School of Communications undertook the formative research for the project. It's task was to conduct a variety of research activities designed to improve both the educational effectiveness and entertainment value of the television shows. The formative research unit included the principal investigator, who was a faculty member, several graduate student assistants for research design and test development, a data analyst, a field coordinator and an administrative assistant.

The East Los Angeles College Foundation organized a community outreach program in the predominantly Mexican-American neighborhoods in the East Los Angeles area. The smallest of the Consortium's components, it consisted of a college administrator and a field coordinator.

The Institute for Social Research of Ann Arbor worked with the Consortium from the beginning serving as the summative evaluator of the project. The role of the Institute differed from that of the other Consortium members in that it was not a participant in the development of materials and indeed it had to demonstrate in the original proposal to NIE how it would maintain the "needed detachment" of an evaluator. This component was headed by a principal investigator who along with his research staff was located in Ann Arbor, although one staff person lived in Los Angeles for a year to document the process by which FREESTYLE was developed. The activities and findings of the summative component are detailed in this volume.

Each of the Consortium's components were represented by one or more of its staff members on the central planning and policy-making committee called CORE. The CORE Committee dealt with consortium-wide administrative and policy issues and reviewed and approved the work of the various components. Another group, the Management Council, was composed of the administrators of several of the organizations which formed the Consortium. The function of this group was to facilitate the work of the Consortium. It also held the right to review and approve its work, but it did not intervene in the day-to-day operation of the project. Finally, the Review Board composed of individual educators and community leaders from across the country was convened about twice a year to review and comment upon the Consortium's work. Its authority, unlike the CORE Committee and the Management Council, was primarily moral and cultural, based on its collective experience and expertise. These groups and individuals worked together to produce FREESTYLE and its supporting materials.

The Development of FREESTYLE

The Consortium produced the FREESTYLE materials in four main phases: planning of the curriculum; production of three experimental pilot television shows and supporting materials; revision of the curriculum; production of the television series and supporting materials. A detailed history and analysis of these four phases can be found in a companion volume (Ettema, 1980). An overview here, however, will enhance the reader's appreciation of the problems encountered and the solutions adopted in the development of FREESTYLE.

The work of the first phase, curriculum planning, centered around the Curriculum Planning Team. The Team carried out day-to-day work on the plan, but it shared power on form and content with the CORE Committee, the Management Council, NIE's project officer and even outside consultants. This broad distribution of power was the result less of the formal structure of the Consortium as specified in its proposal to the funder than of informal organizational factors such as the simple and readily accessible technology of curriculum planning, and the inadequate staffing of the Curriculum Planning

Team. Given these conditions of shared power, it is hardly surprising that the key decisions about the curriculum plan were made in a legislative process in which the various groups and individuals involved met more or less as equals to deliberate and, when necessary, to negotiate the content and form of the plan.

The first curriculum plan to emerge from the many rounds of deliberation and negotiation included an eclectic literature review and the following nine very general "experiential objectives:"

1) Children will practice behaviors such as independence and interdependence, and aggressiveness and yieldness (sic), depending upon the most appropriate behavior for the situation rather than on sex-role stereotyped behaviors.

2) Children will experience a greater variety of work-related activities not previously considered appropriate for their sex roles.

3) Children will experience situations that depict the limitation sex-role stereotyping has placed on both male and female choices and activities.

4) Girls will experience situations that encourage them to take reasonable risks and not give up because of occasional failure.

5) Children will experience situations that counteract the prevailing myth that females will be taken care of by males and will not need to be employed.

6) Children will experience situations that encourage the development of positive attitudes towards girls in leadership roles.

7) Girls will experience situations designed to help them attribute their successes to ability, not solely to luck.

8) Girls will experience situations designed to evoke and reward appropriate degrees of independence, initiative and self-direction.

9) Boys will experience situations that evoke and reward nurturant behavior.

The nine experiential objectives and the literature review were the result of discussion around a variety of issues. One of these was the idea of an "experiential objective." This was introduced into the project by the Curriculum Planning Team over the objections of the formative evaluators who argued that such an objective would hinder the work of the evaluators. The Curriculum Planning Team's position, however, prevailed on this issue due in part to their argument that specifications of experiences rather than learner outcomes would be most useful to the television production personnel.

Another issue of special salience was the treatment of racial and ethnic stereotyping which, according to the original goal, was to have been an important concern of the project. As the project got underway, however, the NIE project officer intervened in an attempt to reduce the importance of the topic. This aroused a good deal of consternation among the Review Board and among several sectors of the Consortium. The issue was bitterly debated and compromise was long in coming. Eventually the notion of treating ethnicity as it "interacts" with sex-role stereotyping was worked out. No experiential objectives outlining this interaction or ethnicity in general were produced, however.

A third issue was, perhaps, the most central with respect to the content of the curriculum plan. Since, promoting career awareness and attacking sex-role stereotypes were seen to be two different topics, the relative importance of each of these topics was briefly weighed by the Curriculum Planning Team in order to determine the primary focus. Sex-role stereotypes were selected as the major priority at least for the time being. Relying heavily upon the guidance of the outside consultants, the Team enumerated the sex-role related attitudes and behaviors to be changed and the alternatives to be developed, and these were incorporated into the nine experiential objectives.

The nine objectives served as the basic subject matter for three experimental pilot television shows which were produced in the next phase of the project. While production of the pilots was the responsibility of KCET-TV in particular the executive producer and his staff -- the formative researchers and the educators also contributed directly to the effort: The evaluators collected and interpreted a variety of data and passed on their conclusions to the executive producer. In addition to providing the curriculum plan, the educators critiqued the scripts and the completed show segments with an eye toward adherence to the plan and acceptability of the shows to other educators. According to the Consortium's proposal, both the scripts and the completed shows were to be subject to review by the CORE Committee, Management Council and Review Board. Unlike the Curriculum Planning Team, however, the executive producer retained complete control over the TV products, because he alone could coordinate the complex television production process.

The executive producer therefore had the final authority on all matters pertaining to the television shows. The formative researchers, educators and others served as advisors to the executive producer rather than as collaborators. They provided advice at those points in the production process when the executive producer was required to make a decision for which their advice could be useful -- e.g., design of the format for the pilots, generation of premise or story ideas, review and selection of scripts and review of completed program segments.

Three quite different plans for the pilots emerged from this collaborative process. The first, designed by the executive producer, was something like a hybrid of Sesame Street and an adult variety show, featuring a number of short film and cartoon segments as well as musical numbers taped in the studio. Its primary focus was to define and illustrate the concept of stereotype. The executive producer first submitted his outline for this pilot to the CORE Committee, whereupon the formative researchers produced certain data suggesting that 9-to-12 year olds were less likely than their younger siblings to be attracted to a program with many fast-paced segments. This led the producer to design, for the second pilot somewhat longer segments that focused on the activities of a continuing set of characters. This plan had continuity and coherence even though the segments still dealt with a variety of concepts extrapolated from the curriculum plan (e.g., nontraditional occupations, risk-taking and attributing success to ability not luck).

While work on the two pilots proceeded, the educators began to push for an entirely different approach for the third pilot. They wanted this pilot to tell a single dramatic story within a format that would be appropriate with respect to both the content of the curriculum plan and the interests of the audience. The educators argued that it would be more effective in the classroom if a show developed only with memorable impact rather than to try to distribute attention over a number of concepts. After much discussion the executive producer devised a show in which a young girl who is interested in auto mechanics asserts herself to obtain a summer job in a gas station. Before long, however, she takes an unreasonable risk by attempting an auto repair for which she is not prepared. She fails but later has the opportunity to learn more about mechanics and when called upon again in an emergency she saves the day in classic fashion. The strategy of this show was to model desirable attitudes and behaviors.

If this pilot was very different from the other two, all three shared one important feature in common. Each was a complete 1/2-hour show designed for home-viewing but each could also be divided into two 1/4-hour episodes for classroom use. This feature was built into the pilots, and into the series as well, based on the educators' conclusion that 1/4-hours suited the needs of classroom teachers who would be asked not only to show the program, but also to conduct introductory and follow-up activities when the program was broadcast. A 1/2-hour show in addition to the other activities was thought to require too much time from any given school day to gain teacher acceptance.

In overview, the advisors made vital contributions to the development of the pilots. Their data and critiques were particularly relevant in steering the executive producer away from potential problems and pitfalls. The executive producer himself designed the formats, generated the premises and oversaw the scripting and production of the shows. The form and content of the shows were, then, fundamentally his personal creative achievement.

As a logical sequence to production, the Consortium planned to test the three pilots and use the test results to choose one pilot as the model for the series. Meanwhile the Consortium turned its attention once more to the curriculum plan. The executive producer had been a particularly harsh critic of the plan arguing that it was too vague to serve as an effective guide for the series. He and others faulted the use of experiential objectives -- as opposed to learner outcome objectives -- for aiding and abetting the vagueness of the plan. Whatever the cause, a lack of conceptual guidance had indeed resulted in several expensive mistakes during the scripting and production of the pilots. Other criticisms of the plan were that because it dwelt too much on the "crippling effects of stereotyping," it was too negative in tone, that it paid too little attention to the needs and interests of boys, and that cognitive goals had been sacrificed to affective goals. The debate concluded with agreement that these were shortcomings that should be corrected. The revision of the plan constituted the third phase of the project.

The first step of the revision process was to obtain consensus among the Consortium on what was to be done and to codify those agreements into a "platform" for change. The key planks of the platform were:

--Retain the concepts in the original plan but detail specific messages.

--Add material to address the needs of boys and to provide a positive tone. Include objectives on cooperation between the sexes and more material on nontraditional activities and behaviors.

--Replace experiential objectives with learner outcome objectives.

--Specify both cognitive and affective outcomes.

In order to develop the "specifics" required by the platform the Consortium retained a consultant to produce a background paper detailing specific messages about each of the general concepts in the original curriculum plan. The consultant, a well-known developmental psychologist, first outlined the three themes which came to constitute the focus of the project. The consultant cited 1) behavioral skills such as leadership and nurturance and 2) pre-occupational interests and activities as the two primary themes of the revised curriculum; and 3) adult work and family roles as the third theme. Within each of these themes she specified a large number of messages to be presented such as the steps to a position of leadership and the benefits of expanded adult roles. This background paper bridged the gap between the more general concepts in the original curriculum plan and the platform and the particularized messages to be presented in the revised plan and the television series.

The final step of revision involved the actual reworking of the objectives and the other materials. This began at a session attended by members of all components of the Consortium where the task was turned over to the Curriculum Planning Team. They rewrote the nine original experiential objectives into six subgoals drawing upon the messages provided by the consultant, and the platform requirement that the concepts from the original plan be retained but that both cognitive and affective learner outcomes be specified. The new subgoals were based directly on the original experiential objectives. The consultant's three content themes were woven throughout the subgoals and the 84 learner outcome objectives. The objectives themselves drew heavily upon the messages specified by the consultant such that excerpts from the consultant's background paper were juxtaposed with the appropriate objectives as interpretive material in the final version of the curriculum plan. The literature review was re-edited but not drastically altered.

On the whole, the legislative process during the curriculum revision phase of the project was more restrained than during the original planning phase. Many of the hard issues had already been resolved and perhaps more importantly, the Consortium was able through skillful politicking to codify its ideas for the revision into a platform which could then serve as a guide for the work of the curriculum planners.

The curriculum revision was not yet complete when the fourth and final phase of project, series design and production, began. The first task of this phase was to select one of the three pilots as the model for the series. The pilots had been tested in four cities. Indications were that while comprehension of the messages in the dramatic format pilot had been the lowest of the three pilots, it was nevertheless the overwhelming favorite of both teachers and their students. Based primarily on this preference data the formative evaluators recommended that the dramatic format be used, and also that steps be taken to make the series messages more explicit and comprehensible. The executive producer welcomed the recommendation: he had come to prefer the dramatic format and had, in fact, begun to make plans for a dramatic series.

The series design would utilize the three themes as the basic content categories for the series. The producer felt that most of the behavioral skills would lend themselves to dramatic portrayal as had assertiveness and reasonable risk-taking in the third pilot. The theme of nontraditional interests and activities would serve as the background to lead into the dramatic events of the stories, just as the young girl's interest in auto mechanics had launched her summer job adventures. The producer termed the relationship between the behavioral skills theme and the non-traditional interests and activities a "figure-ground relationship." The strategy for combining the two themes structured many of the shows in the series: some used adult work and family roles or dramatic non-traditional activities (e.g., sports) as the "figure."

Besides the figure-ground metaphor and its implications for the treatment of the curriculum content in the series, two other major elements took prominence in the series design. In order to make the shows more explicit and comprehensible with respect to role modeling, the producer decided to include in each show one or more scenes in which the modelled attitude or behavior would be labelled and discussed by the characters. The producer called these the "Ah-ha!" scenes because, he hoped children would exclaim, "Ah-ha! Now I understand." The other major factor of the series design was selection of the cast of characters and their social environment. The cast, invented by the producer was a multi-racial group of kids and their families who, for the most part, were already nonstereotypical in interests, activities, attitudes and behaviors. There were a few exceptions who were destined to undergo change and growth in the series.

With design for the series in hand, the producer faced the task of premise generation and scripting. Here, he assembled a Premise Team which included in addition to himself one other member of the television production unit, an advisor from the Curriculum Planning Team and one from the formative evaluation component. This group brainstormed on premise ideas. The producer generated most of the premise ideas which were actually used, and the team provided the essential creative environment in which the ideas took shape. The premise ideas were given to the script writers in the form of elaborate Curriculum Assignment Sheets which detailed the plot and messages of the shows in the series. The Premise Team also reviewed first drafts of the scripts.

The FREESTYLE series which resulted from this process consisted of thirteen 1/2-hour television shows. Each show was divisible into two 1/4-hour episodes in which the first episode ended in a "cliffhanger" and the second resolved the tension. As planned, each show contained one or more "Ah-ha!" scenes and some combination of the content themes. The messages within each of the three content themes dramatized in the series are summarized in Appendix B.

In support of the television series three publications were produced: A teacher's guide, a student activity magazine, and a parents' guide. The teachers' guide laid out a lesson for each episode of each show. These lessons contained a preview activity designed to sensitize the students to key points made in the episode, a list of post-viewing questions designed to elicit class discussion about the key points and suggestions for class activities such as essays or projects designed to promote fuller understanding and application of the points. The student activity magazine had games and puzzles designed to expand upon messages such as the nature of stereotypes, the range of nontraditional activities and occupations open to people, or the linkage between childhood interests and adult careers. The parents' or home-use guide was in the form of a calendar which briefly summarized the messages of the shows and included games and activities.

Two other Consortium products completed the FREESTYLE package of materials. These were materials for a one-day staff development workshop to introduce teachers to the series and supporting materials. This was prepared by the staff of the Office of the Los Angeles County Superintendent of Schools. The workshop introduced the goals and materials of FREESTYLE and provided an opportunity to practice with the materials. The final piece of the FREESTYLE package was a community outreach program in which a number of viewing groups were organized particularly in low income areas of Los Angeles. In these groups parents watched the shows with their children and conducted followup activities. The purpose of this endeavor was to experiment with ways to get greater educational impact out of non-school viewing.

These, then, are the FREESTYLE products evaluated in this report. They represent nearly three years of work by five organizations and dozens of key individuals. Neither the materials produced nor the production process itself is beyond criticism. FREESTYLE has emerged, however, as an important attempt to use television in the pursuit of worthwhile social and educational goals. The success of FREESTYLE in these endeavors is the focus of the remainder of this report.

Chapter Three

DESIGNING AND IMPLEMENTING A "PRODUCT VALIDATION" OF FREESTYLE

The impact of FREESTYLE on children is a major focus of this evaluation. This statement needs some qualification because of the timing of the summative evaluation. The evaluation was conducted in the fall and winter of 1978-1979 during the first season FREESTYLE was broadcast. Thus it came too early in the dissemination and implementation of the series to answer in a definitive way the question: what impact is the series actually having on the nation's children? The question would be appropriate several years from now, after the series had been available for three to four years, and had an opportunity to capture the interest and attention of its target audiences.

For the home viewing version of the series adoption can move fairly rapidly. If the series is characterized by high production values it will draw close to maximum size audiences by the end of its first season on the air. One aspect of the home viewing version would however, lengthen the process of adoption: the designers wanted parents and children to view together at home and discuss the shows. This requires experimentation with scheduling coupled with a planned effort to induce this atypical viewing arrangement. With regard to school use of the series more time is needed to attract the interest of the gatekeepers, classroom teachers. For one thing, they are encouraged to adopt the entire series as opposed to viewing one or two shows. For another, they then need to adapt the materials to their teaching styles and their students' needs. Added to this is the absence of a plan to advertise and promote the series. It was concluded for these reasons that the most appropriate summative evaluation of program impact would be a "product validation" study.

As the term "validation" implies, a test is conducted in a small number of sites which have been carefully prepared to cooperate with the study and to use the materials intensively at a level of use expected after three years of natural adoption and adaptation by interested teachers and parents. If the summative evaluation is purely a product validation then it is has to answer this question: can the series, <u>if used as the designers intend</u>, have sufficient impact to warrant further dissemination and use? The validation design is common in medicine, but to the best of the authors' knowledge, a product validation study has not been used before in summative evaluations of educational interventions. The logic for its use is compelling under the present circumstances however. It might be considered an appropriate design for other summative evaluations as well.[1]

Part I: Design for a "Product Validation"

At its simplest, the basic research design chosen for this evaluation was a pre-post design with both experimental and control groups. In conventional Campbell and Stanley (1963) notation, it looks like this.

$$\begin{array}{l} \text{Experimental group} \quad O_1 \quad X \quad O_2 \\ R\text{------------------} \\ \text{Control group} \quad\quad\quad O_1 \quad\quad O_2 \end{array}$$

Experimental subjects are selected randomly from a population and assigned either to the experimental or control condition. Each group completes an identical pre-test before treatment begins and again when the treatment is complete. Impact is assessed by comparing the scores of the two groups after the treatment is complete, "controlling" for pre-test differences if necessary. The basic schematic, however, is deceptively simple. To be entirely understood it is necessary to see the plans for the treatments which are to be implemented, the plan for the selection of sites where the treatment will be implemented, and the measures which will be used to assess change. The first two of these are presented below. The measures are discussed in a later chapter.

---

[1] In a forthcoming book Cronbach advocates this type of study, calling it a "super-realization." (Cronbach, et al., 1980).

Determining the nature of the treatments to be assessed is difficult given a rich educational package such as FREESTYLE. A total of four separate treatments were chosen to be tested. This number was selected after examining the products and taking into account two factors: (1) what are the "policy" questions of interest and (2) what combinations of the products can reasonably be expected to make a measurable incremental difference in impact? Consider first the available products. As a package FREESTYLE is a multifaceted intervention with many separable components.

> Television show: 13 1/2-hour color television programs, each divisible into two inter-related 1/4-hour shows for classroom use. For school use both 1/4-hour shows are supposed to be used in the same week, separated by one or two days. For home use one 1/2-hour show should be seen each week. The designers hoped it would be broadcast to homes at a time when both children and their parents might view it together.
>
> School Guide: A booklet that provides teachers with an overview of the project, a discussion of the objectives, and complete units for each TV show including suggested discussion topics and student activities.
>
> "Freestyle" Magazine: A 32-page magazine for children designed to stimulate thinking about the objectives in an entertaining and motivating way.
>
> Teacher Training: A self-contained orientation and in-service training program designed to help the school staff work effectively with FREESTYLE in the school setting. One half-day session preceding the airing of the series.
>
> Home Guide: Similar to the School Guide, but designed for use by adults at home. It encourages active adult participation in the project.

While each product is clearly identifiable, they vary in their potential for distinct or additive effects on student impact.

Each of the television shows is a dramatic episode, one half hour in length, and divisible into two stand-alone 1/4-hour shows for instructional use. As a set, the TV shows comprise the strongest single component of the intervention. All of the other components can be viewed as add-ons that augment the influence of this core element of the intervention. There was considerable interest in knowing whether TV alone could influence change in children. After all, the majority of 9-12 year olds might be exposed to FREESTYLE only through the broadcast. Here again, the validation notion comes into consideration. Research has shown that viewing at home is not attentive viewing; there are too many distractions and this results in reduced message processing. Testing those who viewed at home would indicate the show's potential under the normal conditions of home viewing, but viewing at school under the conditions of "captive audience" is by far the superior test of the potential of television alone to influence attitudinal change. Consequently, viewing at home and viewing at school were singled out for separate experimental treatments.

Consider next the supplementary non-broadcast components. The key non-broadcast element is a 32-page multiple-use magazine for students. Other non-broadcast materials include the teacher guide and the parent guide. These latter are not themselves input for the children, only guides to help adults plan program-related activities. By itself it did not seem that the student magazine could induce detectable differences in children so it was not singled out for a separate level of treatment.

In the adult guides the suggested activities for teachers and parents may be divided conceptually into three categories, the first two associated with mediation of the show's messages and the last with extension activities. Mediation is defined as adult interaction with children for the purpose of increasing comprehension of the show's messages. Two types of mediation activities can be distinguished: pre-show setting of context and post-show discussion. The first includes any activities preceding the broadcast which prepare viewers to decode the messages that will be presented. The second includes discussion immediately following the broadcast for the purpose of clarifying the messages of the show. The third category of adult activity is extension. This includes activities designed to expand the effects of the show by creating experiences other than viewing which teach an additional, related lesson. An example is an activity in which children go to a shopping center and note the sex of people in various types of jobs -- sales clerks, managers, etc. -- and later discuss the findings in class. These supplementary activities could augment a child's exposure to FREESTYLE themes by as much as two hours per week. While the content of such intervention is a less-known quantity than a pre-recorded TV show, its presence could add significantly to the overall effect. Accordingly for both the Home and School settings separate treatment levels were singled out in which viewing was supplemented with adult mediation and extension activities.

Balancing off considerations of feasibility -- what is possible for a teacher or parent within the context of other things competing for their time -- and the designers' hopes, four levels of experimental treatment were designated in addition to the control condition.

1) <u>School Full:</u> a) Television show received in a classroom setting during school hours as part of grade 4-6 curriculum. Two broadcasts of 1/4-hour each used every week for 13 weeks. b) School Guide available for teachers. Teachers use guide, conduct some minimal activity with students prior to each airing (5-30 minutes) and conduct a debriefing following the show (20-40 minutes) in which they develop one or more of the "talk topics" suggested in the Guide. Teachers are encouraged to "extend" the themes of the show into other curricular areas (math, language arts) following suggestions in the Guide; minimum recommended is one extension activity per week (30+ minutes). c) The "Freestyle" magazine is distributed to students and used as directed. d) Teacher training as designed by L.A. County Schools is provided for 1/2-day at the beginning of the series (September, 1978).

2) <u>School View Only:</u> Students view the show in classrooms or central school areas, but with no teacher discussion of the content. Viewing frequency is the same as in the two above treatments.

3) <u>School Control:</u> Students do not engage in any viewing or related activities.

4) <u>Home Full:</u> Students do all viewing at home. They are encouraged to view one 1/2-hour show per week for 13 weeks. Their parents are encouraged to view with them, discussing the shows and themes in ways suggested by the Home Guide.

5) <u>Home View Only:</u> Students are encouraged to view one 1/2-hour show per week for 13 weeks. Parents are not given Home Guides and are not encouraged to view with their children.

6) <u>Home Control:</u> Students do not engage in any viewing or related activities.

Two control conditions appear in this chart. They are a result of two considerations. One concerns the requirement we will discuss at a later point -- that school-use and home-use of the series be tested in separate geographical locations. The other concerns the related analytical requirement that children from different cities not be pooled for analytical purposes. Two home conditions appear also, although probably only one is justified. When the Home Guide was conceptualized it was to be a well articulated guide for parents. In its final form it was only a calendar, offering little in the way of structured guidance for parent mediation. It hardly warrants a separate Home Full treatment, but it was too late to adjust the research design.

Assigning Treatments to Sites

Important policy questions center on the different effects associated with school and home use of the series. Ideally, the two types of use should be tested within the same sites using children from the same population. However, open-circuit broadcasting was used to distribute the programs to schools and homes; the ITV version for school use was broadcast during daytime school hours while the ETV version for home use was broadcast during late afternoon or early evening hours.[2] This meant that if a station were to air both the school and home broadcast, then those in a school treatment could go home and view the show again; this is very undesirable given the interest in differentiating between home and school effects. (The reverse need not be true since those in the home treatment could view in school only if the series were being used by the child's classroom teacher.) Whether or not children in a school treatment would actually go home and watch if they had the opportunity is unclear. Given the typical Nielsen viewing data for children's programs on educational stations it is quite possible that only a few of the children would view twice. However, to insure that there was not contamination all but one of the home and school treatments were established in separate broadcast areas. Stations in school treatment cities were asked to broadcast only the ITV version of the series during the Fall of 1978. Stations in home treatment cities could broadcast both versions if they wished

---

[2]Initially stations and schools were to have seven-day record and playback rights. A few days after PBS began feeding the series to the stations new 5-year record and playback rights were announced. By this time it was too late to conceptualize the series as other than open-circuit in its basic design.

but schools cooperating with the research in these locations were asked not to use the series in the classroom during the experimental period.

In assigning school treatments to sites, two different combinations were used. One configuration had two levels in the same site: SCHOOL FULL and SCHOOL CONTROL. The other had three levels: SCHOOL FULL, SCHOOL VIEW-ONLY and SCHOOL CONTROL. A site was to have only one configuration in it, a decision that resulted from the following analytic considerations. The evaluation was addressing three questions. First, was SCHOOL FULL effective in changing the sex-role orientations of children; and, if so, was it differentially effective for various population subgroups? To answer these two questions required a total number of classrooms spread between experimental and control conditions of approximately 70. The third question concerned the relative effectiveness of the FULL and VIEW-ONLY conditions. For this question analyses of population subgroups were not so important; even so, testing two experimental conditions against a control group required approximately 60 classrooms. A number of inquiries to school administrators led to the conclusion that 75 upper elementary classrooms was the limit that could be secured in any one district. Accordingly, the two configurations had to be implemented in separate sites.

It might be argued that this should result in the selection of two sites for testing school use of the series. But two additional considerations led to the doubling of this number to four sites. First, an experiment of this sort is very difficult to implement. After spending six months courting a TV station and school district, participation could be withdrawn at any time (as it almost was in two sites). Any number of other factors could threaten the validity of any one site's efforts. Thus two sites for each configuration provides a margin of safety for the experimenter. Second, since selection and assignment to treatments had to be done within sites, analyses and therefore conclusions had to be limited to a single site. The addition of a second replicate site provides a means of extending the external validity of the design by seeing if relationships observed in one site are replicated in the alternate site. Evidence of the wisdom of this decision is provided in later chapters.

The test of the home use of the series was deemed to be very difficult to implement. The past experience of Educational Testing Service in trying to test the effectiveness of <u>Sesame Street</u> and <u>Electric Company</u> in the home setting was very instructive: despite investment of extensive resources, the amount of viewing in the home condition was insufficient to validate its effects. However, certain policy issues center around the differential effects of home and school use of FREESTYLE. Accordingly, following the advice of a number of experts[3] the home use of this series was tested using a very small number of students who were followed and encouraged to watch the show regularly. For the HOME FULL treatment, the parents of the students were encouraged to view the series with their child and to discuss it with him/her. These students were selected from intact classrooms and then assigned to HOME FULL and HOME VIEW ONLY treatments. To minimize contamination, treatments were assigned separately by school. Thus, one school had classrooms whose students were assigned to the HOME VIEW ONLY condition; another school had only HOME FULL students, and yet another had HOME CONTROL. Ideally CONTROL students would be located in the same schools as the two experimental treatments; however, only a unique site with cable broadcasting that could be carefully manipulated would have permitted this arrangement and none was found.

Measurement points for children included a pre-test and post-test timed within a week of the beginning and end of the complete series. This test is described in Chapter Six. Additional intermediate measurements were taken in two sites to assess comprehension by the children of the series' messages. In addition, each classroom teacher provided information via a pre and post questionnaire (Chapter 4); and each experimental classroom teacher also kept a log of classroom activities as a measure of treatment implementation. A schematic of the design is shown in Figure 3.1.

---

[3]Sam Ball, Educational Testing Service; Keith Mielke, Children's Television Workshop; Saul Rockman, Agency for Instructional Television.

Figure 3.1
Schematic of the Research Design

Site Type 1	O_1	SCHOOL FULL $O_a \ldots O_n$	O_2
	O_1	SCHOOL CONTROL	O_2
Site Type 2	O_1	SCHOOL FULL $O_a \ldots O_n$	O_2
	O_1	SCHOOL VIEW ONLY $O_a \ldots O_n$	O_2
	O_1	SCHOOL CONTROL	O_2
Site Type 3	O_1	HOME FULL	O_2
	O_1	HOME VIEW ONLY	O_2
	O_1	HOME CONTROL	O_2

Where O_1=pretest, O_2=post-test
$O_a \ldots O_n$=intermediate measures

Selecting Sites and Schools

In this project a site was considered to be the A-contour coverage area of a PTV station. This area typically includes a large number of school districts, a few of which have a large number of students and many more which have very small numbers. For pragmatic reasons the selection of 9-12 year olds was done by choosing intact classrooms in elementary schools containing in grades 4-6, and taking all the students in the classroom. This approach was used for all treatments, permitting random assignment of classrooms to treatments. Actually, there is an additional restriction. To avoid contamination, only one treatment was permitted in any one school, so the random assignment was really of schools to treatments, each school having a certain number of teacher-volunteered classrooms.

These considerations are summarized in Table 3.1 which shows the treatments and target sample sizes for each site. The sample sizes in the table are targets, not final expected sample sizes. Consideration of two factors are likely to reduce these numbers appreciably -- normal attrition and variation in treatment implementation. All studies must take into account non-response; in this study the most likely source of non-response is normal student absence. Since the research design calls for pre and post tests on each student, absences at either testing can reduce the sample size. We estimated that attrition for reasons of absence at one time or another would be 20 percent, with a higher rate among some minority groups. Among the experimental subjects with usable data, many would miss some or even most of the television shows, and thus would have to be eliminated because they did not receive full treatment. We estimated this number to be another 20 percent. Thus, the numbers in the table take into account that the likely yield for students in the experimental groups would be only 60 percent of the target numbers.

The list of potential sites to be approached had representation from every region of the country. Such diversity was thought necessary to provide political credibility for the research results, and it would also permit detection of any regional differences in sex-role orientations. Within any one site a number of considerations would determine selection. These included the demographics of the school districts contained within the signal coverage area of the station, the relationship of the local districts to the television station, the extent to which the schools use ITV regularly, and the interest of the television station and schools in cooperating with the research. These considerations are discussed in some detail in the next sections.

PART II: IMPLEMENTING THE PLAN

The research design for validating FREESTYLE's effects was an ambitious one. Successful implementation required an extensive effort to sell FREESTYLE to TV stations and school districts -- an effort complicated by the fact that participation demanded adherence by classroom teachers to a detailed four-month regimen that would compete with other classroom priorities. The

Table 3.1
Targeted Numbers of Sites, Treatments and Respondents

Site	Category	Total	School			Home		
			Full	View Only	Con-trol	Parent Co-View	View Alone	Con-trol
1. School Full: Prime	Schools Teachers Students Parents	30 75 2100 2100	20 50 1400 1400		10 25 700 700			
2. School Full: Replicate	Schools Teachers Students	30 60 1680	20 40 1120		10 20 560			
3. School View-Only: Prime	Schools Teachers Students	30 60 1680	12 25 700	12 25 700	4 10 280			
4. School View-Only: Replicate	Schools Teachers Students	30 60 1680	12 25 700	12 25 700	4 10 280			
5. Home:	Schools Classrooms Students Parents	10 20 325 250				4 8 125 125	4 8 125 125	2 4 125
6. Home: Replicate	Schools Classrooms Students Parents	10 20 325 250				4 8 125 125	4 8 125 125	2 4 125

TOTALS: Students=7790 Teachers=295 Parents=2600
NOTE: Subgroup analyses were slated for site No. 1 only, thus the larger number of students in this site.

remainder of this chapter details the implementation of the plan. The first part describes the procedures used to select the sites, school districts, buildings, classrooms and students: the second part assesses the success of this effort in terms of the characteristics of the obtained sample of participants and their adherence to the regimen of the validation plan.

Securing Test Sites

After nine months of searching for cities and school districts to participate in the study, seven sites were enlisted. Securing a site followed a stepwise procedure. Voluntary cooperation was sought first from the local PBS television station, then from a school district identified by the station. Access to the district was gained by identifying an ally within the district --typically an ITV director or a career education specialist -- who in turn would try to sell the rest of the central administration. Approval at this level led to a meeting with school principals and then with interested teachers.

The identification of sites and the assignment of a given site to a treatment condition was accomplished with the following requirements in mind:

> A. The PBS station is willing to carry FREESTYLE for the entire first run of the series, using the broadcast configuration demanded by the experiment. The station has good relations with local schools.
>
> B. The primary school district(s) in the site have grades four through six in the same buildings.
>
> C. The district has an established instructional television capacity which is regularly utilized by a large proportion of teachers.
>
> D. (For a school test site) As a whole, the district has demographic diversity, both racially and socioeconomically. For a School Full test site, the demographic diversity includes both Blacks and Mexican-Americans.
>
> E. The career education series "Bread and Butterflies" is not used extensively in the district. (This series of movies from the Agency for instructional Television has enough similar goals to contaminate the design.)

F. The district(s) must be large enough to yield at least 60 classrooms for a school site or 20 classrooms for a home site.

G. The district(s) will permit random assignment of teachers to experimental and control conditions.

As may be seen by these criteria, it was not simple for a site to qualify for inclusion in the study; the design imposed a number of conditions which ruled out many sites which might have otherwise participated. A total of nine calendar months were taken up in the process of securing the seven sites. The process of identifying, approaching, and obtaining the cooperation of the station, the district, the principals, and the teachers in any one site required about three months per attempt, and these attempts, not infrequently, ended in failure.

Applying the foregoing requirements to the available sites resulted in the assignment of Milwaukee and Long Beach/Torrance to the School Full vs. Control treatment condition, Worcester and North Kansas City to the School Full vs. School View-Only treatment condition, and Saginaw and Covina to the Home View vs. Control treatment condition. Finally, Ann Arbor was added to the study as a special School Full vs. Control site in which individually administered interviews with the children were conducted to assist in understanding how children process the messages and plots of the shows. Despite the fact that Ann Arbor is a "university town" and therefore somewhat atypical, the students of the Ann Arbor public schools provided the demographic diversity sought in assigning sites to school treatment conditions. Most importantly, however, their proximity greatly facilitated the complicated scheduling arrangements necessary to conduct individual face-to-face interviews. Each of these sites is described in Appendix E.

A southern site was sought in order to broaden geographical coverage in the evaluation, but we failed to secure one. Many states in the southeast are covered by state ITV networks. In almost all cases, these networks determine their fall schedules during December of the preceding year. Because PBS did not commit to carry FREESTYLE until February of 1978, it was impossible to involve schools in these states. An effort was made to find a site in the south central section of the United States. Concerted efforts to involve one or more districts in Texas all resulted in failure because either the delivering television station and/or the school districts refused to cooperate.[4] Another Texas district (Austin) which was known to have cooperated in previous television studies had to be ruled out because grade six students were housed in separate buildings from students in grades four and five. Houston, which may have been willing to cooperate, was identified as a possibility too late to complete the clearance processes before the series was aired.

Selecting The Classrooms, Teachers, and Students

Ideally classrooms are allocated to treatment conditions by random assignment. However, an important pragmatic impediment to purely random allocation of classrooms to treatment condition was the clustering of classrooms within a building. That is, it was most efficient to recruit several teachers from a given building, but it would have been undesirable to assign some classrooms in a building to an experimental treatment condition while assigning other classrooms in the same building to the control condition. Thus, the potential theoretical advantage of a purely random assignment strategy would have been more than offset by the risk of almost certain contamination of control students by the treatment students. The compromise solution was to randomly assign school buildings to treatment conditions, resulting in a situation where all classrooms within the same building were assigned to the same treatment.

To accomplish this, a pool of candidate schools which contained two or more classrooms at the fourth and sixth grades was established. Next, each building in the pool was checked to be sure it possessed the necessary television hardware and that recent ITV usage by teachers in the building was reasonably high. Following this, each building was checked to be sure that the A.I.T. series "Bread and Butterflies" had not been used regularly by teachers. (The latter step was taken because this series had enough

---

[4]Unsuccessful attempts of this sort involved Dallas, Fort Worth, Odessa, and San Antonio.

substantive overlap with FREESTYLE to present difficulty in interpreting any observable impacts to the FREESTYLE series alone.)

After these screening procedures had been completed and the principals' approval to approach the teachers had been obtained, invitations were issued to teachers to participate in the study. These invitations were accompanied by materials describing the series, the non-broadcast materials, the evaluation study, and the commitment involved. A local coordinator was available in each site to facilitate this procedure. The commitment by a teacher to participate in the study was made without knowledge of the specific treatment condition to which the teacher's classroom would be assigned. This was necessary because not all of the relevant information had been assembled at that time to permit the assignment of classroom to treatment level or condition. Additionally, it was important to distribute equally to the experimental and control conditions those teachers who were supportive of FREESTYLE's goals, so as not to confound teacher interest or support with treatment.

The next step was to secure school building level information on the demographic and racial/ethnic composition of the student body in the remaining pool of schools. These data were estimates provided by central administrative office personnel, by building principals and, in a few sites, information on file in the central district office. Using these data, the participating buildings were sorted into three categories according to the predominant ethnic background of the student body. For convenience, we shall refer to these categories as White, Black, and Hispanic, though in most cases some considerable mixture of ethnic backgrounds was encountered within the school. Within each of these three categories, the schools were ranked from high to low on the average socio-economic level and reading level of the whole school population. As before, data from office records were used wherever possible; in other cases, estimates were obtained from central office personnel or building principals, and cross-validated with the other source. The final step in the assignment of school building to treatment condition was then accomplished by applying the allocation ratios given in the Table 3.2 to the schools within each of the three categories. For example, if there were six schools on the ranked list of schools within the Hispanic category of a "B" site, the first two would be assigned to the School Full treatment condition, and the next one to the School Control condition. The actual number of participating classrooms assigned to the various treatment conditions is given in Table 3.3.

Table 3.2
Allocation Ratios For Assignment of School Building to Treatment

Site Type	Number of Sites	Allocation Ratio
A-School Full/View Only/Control	2*	2:2:1
B-School Full/Control	3	2:1
C-Home Co-View/View Alone/Control	2	2:2:1

*Because the yield of classrooms in one of these sites was considerably less than expected, no control classrooms were involved in this site. Thus, the allocation ratio used for classrooms in this site was 1 School Full to 1 School View Only.

All students in the 268 classrooms enumerated in Table 3.3 were invited to participate in the evaluation study. The recommendation of local school administrators were followed for extending these invitations and contacting parents. At both the pre-test and post-test students were read a statement reminding them that completion of the questionnaire was voluntary.

The number of students in these classrooms at the time the study began (Fall, 1978) is given in Table 3.4 below. This table shows the maximum numbers of students available before the FREESTYLE experiment began. The cells of the table give the maximum numbers of students per site by grade level and viewing condition. In all cases, these numbers are large enough to permit overall treatment comparisons and detailed analyses by sex and grade with assurance of reasonable subsample sizes. In the School Full/Control sites -- Long Beach and Milwaukee -- the numbers are large enough to permit analyses by race as well.

Table 3.3
Number of Participating Schools and Classrooms
by Treatment Condition Within Site

		Number of Classrooms					
		School			Home		
Site Type	Site Name	Full (SF)	View Only (SV)	Control (SC)	Parent Co-View (HCV)	View Alone (HVA)	Control (HC)
A	Worcester, Mass.	5/30	5/24	3/13			
A	N. Kansas City, Mo.	6/17	6/17				
B	Milwaukee, Wisc.	14/44		6/18			
B	Long Beach/ Torrance, CA	13/29		7/16			
B	Ann Arbor, Mich.	7/21		2/5			
C	Saginaw, Mich.				3/6	3/7	2/4
C	Covina, Calif.				3/6	3/6	2/4
	TOTAL	45/141	11/41	18/52	6/12	6/13	4/8

NOTE: 5/30 indicates 5 schools yielding 30 classrooms.

As described above, these numbers are maximums because they are based upon the number of students in the selected classrooms at the time the study began. However, most of the important analytic questions require complete data from students both before and after the series was aired. Thus, the actual number of students upon whom we will have complete pre-test and post-test data will be somewhat lower primarily as a function of (1) absence on the pre or post testing day and (2) family movement out of the district during the period of study. Students were "oversampled" to compensate for the expected attrition due to these factors. The actual numbers of students that resulted

Table 3.4

Numbers of Available Students by Grade and Viewing Condition

Site Type and City	Grade	School			Home			TOTAL
		Full	View Only	Control	Parent Co-View	View Along	Control	
(A)Worcester	4	247	195	109				551
	5	224	207	114				545
	6	221	190	118				529
	Other*	10	1	0				1
	Total	702	593	341				1636
(A)N. Kansas City	4	158	147					305
	5	129	127					256
	6	162	139					301
	Other*	0	1					1
	Total	449	414					863
(B)Long Beach/ Torrance	4	310		167				477
	5	255		148				403
	6	390		222				612
	Other*	0		0				0
	Total	955		537				1492
(B)Milwaukee	4	428		157				585
	5	415		142				557
	6	478		185				663
	Other*	2		0				2
	Total	1323		484				1807
(B)Ann Arbor	4	212		50				262
	5	105		10				115
	6	230		71				301
	Other*	0		0				0
	Total	547		131				678

Table 3.4 (Cont.)

Numbers of Available Students by Grade and Viewing Condition

Site Type and City	Grade	School			Home			TOTAL
		Full	View Only	Control	Parent Co-View	View Along	Control	
(C)Covina	4				97	97	68	262
	5				0	0	0	0
	6				105	99	68	272
	Other*				0	0	0	0
Total					202	196	136	534
(C)Saginaw	4				83	72	61	216
	5				0	9	0	9
	6				89	50	56	195
	Other*				0	12	0	12
Total					172	193	117	482
Grand Totals**	4	1355	342	483	180	169	129	2658
	5	1128	334	414	0	59	0	1935
	6	1481	329	596	194	149	124	2873
	Other*	12	2	0	0	2	0	26
Totals		3976	1007	1493	374	389	253	7492

*Students whose grade level is not known and students in mixed grade classrooms whose individual grade level was outside the 4-6 range are classified in this table as "Other."

**These "Grand Totals" are presented solely for information purposes. As described in the above text, no analyses are performed upon aggregations of students across sites.

from this multistage selection strategy are described in later chapters of this report.

Comparability of Experimental and Control Students

The procedures for assigning the school buildings (and hence, the teachers and students) to the treatment conditions within a site were intended to produce essentially comparable groups of students in each of the treatment conditions. The achievement of this objective can be assessed by examining the distributions of the grade level, sex, and ethnicity of the students within the various treatment groups of each site.

Before examining these data a re-examination of the data in Tables 3.3 and 3.4 will be useful. Consider the first site, Worcester, as an example. Table 3.3 indicates that the 2:2:1 allocation ratio was not implemented exactly as planned. The actual number of classrooms assigned to the three treatment conditions was 30, 24, and 13. Table 3.3 indicates that the number of students in the three viewing conditions was 702, 593, and 341 respectively. However, with regard to the key question concerning the grade distributions of the students in thee treatment condition, it is clear that no major differences are observable. Therefore, grade differences (should they exist) are not confounded with treatment differences.

Table 3.5 below presents the analyses of grade distributions by treatment. By and large, the percentage distributions suggest few differences from one treatment condition to another within these sites. The two major exceptions to this overall observation occur in the Saginaw and Ann Arbor sites. The analysis strategy to be used with the Ann Arbor data makes the observed differences relatively unimportant. In Saginaw caution will be necessary in the interpretation of analyses. In the other five sites, the grade distributions are very comparable across the viewing conditions. Analyses involving treatment comparisons may, then, proceed with reasonable assurance that treatment is not confounded with grade differences.

Similar data on sex distributions are given in Table 3.6. Here we see remarkably similar distributions across treatment conditions within each of the sites. The single exception is that in Covina a much larger proportion of

Table 3.5
Percentage Distributions Across Grades
By Viewing Condition Within Site

Site Type	Site Name	Grade	SF	SV	SC	HCV	HVA	HC
A	Worcester	4	36	33	32			
		5	32	35	33			
		6	32	32	35			
A	N. Kansas City	4	35	36				
		5	29	31				
		6	36	34				
B	Milwaukee	4	32		32			
		5	31		29			
		6	36		38			
B	Long Beach/ Torrance	4	32		31			
		5	27		28			
		6	41		41			
B	Ann Arbor	4	39		38			
		5	19		8			
		6	42		54			
C	Saginaw	4				48	40	52
		5				0	33	0
		6				52	28	48
C	Covina	4				48	50	50
		5				0	0	0
		6				52	51	50

the students in the Co-View (53%) and control (52%) conditions than in the View-Alone condition (46%) are male. Thus, comparative analyses of these two treatment conditions in this site will have to be sensitive to a possible confounding of sex differences with treatment.

Ethnic distributions are displayed in Table 3.7. Here it is apparent that the procedures were much less successful in obtaining comparability of students across treatment conditions -- but the only requirement is that the distribution be comparable in the School Full/Control sites. The better racial balance of Long Beach over Milwaukee was a major factor in assigning

Long Beach to the role of prime School Full site and Milwaukee to the role of replicate site.

Table 3.6
Percentage Distributions Across Sex
By Viewing Condition Within Site

Site Type	Site Name	Sex	SF	SV	SC	HCA	HVA	HC
A	Worcester	Female	49	49	49			
A	Worcester	Male	51	51	51			
A	N. Kansas City	Female	51	54				
A	N. Kansas City	Male	49	46				
B	Milwaukee	Female	51		51			
B	Milwaukee	Male	49		49			
B	Long Beach/ Torrance	Female	47		49			
B	Long Beach/ Torrance	Male	54		51			
B	Ann Arbor	Female	46		49			
B	Ann Arbor	Male	54		51			
C	Saginaw	Female				53	52	49
C	Saginaw	Male				47	48	51
C	Covina	Female				47	54	48
C	Covina	Male				53	46	52

Characteristics of Participating Teachers

At the last stage of selection, volunteer teachers were solicited. It was expected that in the aggregate the volunteers would be typical of the teachers in the district with the exception that their use of instructional television might be higher than normal. The demographics of the selected teachers in each site is shown in Table 3.8. Typical of elementary schools, the majority were women. Racially they show a dominance of Whites, but no more so than the racial distribution of elementary teachers throughout each of

Table 3.7
Percentage Distributions Across Ethnicity
By Viewing Condition Within Site

Site Type	Site Name	Ethnicity	SF	SV	SC	HCV	HVA	HC
A	Worcester	Hispanic	9	12	1			
		Black	6	6	2			
		White	86	81	97			
A	N. Kansas City	Hispanic		2				
		Black	1	1				
		White	98	97				
B	Milwaukee	Hispanic	12		29			
		Black	35		25			
		White	53		46			
B	Long Beach/ Torrance	Hispanic	18		17			
		Black	21		17			
		White	62		66			
B	Ann Arbor	Hispanic	2		0			
		Black	30		19			
		White	68		81			
C	Saginaw	Hispanic				7	4	8
		Black				18	30	3
		White				74	66	89
C	Covina	Hispanic				19	34	16
		Black				2	2	1
		White				80	64	83

*For this table Hispanic students of Mexican descent have been combined with other Hispanics, and students with ethnic backgrounds other than Hispanic, Black, or White have been excluded.

the districts. As for years of teaching experience, the volunteers were on the average slightly more experienced than the district average.

Table 3.8
Demographics of Participating Teachers

		Total	Sex		Race				Ave. Yrs. Teaching
			Fem.	Male	White	Black	Hisp.	Other	
Worcester	n	68	37	31	67	0	1	0	15.5
	%	100	54	46	98	0	2	0	
North Kansas City	n	34	31	3	32	1	0	1	10.7
	%	100	91	9	94	3	0	3	
Milwaukee	n	61	42	19	50	7	4	0	14.8
	%	100	69	31	82	12	7	0	
Long Beach/ Torrance	n	45	40	5	39	3	1	2	13.3
	%	100	89	11	87	7	2	4	
Ann Arbor	n	27	21	6	17	10	0	0	10.7
	%	100	78	22	63	37	0	0	
Saginaw	n	14	10	4	10	3	0	1	13.7
	%	100	71	29	71	21	0	7	
Covina	n	16	12	4	14	0	1	1	16.2
	%	100	75	25	88	0	6	6	
TOTAL	n	265	193	72	229	24	7	5	13.8
	%	100	73	27	86	9	3	2	

Training Teachers to Adhere to the FREESTYLE Regimen.

Central to the "product validation" model of evaluation is the delivery of the product at a high "dosage" level and in a replicable way to all students. While the television shows are clearly a known quantity, the way in which teachers discuss the shows is not. No amount of training could secure uniformity in how the topics were emphasized and discussed in class. It was expected that a one-day teacher training program could at least guarantee that a similar set of activities would be followed in every classroom. For School Full teachers this would entail such things as viewing twice a week and post-viewing discussion built around discussion questions in the teacher guide.

Another issue concerning procedural integrity is in the collection of the evaluation data. The teachers were to be administrators of the student questionnaire, and were themselves to complete several forms. To insure that administration of these questionnaires was uniform across classrooms, a training session was also needed.

A one-day workshop was developed for all participating teachers. The first one-third was devoted to introducing teachers to the expectations of the evaluation study. This part was conducted by staff from the Institute for Social Research. It included training in questionnaire administration and a detailing of the weekly regimen. For School Full teachers this regimen was fairly detailed, for School View-Only less so; and for all other types of classrooms it involved little more than training in administration of student questionnaires.

The second two-thirds of the workshop for School Full teachers was conducted by trainers from the Office of the Los Angeles County Superintendent of Schools. They introduced teachers to the concepts behind FREESTYLE and gave them opportunities to practice recommended methods of using the TV shows effectively in the classroom. An outline of their training program appears in Appendix G.

Each training session was conducted in a hotel so that food could be provided. This hospitality was the only extrinsic reward given to teachers for contributing so much of their time. Training sessions were conducted on school days in most sites and the district was compensated for the cost of substitute teachers. In Milwaukee the choice was made to conduct the training on a Saturday, so the compensation went directly to participating teachers instead of substitutes. Training lasted about seven hours for School Full teachers and two-and-a-half hours for others. The training program was very well received by participating teachers, especially the sections conducted by the L.A. County trainers which related to better methods of classroom teaching.

Adherence to the FREESTYLE Regimen

Accumulated wisdom and experience from previous evaluation studies suggests that there often exists a wide disparity between an assigned experimental treatment condition and what actually happens when a teacher attempts to implement the assigned treatment within a classroom. To assess the latter (which obviously constituted the "real" experimental condition) some special procedures were designed.

Each classroom assigned to either the School Full or the School View-Only condition was given a "FREESTYLE Activity Log." In this log, records on each 15-minute episode were kept for four types of activities; (1) Introduction to the show, (2) Viewing the show, (3) Discussion after the show, and (4) Other classroom activities. For each of these activity types, information was requested concerning whether or not any class time was spent on the activity, and, if it was, how much time was spent. General instructions on completing the log, including definitions of each of the activity types, were provided. Teachers were encouraged to complete the log at least weekly, if not after each episode. During training the suggestion was given to train two or three students to regularly maintain the record. Figure 3.2 is a reproduction of one page from the Activity Log corresponding to the first 15-minute episode of the show entitled "Partners." Here it is apparent that completion of the log was not burdensome on the teachers, especially if they trained selected students to keep the log up to date.

The authors believe that the log provides a reasonably accurate picture of the true implementation level for most classrooms. This belief is based upon several factors. First, the written instructions on completing the log, reinforced by verbal appeals at the training session, specifically attempted to reduce bias due to social-desirability. For example, the instructions stated: "We are well aware that there is often a difference between the amount of time you plan to spend on an activity and the amount of time you actually end up spending on that activity. It is very important that this log contain a record of time actually spent." Verbally an appeal was made to be honest with the researchers and numerous assurances were given that no data on individual classroom or school performance would be seen by anyone within the district.

Figure 3.2
Example of FREESTYLE Activity Log for "Partners" (first half)

Activity type	Was any class time spent on this activity?	If any class time was spent, please indicate:		
		Dates(s)	Time started	Time ended
1-Introduction to the show	No [ ] Yes [ ] →			
2-Viewing the show	No [ ] Yes [ ] →			
3-Discussion after the show	No [ ] Yes [ ] →			
4-Other classroom activities	No [ ] Yes [ ] →			

A second reason for belief in the reliability of these data is based on contacts made with selected teachers by the site coordinator in several sites. Two such contacts were made; one about half way through the series and the other at its conclusion. The coordinators -- chosen because they were known in the district -- asked these teachers whether they felt they were being candid in the Logs. Although only 20 teachers were contacted, the coordinators felt that candor had characterized all of the Logs.

A third reason for belief in the credibility of these records is provided by the data. Inspection of the Activity Logs for each of the teachers whose classrooms were assigned to the School Full or School View Only conditions revealed very few instances of records which matched "idealized" records. Furthermore, there was evidence in almost every Log of at least occasional non-compliance and this followed a haphazard (and thus believable) pattern.

In order to simplify analyses using the implementation data, the Activity Log for each classroom was summarized into a single index score referred to as the "Implementation Score." It was calculated for each classroom by aggregating the Activity Log data according to the algorithm described in Figure 3.3. The Implementation Score was created by a two-step procedure. The first step was to assign to each episode a score, ranging from zero to four, which represented how many of the four activity types were actually engaged in for the episode in question. As described above, a teacher assigned to the School Full treatment should have engaged in all four activity types for the episode and thus (theoretically) would have a score of "4", whereas a School View-Only classroom should have done nothing except view the episode, resulting (again theoretically) in a score of "1". Once the actual implementation score had been calculated for each of the 26 episodes, the second step consisted merely of adding the episode scores, producing (theoretical) maximum scores of 26x4=104 for a School Full teacher and 26x1=26 for a School View Only teacher. In reality, however, a School View Only teacher could have engaged -- at least on occasion -- in one or more of the other activities; thus, the actual maximum score for such a teacher could exceed the theoretical maximum of 26.

Figure 3.3

Implementation Score Algorithm for Activity Log Data

Step 1 -- Create a summary score (0-4) for each 15-minute episode.

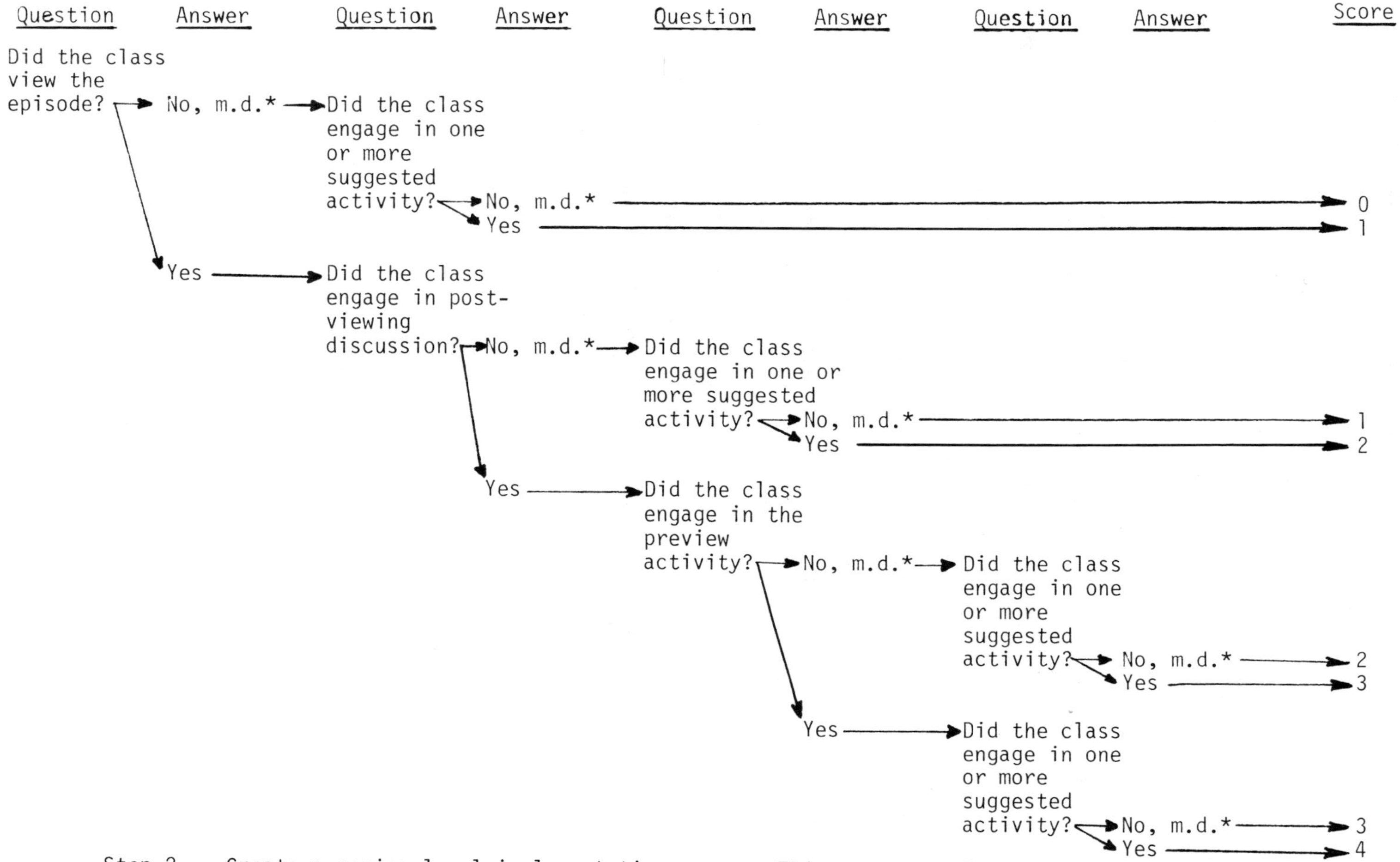

Question	Answer	Question	Answer	Question	Answer	Question	Answer	Score
Did the class view the episode?	No, m.d.*	Did the class engage in one or more suggested activity?	No, m.d.*					0
			Yes					1
	Yes	Did the class engage in post-viewing discussion?	No, m.d.*	Did the class engage in one or more suggested activity?	No, m.d.*			1
					Yes			2
			Yes	Did the class engage in the preview activity?	No, m.d.*	Did the class engage in one or more suggested activity?	No, m.d.*	2
							Yes	3
					Yes	Did the class engage in one or more suggested activity?	No, m.d.*	3
							Yes	4

Step 2 -- Create a series level implementation score. This was accomplished by a simple summation of the episode scores across the 26 episodes comprising the series. The potential range of the resulting series scores is from 0 to 104.

---

*m.d. is used to designate records which were left blank or were otherwise ambiguous.

The application of this algorithm to the Viewing Log records thus produced a single implementation score for each classroom assigned to the School Full or School View-Only treatment condition. The mean implementation score of the 141 School Full classrooms was just less than 77, a figure well below the idealized score of 104. For the 41 School View Only classrooms, the mean score was just greater than 23, a figure very close to the idealized value of 26. In both cases, there is substantial variability around the average; clearly it cannot be assumed that all teachers implemented the treatment condition exactly as it was assigned to them.

To simplify later analyses, classrooms were divided into groups according to the extent they had implemented the treatment. Because extensive use is made of these groupings in subsequent sections of the report, it will be useful to look now in some detail at their characteristics. Table 3.9 describes the average activity levels for each group. In the top half of the table are the data for the 141 School Full classrooms. Looking first at the row labelled "Average," the overall mean number of segments viewed by these classrooms was just over 24, a figure very close to the maximum of 26. The data in the "Segments Seen" column reveal the hardly surprising fact that the average number of segments seen is a monotonic function of the bracketed implementation score. The other column distributions in this table also reveal similar monotonic relationships. The only exception is the somewhat idiosyncratic pattern of the sole classroom whose bracketed implementation score was at level 2. Examining the "Average" scores for the other activities, we observe that compliance rates for introducing and discussing the shows (mean scores just under 22 out of the maximum possible of 26) are slightly lower than the average for viewing, but nonetheless represent rather impressive average levels of implementation. The average for using one or more of the suggested post-viewing extension activities, however, is a little less than 10; the ideal was 13 or one per week.

This "drop-off" for supplementary activities is understandable for at least two reasons. First of all, the suggested extension activities involve planning and conducting classroom activities at a time completely independent of the introduction-viewing-discussion activities; thus, requests for teachers

Table 3.9

Aggregate Mean Activity Levels for Different Implementation Groups

Implementation Group[1]	No. of Class-rooms	School Full Classrooms			
		Mean Number of			
		Segments Seen	Segments Introduced	Segments Discussed	Supplementary Activities
2 (0-20)	1	14.0	14.0	0.0	0.0
3 (21-40)	6	17.3	12.7	8.2	4.5
4 (41-60)	18	22.3	12.9	14.3	4.8
5 (61-80)*	57	24.5	22.2	22.8	4.5
6 (81-104)*	59	25.4	24.9	25.0	17.1
Average		24.2	21.7	21.8	9.7
n	141	141	141	141	141

		School View Only			
2 (0-15)	5	1.4	0.0	0.0	0.0
3 (16-23)	6	20.2	0.0	0.3	0.3
4 (24-25)*	8	24.5	0.6	0.1	0.0
5 (26-26)*	21	26.0	0.0	0.0	0.0
6 (>26)	1	26.0	26.0	25.0	13.0
Average		21.8	0.8	0.7	0.4
n	41	41	41	41	41

[1]For both school full and school view only, group #1 is the control group which had no FREESTYLE activity at all. In parenthesis after each group is the range of Implementation Scores contained in the group

*The analyses in Chapters Seven and Eight are based on children in these classrooms only.

to utilize such activities routinely and regularly place a qualitatively different and quantitatively greater demand upon teachers in the School Full condition. The data suggest, in fact, that many of the teachers who were otherwise fully cooperative failed to utilize these activities on a regular basis. A second reason for the sizable drop in average frequency is that teachers were asked to utilize such activities a minimum of once after each <u>pair</u> of episodes had been viewed. A teacher who complied literally with this minimum would have an upper score of 13 for this component (as opposed to 26 for the other components). Of course, teachers were not constrained to use only one activity per week, as suggested in the training sessions, and in fact the Activity Log was designed to measure any use they made of such activities after each 15 minute episode. The reality of the situation is that a few teachers did, in fact, follow each of the 26 episodes with one or more of these activities, and thus achieve "perfect" implementation scores of 104. In the main, however, the ambiguity in the request coupled with the logistics of regularly scheduling and complying with the request resulted in a significantly lower average level of implementation for this component. In short, this was the most demanding aspect of the School Full treatment; therefore, it should come as no surprise to learn that it was the aspect that had the lowest implementation level. Indeed, had the data indicated otherwise, their credibility would have been questioned.

In the bottom half of this same table are the average activity levels for School View-Only classrooms. With one notable exception the variation in implementation is associated entirely with viewing fewer broadcasts than they were asked. The lone exception is a classroom in which the teacher decided that FREESTYLE was too valuable an addition to the curriculum and went ahead and used it very extensively.

In Table 3.9 there are asterisks by the groups which were selected for analyses in Chapters Seven and Eight. By including only these high level implementers in the analysis of FREESTYLE's effects the series will be given its fairest test of potential effects. Table 3.10 shows the number of schools and classrooms that remain after two filters were used: (1) classrooms where students provided both pre and post data and (2) where the teacher implemented

FREESTYLE at the asterisked level. Comparisons with Table 3.3 show that the losses are quite small in terms of the distribution of schools and classrooms.

Table 3.10
Number of Schools and Classrooms
in Sample Used for Analyses

		Number of Classrooms					
		School			Home		
Site Type	Site Name	Full (SF)	View Only (SV)	Control (SC)	Parent Co-View (HCV)	View Alone (HVA)	Control (HC)
A	Worcester, Mass.	5/23	5/15	3/12			
A	N. Kansas City, Mo.	6/14	6/12				
B	Milwaukee, Wisc.	13/36		5/14			
B	Long Beach/ Torrance, CA	13/25		7/16			
B	Ann Arbor, Mich.	7/16		2/5			
C	Saginaw, Mich.				3/5	3/6	2/4
C	Covina, Calif.				3/5	3/6	2/4
	TOTAL	44/114	11/27	17/47	6/10	6/12	4/8

NOTE: Losses of classrooms or schools resulted from elimination of classrooms for which there was not both pre and post data and in which the interventions was not implemented at the starred levels in Table 3.9. Cell entries are the number of schools followed by the number of classrooms.

The FREESTYLE Home Viewing Record

In the home viewing conditions the procedure for assessing the implementation level of the assigned treatment involved the use of an instrument called the FREESTYLE Viewing Record. In each classroom where the students were to view the series at home (either alone or with a parent), a chart was posted by the teacher in a prominent place within the classroom. The chart contained a row for each student and a set of fourteen columns, one for each of the thirteen shows and an additional one for the student magazine. At a convenient point during the first school day after the airing of each show, students were asked by the teacher to make an entry on the chart to indicate whether they had (1) watched the show with one or both parents (coded WP on the chart) (2) watched the show alone or with someone other than a parent (coded WA), or (3) not watched the show at all (coded X).

As was the case with the school viewing condition, these Viewing Records yielded data which are most believable. Reporting of extensive non-viewing by students characterizes these data; this is consistent with the previous large-scale evaluations of home viewing of children's television. Furthermore, there is evidence of some consistency across time in a given student's viewing behavior; some students viewed with considerable regularity whereas others viewed only rarely or never. This, too, is consistent with findings from previous studies. In short, the patterns of both individual and aggregate student viewing behavior conform to expectations based on earlier evaluation efforts; furthermore, it would be difficult, if not impossible, to explain these patterns solely on a social-desirability basis.

Further information on the credibility of the data supplied by the Viewing Records was obtained in one site where interviews were conducted with several students. These interviews indicated that even when these charts were not completed on a weekly basis as requested, students could readily recall details of shows they had seen over three months earlier. Thus it is likely that even when teacher forgetfulness and/or student absence introduced delays in the completion of the Viewing Record, little if any error was introduced into the data that were eventually reported. The level of viewing obtained in the home sites is described in Chapter Eight.

Summary

In this chapter the research design and its implementation have been described in great detail -- probably more detail than the typical reader needs. Nonetheless, it is essential to archive all of these facts because the conclusions drawn in later chapters depend very heavily on the nature and quality of the design which yielded the data.

Chapter Four

TEACHERS RATE FREESTYLE FOR CLASSROOM USE

What were the reactions of teachers to the FREESTYLE package of materials? Based on the assessments of experienced teachers in the seven different test sites across the country, teachers are very enthusiastic about the products. This is critical for school use of the series, since teachers are the primary gatekeepers who determine whether FREESTYLE will reach the intended audience of 9-12 year olds. In this chapter teacher reactions are examined in some detail.

The chapter is divided into three sections. The first tells how teachers rate the products -- the TV shows and print materials. The second describes how FREESTYLE fits into the school curriculum. The third discusses certain innovative features of the FREESTYLE TV series: e.g., the format of the shows and the production strategies used to convey the educational messages of the series.

As detailed in Chapter Three, the present evaluation is a "product validation." This means that the assessments described here come from teachers who used the series extensively with their students for 13 weeks. In every city the teachers represented the broad spectrum of their 4th - 6th grade colleagues in the district. As volunteers, however, they were somewhat supportive of the goals of FREESTYLE to begin with. For this reason their assessment probably somewhat overstates the level of support of teachers throughout an entire district.

The evaluation involved a total of 268 teachers. Recall that teachers were assigned to one of four different test groups and given training in the role they were to play. Eighty-five taught classes whose students did not view at all (control group) or who viewed at home. Another 41 had School View-Only classes; their students watched the series in the classroom as a captive audience, but the teachers were expressly restricted from discussing the programs. Some reactions to the series were collected from these teachers. The bulk of teacher assessments comes from a special group of 142 teachers who taught the School Full classes (extensive use of FREESTYLE with students for 13 weeks). To appreciate the extent of their familiarity with the product, it will be helpful to briefly review the FREESTYLE curriculum products. Each TV show consists of two interrelated quarter-hour segments, designed to be viewed on separate days within the same week. For each segment, teachers conducted a preview activity, watched the segment with their students, and then led a discussion for 20 minutes or more, using one or more discussion questions suggested in the Guide. They did this twice a week, once for each quarter-hour segment. Once a week, in addition, teachers conducted an activity related to the theme of the week's show. This was in a curricular area of their choice, for example, leadership or stereotyping. The activity was chosen from the large collection in the Teachers' Guide. Then, at some point during the 13 weeks the teachers introduced the Freestyle Magazine and had their students read it and do some of the games and puzzles described in it. At the end of the experiment these 142 teachers were asked to provide a detailed assessment of each of the products and describe how the whole package fit into the school curriculum.

PART I. HOW GOOD ARE THE PRODUCTS?

Teachers were **very** enthusiastic after one semester of experience with FREESTYLE. It is difficult to imagine a single new curricular product being received with more uniformly positive comments from such a broad representation of teachers. One Kansas City teacher described her impressionss this way:

> The entire Freestyle program was terrific from the Freestyle Guide to the programs themselves. The content and presentation of the various segments were of such high quality. There were no "duds." There were no programs that did not stimulate discussion among the children. They literally begged to see it. Some of my "hardest to motivate" students ask when we were going to see Freestyle and would participate in the discussions and activities. I can't say enough good things. It has brought my children closer together as a group. They care more about each other. This is an added bonus. Freestyle -- we'll miss you!

In response too the single question (Question F1) which asked teachers the extent to which they would recommend FREESTYLE to other teachers in their district, seventy-one percent recommended the package "strongly" or "very strongly;" another 24 percent recommended it with "some reservations." Only four percent had serious reservations and just one did not recommend it. (The question and response distribution for F1 and other questions referred to in this chapter can be found in Appendix H.)

What are the dimensions of success for a show like this? The answer is captured in the written comments of the 71 percent who recommended the series without reservation. Four types of responses emerged. Some noted how well the shows dealt with the various topics, noting high production values and good acting.

> I found it a series that was well acted, with believable situations, [actors] my children could identify with, interesting format and good subject areas.

> ...it should be a success because it was entertaining while getting across its message. This was a prime reason for success.

Some noted that the themes were very relevant and needed in today's world. A third group focussed on the changed behaviors of their students, noting increased awareness of non-traditional possibilities for youth and adults.

> I think my students are much more aware of stereotyping and its results. Many changed their way of thinking or at least became more aware of stereotyping.

> Some of the things stressed in the shows stimulated a lot of them "thinking" and exploring the possibility of doing things on their own and showing more independence.

> Freestyle was a very valuable tool for myself and my class as members of a minority group (Puerto Ricans).

> During the bilingual episode, my _very_ shy bilingual students blossomed. When I wrote all the possible careers they could go into on the board, and especially said, "Just think, Irene, these are all _your_ possibilities when you grow up" -- I've never seen this child look so pleased and proud. It was really touching and I'm sure they will tuck this information into their memory bank.

The fourth group seemed to endorse FREESTYLE because of how much the students enjoyed the shows and the discussions.

> My class ask every week if we are going to view Freestyle. For many children, they claim it's their favorite part of the school day.

> The children were highly motivated to watch 'Freestyle.' In fact, if a child was absent he/she would take it upon themselves to watch the missed session at home or with another class.

> The shows certainly held the interest of the children. During viewing time, even though there were three classes (75 pupils) viewing at the same time you could hear a pin drop. The children loved the programs and were very attentive.

It has been said that boredom is the deadly enemy of education. If that is true, then these teachers may be showing their pleasure in finding relief from that condition.

What about teachers who were not so enthusiastic? Three of the eight teachers with serious reservations encountered technical problems receiving the TV programs and were dubious that it could be used easily by teachers. The other five found the themes too repetitious, too feminist, or didn't like something about the portrayal of the children.

Those who recommended it, but with "some reservations," form three groups. Nineteen them had some reservations about the content, but their comments did not fall into any discernible pattern. Eleven others responded, not to the FREESTYLE content, but rather to the curriculum overload that it represented. A small group had technical problems receiving the programs and this caused them some concern regarding continual classroom use. The fact that the negative comments were mostly idiosyncratic and did not indicate a common theme reflects well on the success of the producers. While their comments should be looked at, they nonetheless did not appear to be salient issues for the vast majority of teachers.

Grading the Products

The teachers were asked to rate each of the FREESTYLE products -- the thirteen shows, the guides, and the magazine for students -- on a number of dimensions, using the familiar report card letter grades for their ratings.

The results are summarized in Table 4.1. The TV shows receive very high marks for their ability to hold the attention of children, and receive marks which are about as high for conveying messages in a way that is clear to the viewers. The grades are somewhat lower for "believability" of the shows, and for the ability of the shows to stimulate class discussion -- 53 percent choosing "B" or "C". However, the average grade across the four dimensions is A-minus --slightly below "superior."

The findings on believability are important, especially if the children assess the show's believability in a comparable fashion. The foremost educational strategy employed in FREESTYLE is that of positive role modeling, a technique that depends on believability of the central characters for its effect. Here are some of the comments from teachers on this issue. First, on the positive side:

> My class has many Latin and Mexican Americans and their representation through Ramon [one of the leading characters in the series] was good.

> They do seem to relate to these characters a few years older than themselves. They surely find the situations believable, for after each show they're eager to share their own similar experiences. I can't recall a single comment to the effect that a situation seemed contrived.

However, compare these comments with the following:

> After awhile my class was able to predict the endings. The girl always saved the day. They were frankly getting tired of it.

> Some of the situations were very realistic -- others were a bit too good to be true.

A comment by a Milwaukee teacher shows the difficulty that an adult may have in determining how believable the shows are to children.

> Although the children related well to the kids on the telecast I had trouble feeling they were believable. They were "too good." I did hear this comment, but it may have been a reflection of my attitude. I wonder if 7th and 8th graders would be as accepting as my 5th and 6th graders were of such wholesome, ideal teen-agers?

FREESTYLE Guide. The "FREESTYLE Guide" is designed for teachers. The first half of the book is keyed to each of the 26 quarter-hour segments. Each segment has its own page with a "Highlights" section which summarizes the

Table 4.1

Teachers "Grade" the Products

The FREESTYLE Product	Average Grade	Percent Assigning Each Grade				
		A	B	C	D	E
I. The Television Shows						
How well do they convey messages in a way that...						
1 holds the att'n of children?	A−	76	19	5	·	·
2 is clear?	A−	68	27	5	·	·
3 is believable?	B+	48	42	10	·	·
4 stimulates class discussion?	B+	47	43	10	*	·
Average of four grades	A−					
II. The FREESTYLE Guide for Teachers						
1 Overall, what grade would you give the guide as an aid for teachers?	A−	65	27	8	·	·
III. The FREESTYLE Student Magazine						
1 Appeal of the art	B+	56	35	9	·	*
2 Clarity of language	B+	34	50	16	·	*
3 Intrinsic interest of stories and activities	B	29	53	16	2	*
Average of three grades	B+					

*=less than 1 percent.

plot, a "Preview Activity," a list of "Talk Topics" to focus post-viewing discussion, and a list of activities correlated to the show's theme. The second half of the book contains detailed descriptions of the activities themselves.

The guide is attractively packaged with a glossy, cover in color. Asked to grade the guide as a teaching aid, the teachers assigned an overall grade of A-minus. They were asked also to rate how much they used each section and how helpful they found it when they did. The parts associated with each show ("Highlights," "Preview Activity," and "Talk Topics") were used for most shows by at least three-quarters of the teachers. Eighty percent found each section "quite" or "very" helpful. As expected, the "More to Come" activities were used less often; only one-third of the teachers used these regularly. There was a wide range of reaction to how helpful these activities are, but still the average rating is "quite" helpful.

The highest ratings are exemplified by the comment of one Long Beach teacher: "Very superior teacher's guide. The guide is the best I've seen in many years -- easy to use because it gives us a _few good_ choices and doesn't overwhelm us with too much to consider. I tend to put aside guides that are three inches thick until I have time to deal with so much and end by not using them at all." But to illustrate how difficult it is to develop a guide which meets every teacher's needs, consider this comment by a teacher in the same school system. "The guide was in a format which I did not personally like. The preview activities could be improved on, and the questions in the Talk Topics should be more precise -- too wordy for busy teachers."

Student Magazine. While its exact function has not been clearly specified in official project statements, the student magazine potentially serves two functions. One is to enhance interest in the television series and the themes with which it deals, the other is to provide extension material for four of the project's goal areas beyond the treatment given in the TV shows. It was intended by the designers that the magazine perform a task which the TV shows could not adequately handle -- to help students apply some of the lessons to themselves (e.g., "which non-traditional activities are _you_ interested in?").

The teachers were asked to grade the magazine on three dimensions: art appeal, language clarity, and intrinsic interest for students (Table 4.1). Ratings for art appeal were highest, averaging a B-plus. On "clarity of language" and "intrinsic interest of stories and activities" they averaged B-plus and B respectively. The ratings are on the whole quite respectable, although lower than those for the TV shows. This may be partly due to ambiguity among the teachers regarding the magazine's role in achieving FREESTYLE's goals. When asked how important "using the magazine is for achieving the goals of FREESTYLE," the teachers were split. Forty-nine percent said "not at all" or "not very important," while 44 percent rated it "somewhat important." Only seven percent said it was "very important." A similar split occurred when the teachers were asked to rate how much they thought "the magazine contributed to student understanding" of the four goal areas it was trying to cover (Question D8). Teachers thought the magazine was the most effective in helping students understand "what people do in various adult occupations;" sixty-three percent thought it contributed "quite a bit" or "a great deal." The ratings declined steadily through the other three goal areas: student understanding of the range of activities and interests 9-12 year olds can pursue right now; how pervasive sex-role stereotypes are; and the relationship between childhood interests and adult occupations.

How should the magazine ratings be interpreted overall? It is the evaluators' assessment that the magazine fills a need for many, but not all, teachers. Its value probably depends on style of teaching and the degree to which the teacher judges that the students need to be motivated by a colorful comic book or can profit by the explorations contained in the magazine's content. When a group of teachers in Worcester were interviewed at the end of the project they were asked if they could do without the magazine if they were teaching FREESTYLE again. Their reply was, "We could do without it, but the students wouldn't let us!." The comment indicates that many teachers feel that the students are very enthused by it and for this reason alone it is a valuable adjunct. Because the magazine was provided at no cost to the teachers, it is unclear whether they would feel any differently if a portion of the classroom or school budget had to be allocated to their purchase.

     Teacher Training Package. The Office of the Los Angeles County Superintendent of Schools developed a teacher training package which introduces teachers to the basic concepts behind FREESTYLE and gives them practice in ways to use the shows effectively in different teaching situations. The program can last for either a half or full day. The half day version was used to train School Full teachers. While it was not formally evaluated by the evaluation team, it was noted that the teachers and administrators were quite enthused by the program. A number of comments made to the evaluator were to the effect that it represented one of the best inservice programs presented in the district. This was more true after some of the "bugs" were worked out subsequent to the first training session. Realistically, it is doubtful that a one-day teacher training program can change appreciably the way in which a teacher presents material. Most teachers have behind them many years of habit. If the training is consonant with how they would normally present the materials, then it may not make much difference. If the training presents new ways to instruct with television, change is not likely to be appreciable in classroom presentations occurring days or possibly even months after the training is over. However, if the training offers a good source of instructional ideas, it may be worthwhile. More importantly, if it engenders enthusiasm for sex-fair career education and for the FREESTYLE materials, then it may be a very important tool to get teachers to try out the series and continue using it once tried. Details of the training program may be found in Appendix G of this report. A detailed evaluation of the program by participating teachers can be obtained from the Los Angeles County Schools.

PART II. WHERE DOES FREESTYLE FIT IN THE SCHOOL CURRICULUM?

     No matter how much one may value the goals of FREESTYLE, teachers and administrators considering its use in school must look at the question: how can several hours per week spent on FREESTYLE be justified within the curricular priorities of the upper elementary school? To answer this question, one must begin with a number of other questions. What is the subject matter of FREESTYLE? How does this classification fit into the curricular priorities of the school system? What is the overlap between FREESTYLE and other subject matter areas which may be of higher priority?

The teachers were asked how well FREESTYLE fits into each of a list of standard curricular areas.[1] As expected, they see it fitting best into career education. For schools that do not recognize this category in the upper elementary curriculum, FREESTYLE is seen as fitting "pretty well" into social studies and language arts, and "a little bit" into physical education, science, and math. A Long Beach teacher noted, "Good extension into Language Arts particularly -- ideas pop up in other areas such as films and books where they see situations of bias or prejudice in job situations." The good fit with language arts had special salience in the minds of the designers. They envisioned that FREESTYLE themes could be "infused" into other curricular areas as their content. For example, if critical thinking is a skill to be taught there is no reason why the content of that skill practice cannot be an analysis of a FREESTYLE drama -- discussion of the motives and messages in the story. Similarly, as the "More to Come" activities illustrate, one can assign themes, research projects, and even computational activities (e.g., graph the percent of men and women in each of six occupations) that meet the needs of implicit skill goals and cover non-traditional sex-role behavior as well. In principle this is an exciting concept, suggesting that goals for instructional skills (reading, writing, arithmetic) might remain fixed while the content to which the skills are applied might shift according to the value priorities of the community. In practice this is not simple. Skills and content are to some degree wedded in teachers' minds. To illustrate, the teachers were asked the following. "For this experiment FREESTYLE may have fit perfectly into some parts of your curriculum. On the other hand you might have found yourself having to 'steal time' from some curricular area because it did not fit perfectly. How much did you have to 'steal time'?" In response, 36 percent indicated that they stole "some" and another 20 percent said "a lot." A Long Beach teacher described the problem this way:

> It made learning fun and motivated many creative writing and art projects for us. It was such a good springboard for class discussions

---

[1] See Question E3 in the Teacher Post Questionnaire in the Appendix H.

and we looked forward to each new show. If we were not held to keeping class profiles...on the 3 R's I would have spent even more time on "Freestyle" activities.

Clearly, future dissemination and full utilization of FREESTYLE and similar programs hinge to a large extent upon dealing successfully with this issue.

FREESTYLE is strongly endorsed as an addition to the curriculum in grades five, six, seven and above (Question E5). The present evaluation was conducted in grades four through six, based on the recommendations of the product designers. There is clearly some support for using FREESTYLE in junior high school as well. The assistant superintendent for curriculum in one of the test cities is recommending the series for grades seven through nine as well as upper elementary. Regarding support for use of FREESTYLE in grade four there arose some reservation and difference of opinion. Examinination of the written comments of teachers suggests that there is wide variation in the maturity of fourth graders, and that adoption at this grade level should be more carefully weighed than at higher grades.

FREESTYLE can be classified as a career education/social studies curriculum. As such, the question can be put, how well does it fit with the curricular priorities of most school districts? When the teachers who had spent over two hours a week on the series were asked this question (Question E6), seventy-two percent felt the curricular priorities permitted spending the time needed for FREESTYLE or more. Only three teachers indicated that they could not include FREESTYLE in the curriculum under normal conditions, i.e., if they were not participating in the evaluation.

Due to the fact that the goals of FREESTYLE -- encouraging the acceptance of non-traditional behaviors in boys and girls, men and women -- might be seen by some as controversial, teachers were asked how supportive they felt certain groups of people were of the goals of FREESTYLE. The five groups to be considered were: other teachers in the building, the principal, central administration, the school board, and parents of school-aged children. With some variation, teachers reported that each of these groups would be "moderately" to "very" supportive. Nowhere did we find evidence -- including in a subsequent set of group interviews with teachers -- that any groups in our test cities would be opposed to the FREESTYLE messages.[2]

PART III. HOW GOOD ARE FREESTYLE'S INNOVATIONS IN INSTRUCTIONAL DESIGN?

Configuring the TV Shows

Quarter vs. half hours. FREESTYLE is available in both half-hour versions for home use and quarter-hours for school use. The decision to produce the series in two formats was a central issue in the development of the series. To produce half-hour dramas that reached a climactic breaking point half-way through was no small feat for writers and producers. The school people among the series' designers argued that teachers want quarter-hour shows, because with half-hour shows there is no opportunity for classroom discussion of the content. All the teachers in the evaluation used the quarter-hour version, but they were nevertheless asked for their preference. About two-thirds favored the quarter hours, with the remaining third in favor of half-hours. Thus a clear majority agreed with the production decision, and the numbers might be higher if the technological limitations could be overcome. A Milwaukee teacher commented, "The two part idea was superb and it really held the students attention. (Also the teacher's too)!"

Several teachers who expressed a preference for a half-hour format were contacted; they explained their decision in one of two ways. For some it was a matter of reducing the amount of time devoted to FREESTYLE themes. For others the time factor was complicated by TV viewing conditions. Typically, they had to view in a location other than their classroom. This meant time for relocating and, consequently, some loss of impact when the viewing and discussion were interrupted by the room-to-room shuffle. One Worcester

---

[2] In our attempt to get test sites we tried very hard to have a representative from Southeast or South Central United States -- locations which stereotypically might be expected to be more resistant to messages of changing roles for women. One Texas city declined to participate largely because the messages were not acceptable in that community. This is suggestive that some areas of the country might not be receptive to the FREESTYLE messages.

teacher who was adamant about her preference for a half-hour show once a week explained that in order to view the show her class had to walk through three buildings to get to a cafeteria. Here they viewed the show with several other classes on a single monitor. (This situation was a rare exception in this study, but nonetheless one that is faced by many teachers in districts that do not have extensive ITV capabilities.) The teacher was asked how she might vote if she had a videotape playback unit in her own classroom and access to cassettes of the shows; given this alternative she chose quarter-hours twice a week. Apparently, the decision to make both versions available was a wise one. Indeed, in the next chapter it will be noted that Fall 1979 broadcast plans for Worcester schools call for transmission of only the half-hour version; other sites will broadcast quarter hours for school use.

Frequency of broadcast. The teachers voted on both the issue of show length and broadcast frequency. Ninety-one percent of the teachers desired weekly broadcasts. This suggests that teachers see weekly treatment of the subject as necessary for continuity of theme development.

Length of the series. For school use, FREESTYLE consists of 26 quarter-hours designed to be used twice a week over a 13-week period. For open air broadcasting in the fall semester this amounts to one term of school time, because the feed from PBS does not begin until October and two vacation periods break up the continuity of the school term. A typical fall term broadcast period for the series would begin the first week of October and end around the middle of January. The teachers were asked, "Ignoring the number of shows currently available, over what span of time would you like to use FREESTYLE in your curriculum (Question B5)?" About half the teachers would choose the same amount of time, and only nine percent wanted it to be shorter. Of real interest is the fact that 45 percent wanted FREESTYLE to last longer. Thirty-six percent voted for a full school year. A Long Beach teacher commented:

> They really looked forward to a new situation each week -- they were really disappointed that there were only 13 episodes. They even requested to see the series again the second semester.

Additional shows. Matching the interest in using FREESTYLE for a longer portion of the school year is the preference by 39 percent of the teachers to have more TV shows available (Question B3). Their preference for the topics of the additional shows was ascertained by a question which required them first to consider FREESTYLE's three topic areas and then vote which one(s) they would like to see receive more emphasis (Question B4). Their response indicates that they felt satisfied with the present emphasis regarding the themes of acceptance of adults in non-traditional job and family roles. They would like slightly more emphasis upon encouragment of boys and girls to explore activities which would be non-traditional for their sex. The major area they would most like to see expanded is the development of "behavioral skills" such as leadership, independence, assertiveness, helping skills, cooperation, and reasonable risk-taking. Forty-three percent of the teachers would like to see more emphasis in this area. This preference is understandable considering that most topics in the behavioral skills category took up only one, or at most two, episodes. Yet each behavioral skill is a complex behavior which must be depicted not only in the terms of its stereotype (e.g., girls stereotypically are less assertive than boys), but also in terms of the components for its proper expression. This content is difficult to cover adequately in two quarter-hour shows and associated class discussion. These skills also require some practice time if children are to master them. A Long Beach teacher summed it up this way:

> The chidren's favorite programs -- and those that sparked the most interesting discussions -- were those focussed on 'behavioral skills.' Discussions about non-traditional activities and stereotyping were interesting at first, but now this topic has become repetitive and our most recent discussions have lagged.

Interestingly, measures of the impact of FREESTYLE on children show that the series did not effect much change in the area of behavioral skills (see Chapter Seven).

Alternative Delivery of Shows

In the National Institue of Education's "request for proposals" which authorized the creation of FREESTYLE it was argued that both a school and home version of the show was needed. The rationale was that, while the school might provide the most systematic instruction, the values being challenged in the series were deeply rooted in the family. It was important therefore to broadcast a show which parents could watch with their children as well as one which students could view and discuss with their teachers.

At the time that the evaluation was being designed it became apparent that the home broadcast was an attractive design feature. Districts that were approached to be part of the evaluation made it quite clear that the upper elementary curriculum was quite full and that FREESTYLE's biggest problem would be gaining access to it. Thus a series which might be endorsed by the school but which might also be delivered to students through the home presented an intriguing variation to most curriculum development projects.

Several issues stand in the way of taking advantage of this option. If we assume that teacher-mediated in-class viewing is the most potent form of delivering the message, will there be a sufficiently large impact on students viewing it on their own? This question is addressed later in this report. A second issue has to do with delivery: would teachers endorse any other method of delivery and still consider FREESTYLE to be part of their curriculum? Teachers in the evaluation were presented with five options and asked how willing they would be to use FREESTYLE in each of those ways (Questions F2-F6 of Teacher Post Questionnaire in the Appendix). One option was the equivalent of the School Full treatment of the present evaluation, requiring two or more hours of class time per week. At the other extreme was an option to have the viewing done entirely at home, with parents encouraged by the school to watch and discuss the shows with their children: this is the equivalent of the Home Full treatment. Intermediate options included the equivalent of School View-Only, and one in which the teacher conducts a lesson in school but the children do their viewing at home. Support for these options was solicited from all teachers in the evaluation whose children used FREESTYLE in any form. The single option receiving clearcut endorsement from all teachers is School Full. The lack of interest in other options is not especially surprising since the School Full option is the only one which models how teachers actually use TV in the classroom (or think it should be used). It follows the norm for elementary teaching, keeping the teacher in the central role delivering and mediating the messages of the series. The other four options have a modal teacher response at the "maybe" point on the scale of willingness.

Most significantly, perhaps, the other options represent true innovations in instructional design. An administrator in Covina (a home viewing test site) noted that the previous year there had been an outstanding dramatic play on the local PBS station. A month before the broadcast the school created the expectation that high school children and their parents would be expected to view the show at home. Teachers were given discussion guides and time was set aside to discuss how the show might fit into class time. The experiment was well received by parents, students, and teachers alike. The administrator's point was that this type of implementation plan does not currently exist in FREESTYLE.

In one of the test sites, the quality of the equipment, and experience of teachers with ITV was considerably lower than foreseen. In two schools TVs were scarce. While this was atypical of the rest of the test sites, it was probably quite typical of the majority of school districts. A comment from one teacher might be remembered when the time comes to think about the appropriateness of delivering FREESTYLE's messages entirely through classroom television.

> The only negative comment I can make on the Freestyle Program is the poor viewing conditions. All the viewing for my school took place in my classroom. Teachers tried to be as 'cooperative' as possible. However, reception and sound on TV was very poor many times. When the audience was packed, some children could not see the small screen. They were interested in the viewing, but these poor viewing conditions turned them 'off'.

Summary

In the eyes of teachers, then, FREESTYLE is an exciting new curricular product that fits fairly well into several different areas of the grade 4-6 curriculum. While its content is somewhat different from the typical fare taught in those grades, there seems to be an emerging demand -- at least in the test cities -- for materials that develop career awareness in a way that counters existing sex-role stereotypes. Indeed, there is a demand from a large proportion of the teachers polled to have more FREESTYLE materials than currently exist.

Chapter Five

STATION CARRIAGE AND MARKET RATINGS OF FREESTYLE

One measure of the success of FREESTYLE is the response of its many gatekeepers. This includes carriage by the Public Broadcasting Service (PBS), carriage by each of the 265 stations affiliated with PBS, and the response of home and school viewers to its availability. This chapter details the carriage and viewing data available in Spring of 1979 and projects the possible response for the fall of 1979.

FREESTYLE had widespread use by PBS stations, making the shows available to approximately three-fourths of American households. The series was carried by 185 stations when it began in October, increasing in November to 230 or 86.5 percent of the 265 PBS stations. Thus the majority of stations chose to carry the series -- and most of them aired each episode two or three times.

As the number of stations carrying the series increased so did the Nielsen ratings, from 1.1 in October to 2.2 in November. These ratings indicate the percent of TV homes that tune into the first six minutes of any episode. Each rating point represents 745,000 homes, making a November audience of about 1,640,000 homes.

Overall, FREESTYLE maintained something above a 2.0 rating which is high for a PBS series and especially high for a series aired for the first time. Among children's PBS programs, FREESTYLE compared favorably, falling at the midpoint in the ratings. The December 1978 survey done by the research department of PBS indicates the following ratings for other children's programs: Sesame Street, 13.2; Electric Company, 7.6; Zoom, 3.4; Feeling Free (new series in Spring, 1978), 0.9; Infinity Factory, 0.6; and Villa Allegre, (did not receive a large enough audience to measure). It is important to bear in mind that, in these cases, programs that received the higher ratings were carried by a larger number of stations and/or were telecast more times per week each week than those programs with lower ratings.

Aimed at 4th to 6th grade children, 5.5 percent of homes with children aged 6 to 11 watched the FREESTYLE series. The highest viewing rate (9.3) was in homes with children less than six years old -- understandable since many stations scheduled FREESTYLE in the "Kiddie Block." Most of the programs in this block are geared to the younger age group, and FREESTYLE could have been watched by the overflow of children who had already tuned in the PBS channel. Another explanation is that many older children who watched were joined by younger brothers and sisters, in which case these homes would be counted in both lower and higher age groups.

The FREESTYLE audience appears to be somewhat atypical when compared to the viewing audience for most children's programs on PBS. Household heads of the typical viewing families have 1-4 years of college. In occupation and income they are distributed about equally between semi-skilled jobs with incomes in the $10,000-$15,000 range and professional jobs with higher than average incomes. This makes for a relatively flat audience profile for occupation and income, beginning at the medium levels of job status and income. Audience profiles do vary for some of the more cultural offerings on PBS, with these offerings drawing more heavily from the upper level of job status and income. This pattern did hold true in homes of FREESTYLE viewers. FREESTYLE did attract families within the typical education range, but it also attracted a larger than average number of families with skilled and semi-skilled jobs within the $10-$15,000 income range. Thus drawing from the low end of the occupation and income scale. FREESTYLE's appeal to non-white families is unclear from the available data. Non-White viewers comprise only about 10 percent of the total public TV audience, and the percentage viewing a single series is very low. In the case of FREEESTYLE this figure was, in fact, too low to measure. With a total audience the size of FREESTYLE there is a large margin of error in the estimates for demographic subgroups. The only thing that is clear is that FREESTYLE did not draw a disproportionately large number of non-White viewers.

Plans for Future Use of FREESTYLE

Station carriage during a premiere session is not a strong test of station response. Accordingly, the stations in the FREESTYLE test sites were asked in June of 1979 what their plans were for the Fall of 1979. Similarly, the school districts in the test sites were asked about their plans for use of FREESTYLE in the upper elementary curriculum beginning in the Fall of 1979.

FREESTYLE will be aired again in the Fall of 1979 over all the PBS stations that cooperated with the study. In many cases it was already aired a second time in Spring of 1979, and thus the Fall broadcast will represent a third airing. The reasons given by every station for carrying the program again were the strong and positive response from schools, the wish to accommodate the school districts' needs, and the program departments' own favorable impressions of the show.

Frequency of broadcast depends largely on the facilities for replay within the local school systems. In cases where the school system can tape the programs and use them at their own convenience the programs need be broadcast on the local public broadcasting station only once.

Time slots for the programs vary from site to site and some stations will broadcast at both home and school times while others will broadcast at only one of these times. Both the 1/4-hour and the 1/2-hour versions are being considered for school time use. Again, these decisions are based largely on the wishes and needs of the schools being served. They also depend on other pre-existing schedule commitments of the stations.

Following are the detailed projections of the stations involved in the study:

KCPT in Kansas City will carry the 1/4-hour version -- a decision arrived at in a meeting with the stations's Elementary Curriculum Committee. They will not have multiple broadcasts because the schools in their service area have recording equipment and can replay the programs to suit themselves. KCPT is not able to conduct a teachers in-service workshop on the use of individual programs, but the station does conduct more general workshops which would include ways to use the FREESTYLE programs. They are considering doing some teacher training on the air.

MET, the Massachusetts Educational Television Network, is connected with WGBH, the public broadcasting station that serves the Worcester site. It aired the 1/2-hour version for the second time in the Spring of 1979. Broadcast time was every Friday at 10:00 a.m. While afternoon is the intended time for such broadcasts, previous scheduling interfered. In any case, Friday was considered a good day. MET staff feels the programs are of exceptional quality and is planning to carry the 1/2-hour version again in the Fall of 1979 and also the following semester -- in twice weekly broadcasts. The 1/2-hour version is their preference for an on-air format.

One of MET's strong functions is teacher training. Training in the use of FREESTYLE is considered a "staple" in their workshops as they feel this series can be used at many levels and in many subjects. MET will produce its own teacher guide if they are unable to get anything through other channels, supplying it free to districts.

KCET in Los Angeles, the producer of the series, broadcast both the 1/2-hour and the 1/4-hour versions of the series for the second time in Spring of 1979 following completion of the first run. The 1/2-hour version was broadcast on Friday evenings and twice over the weekends. Each segment of the 1/4-hour versions was broadcast twice a week during school time, first in the morning (10:00 a.m.) and then repeated in the afternoon (1:00 p.m.) of the following day. KCET will be broadcasting both versions of the series again next fall following a very similar schedule and they hope to air it the following January as well. Teacher training is well-covered by the L.A. County Schools so KCET would not be directly involved in this.

WMVS-TV in Milwaukee has not yet slotted a time for the series, but is planning to carry the 1/2-hour version, probably airing it once a week in the early evening over the weekend. Positive response to the series in this district was encouragement to air the programs. The school's own system will replay tapes, making it unnecessary for the public broadcasting station to carry the program during school time. Teacher training sessions would be conducted at the ITV level as well.

WUCM in Saginaw carried the program again last spring because of interest generated by the project in the fall. Next fall they will probably carry both the home and school versions with multiple broadcasts since Saginaw does not have facilities for taping and replay. The school broadcasts would follow a morning/afternoon pattern with back-to-back broadcasts of the introductory segment aired on Wednesday and the concluding segment on Thursday. For home broadcasts the first choice for a time slot (7:00 on a weekday evening) is not available because of other programming, so FREESTYLE will probably be aired over the weekend. WUCM is not equipped to do teacher training, but would supply teacher guides on request if they received them from KCET. Encouragement to use the programs would be the responsibility of the school system.

These data on station carriage are suggestive of great success in producing a popular series, but future delivery of the series on PBS are limited by contract arrangements. PBS is to feed the series to stations only four times in three years. Stations can in turn broadcast the series only four times. The third feed for PBS will be used in the Fall of 1979, and for many stations this will also be their third broadcast. FREESTYLE could be unavailable to the public in a very short time -- well prior to many viewers even discovering its existence.

What about use of FREESTYLE in school settings? The FREESTYLE series may be taped and held for in-school use at any time until October 1, 1983. This means schools can make FREESTYLE available for classroom use at more frequent and convenient times than is allowed for by most PBS schedules. In the districts that participated in the study this is done via a closed circuit system which presents the programs in all schools simultaneously or simply by lending tapes to teachers to play back on video equipment in their schools. The process of getting a series such as FREESTYLE incorporated into the school network involves the dedication of at least one administrator. In the case of FREESTYLE, this might be someone from career education, the curriculum division, the audio-visual department or a combination of these people working together. They obtain the endorsement of other staff, arrange to make use of whatever in-school audio-visual facilities are available, encourage teacher use and communicate with the local public TV station. Plans for using FREESTYLE in Fall 1979 vary from site to site and are described below.

In Worcester Schools, the decision to schedule FREESTYLE for the fall of 1979 was made by the Instructional Resource Center staff who saw FREESTYLE as a good program with good response. Beginning in the Fall of 1979, the center is planning a program for their school cable system which includes FREESTYLE. The center will work with schools to arrange the best times for delivery of the shows, and will promote the series via the schedule they put out (as will the state-wide ITV network). They plan to help with distribution of teacher guides if they are available.

In North Kansas City Schools, decisions regarding FREESTYLE were arrived at through meetings with the public TV station and school district curriculum advisors. The schools requested that KCPT-TV air the 1/4-hour version of the program. These programs in turn will be recorded by the school districts' library facilities and added to their tapes under career education and sexism classification. Teachers can then order individual programs from the library to play in their classroom, or watch the KCPT broadcast if the time is convenient. Teachers were already doing this during the Spring semester.

In Milwaukee Schools, because of teacher demand, the Instructional Resources Center has already played the FREESTYLE series a second time (Spring, 1979) over its closed circuit (ITFS) system. They will repeat the series in the fall. For the research project one of their four channels carried continual broadcasts of FREESTYLE twice a week during the study. This allowed for eight plays a week of each segment. The 1/4-hour version was used, again because of teacher preference. The same schedule was followed in the Spring and will be followed in the Fall. Before the 1979 Fall term begins, the Instructional Resources Center will hold a short inservice for teachers to preview the entire schedule of shows to be aired. This will include FREESTYLE. They are recommending FREESTYLE for use at the 5th grade level, and another career education program at the 6th grade level.

In the Los Angeles area the Regional Educational Television Advisory Council (RETAC) contracts with nearby county school districts to present educational programs and provide teacher training. Staff from this organization developed and conducted the teacher training workshops held at the beginning of the field study. (The complete workshop, or just the print and audio-visual materials, are available to districts anywhere in the U.S. for a fee from L. A. County Schools.) They have continued to conduct these workshops and promote the program and will do so as long as their budget allows. Their broadcast schedule for FREESTYLE and the KCET-TV schedule are one and the same.

In addition to the KCET/RETAC schedule, local school districts can record and replay FREESTYLE on their closed circuit systems. Because reactions to the programs have been so good the TV and Film Services in the Torrance School districts have chosen to relay the KCET/RETAC broadcasts in the Fall. In addition, they have two channels on which they can record/replay the programs upon teacher request. They can play up to ten programs a week this way. As part of their utilization effort they will encourage the programs to be used for career education purposes. Already they have held a workshop that included the FREESTYLE programs. They expect to use the 1/4-hour version which most teachers prefer.

Similarly, the career education consultant and the assistant superintendent of the elementary division in Long Beach Schools are requesting that FREESTYLE be shown over their closed circuit system in the Fall.

In Covina Schools, use of the programs will depend on the individual schools and teachers. Those interested will be able to watch the KCET/RETAC broadcasts. Some schools also have the ability to record the programs and replay them later if teachers request it.

In Ann Arbor Schools, FREESTYLE will be made available at the recommendation of the career education advisor who, during a meeting with the board, requested approval of the series as supplemental material. As a result of this, all elementary schools will be able to receive FREESTYLE via cable next fall. The school district's Instructional Materials Center will provide tapes. There will be multiple airings of the 1/4-hour segments and schools without cable hook-up will be able to borrow tapes from the Instructional Materials Center to play on their own equipment. Teacher training will take place under the direction of the career guidance advisor who will supply teacher guides to those using the programs.

Saginaw Schools will rely largely on the public TV broadcasts, although tapes are also available for playback in schools.

In sum, FREESTYLE received wide coverage, a wide audience, and wide approval during its first season. TV station personnel in the research sites were encouraged by the response of schools and, in turn, school district administrators were encouraged by teacher response. In both cases they were impressed with the overall quality of the TV series. For these reasons, FREESTYLE will be seen on both local public TV stations and over school system equipment during the Fall 1979 semester in these sites. Beyond this, its future is less certain unless additional action is taken to renegotiate broadcast rights.

Incorporating FREESTYLE into school district plans has required the efforts of at least one interested school administrator who promoted the series and acted as liaison between different administrative departments and the local public TV station. In some cases the TV station had a department for the utilization of educational TV in schools. Where this was so, these people also promoted the series in schools and encouraged its use. Naturally, some districts had more resources available to them than others (especially with regard to audio/visual equipment). FREESTYLE consequently will be more easily available to teachers in those sites, and will receive more support in terms of workshops, and so on. However, in all sites a workable arrangement has been made so that all interested teachers can use the series.

Chapter Six

MEASUREMENT OF FREESTYLE OUTCOMES

The goal of the FREESTYLE project, according to the funder's original statement of aim, was to make sex and ethnicity less powerful predictors of the pre-occupational interests and activities of fourth to sixth graders. This general goal was developed by the curriculum planning team into an extensive list of subgoals and outcome objectives. Recall that these included affective, cognitive and some behavioral outcome objectives within the content domains of pre-occupational activities, behavioral skills and adult work and family roles (Chapter Two). The executive producer and his advisors selected a subset of objectives within each of the subgoals and formulated them into the messages which appeared in the shows and supporting materials. It is from these messages and the objectives and subgoals upon which they are based that the outcomes or dependent variables used in the evaluation of FREESTYLE are derived. In addition, the goal of having impact upon fourth to sixth graders of both sexes and all races suggests that age, sex and race as well as participation in the intervention itself must all be included as independent variables in the analysis of FREESTYLE. The techniques for measuring these variables are discussed in this chapter.

The Effects of FREESTYLE: The Dependent Variables

The curriculum plan for the project included cognitive and affective as well as a few behavioral outcome objectives. It was the affective outcomes which contributed most to the messages in the FREESTYLE materials however. These messages (Chapter Two and Appendix C) were, for the most part, directed toward expanding children's interest in nontraditional pursuits and toward imparting the attitude that these pursuits are appropriate. The messages contained little new information about the pursuits themselves beyond the attractive images of children or adults competently engaging in them. For example, the episode designed to interest girls in mechanical activities includes montages of an attractive girl engaged in auto repair work who eventually is rewarded for her efforts. The show is definitely not a lesson in auto mechanics or in the specifics of mechanical hobbies. Rather, they are clearly oriented toward affective outcomes -- changed attitudes and expanded interests. The dependent variables developed for the evaluation reflect this orientation.

While affective outcomes play the major role in the evaluation of FREESTYLE, cognitive outcomes of a particular sort also have a part. A good deal of theory and research on attitudes focuses on the relationship between affect and cognition. One of the best known theorists in this area is Martin Fishbein (Fishbein and Ajzen, 1975) who holds that attitudes rest on clusters of cognitions which he labels beliefs. Fishbein defines a belief as a judgment about the probability of a linkage between an object and some other object or attribute. For example, someone may judge it to be highly probable that a female auto mechanic (object) will do inferior quality work (attribute). This cognition is a single, specific belief about auto repair work done by females.

Fishbein goes on to define an attitude as the rating of an object on some evaluative dimension such as good-bad or right-wrong. A central tenet of Fishbein's theory is that an attitude toward an object can be predicted from beliefs about that object. To change an attitude the underlying beliefs must first be changed. In the example of female auto mechanics, it is reasonable to expect that anyone who holds the particular belief is also likely to hold a negative attitude toward female mechanics and that for the attitude to change the belief must first change. Fishbein has developed this basic idea into his "value expectancy theory" which generates quantitative predictions about attitudes based on information about beliefs. The theory also relates attitudes to behavioral intent and behavior itself.

While Fishbein's work is notable for the clarity of his definitions of belief and attitude and his specification of the linkage between them, it is not the only work on the cognitive-affective relationship. Social psychologists (e.g. McGuire, 1972; Triandis, 1971) as well as students of diffusion of innovations (e.g., Rogers and Shoemaker, 1971) and marketing (e.g., Ray, 1973; Rothschild and Ray, 1974) have all contributed theory and research on this topic. Most of the researchers along with Fishbein have focused on a sequence in which learning is followed by attitude change which, in turn, is followed by behavioral change. This, however, is not the only conceivable sequence.

Ray and his associates label the well studied cognitive-affective-conative sequence the "learning hierarchy." They argue that this classic hierarchy adequately describes the sequence necessary to change firmly held attitudes and the behavior mediated by such attitudes, but it is not the only hierarchy. Ray provides evidence that other hierarchies are found in other contexts when behavior is not mediated by a firmly held attitude. For example, in some cases changing a loosely held attitude can lead to changed beliefs which in turn leads to changed behavior. While it is not clear which hierarchy is most applicable in the case of FREESTYLE, Ray's theory and research displays the intimate linkage between cognition and affect. Any evaluation of the effectiveness of an attempt to change attitudes and expand interests cannot afford to ignore the beliefs related to these attitudes and interests.

Interest in beliefs is reinforced by extensive research on the effects of the mass media indicating that the media are not especially successful in changing attitudes but are considerably successful in disseminating information or beliefs about what is true of the world (e.g., Clarke and Kline, 1974; McClure and Patterson, 1974). Indeed Clarke and Kline note a major shift in interest among communication researchers from attitude change to learning. In the case of FREESTYLE, beliefs about what is true of boys and girls may be formed or changed even when attitudes about what is appropriate for them are not. For example, as a result of FREESTYLE's many images of children and adults excelling in nontraditional pursuits the audience may come to hold new beliefs about the competencies of the opposite sex.

The concept of belief emerges as important for two reasons. First, new and changed beliefs are a potential effect of FREESTYLE worthy of study in their own right. Second, beliefs are likely to be centrally involved in the attitude change and interest expansion sought by FREESTYLE. Changing boys' attitudes towards girls' participation in athletics may first require a change in their beliefs about girls' athletic prowess. Similarly, to interest girls in athletics may first require a more positive attitude toward girls participation which may, in turn, require the belief that girls can and do participate successfully in sports. Following Ray, the hierarchies posited here are belief-attitude and belief-attitude-interest.

Based on these arguments, beliefs join attitudes and interests to produce three categories of dependent variables. These three categories emerge from the messages and objectives of FREESTYLE as well as from relevant theory. At the same time three content categories also emerge from the messages and objectives of FREESTYLE. These are the three major content themes reviewed in Chapter Two: childhood activities, behavioral skills, and adult work and family roles. Within each of these three content themes the developers of FREESTYLE sought attitude change, interest expansion or both. In addition, as argued above, changed beliefs are likely to be associated with changed attitudes and expanded interests. The three content themes are thus orthogonal to the three categories of dependent variables and together they yield the typology of FREESTYLE outcomes shown in Figure 6.1.

The figure provides an overview of the approach to measuring the effect of FREESTYLE on children's sex-role orientations. For each type of outcome shown in the matrix, indices were developed as dictated by the specific objectives and messages as well as several measurement principles reviewed below. These indices are located in the appropriate cells of the figure. Information on the specific questionnaire items which comprise the indices is contained in the Glossary.

Five principles or rules were followed in generating the measures listed in Figure 6.1. The first was that the measures must be composed of closed-ended (i.e. multiple choice) rather than open-ended items. This rule was necessitated by the plan to have teachers administer the questionnaire to their class as a group. Recording of individual answers to open-ended

Figure 6.1
Typology of Dependent Measures

	Beliefs About	Attitudes Toward	Interest In
Childhood Pre-occup. Activities	Boys in helping roles Girls in athletics Girls doing mechanics ...	Boys in helping roles Girls in athletics Girls doing mechanics ...	helping athletics mechanics
Childhood Behavioral Skills	Girls as leaders Girls being independent Girls being assertive Girls taking risks	Girls as leaders Girls being independent Girls being assertive Girls taking risks	... ...
Adult Work and Family Roles	Extent "male" jobs are done only by men	More women in "male" jobs	"male" jobs
	Extent "female" jobs are done only by women	More men in "female" jobs	"female" jobs
	Extent "male" household tasks are done by husbands	Wives doing more male household tasks	...
	Extent "female" household tasks are done by wives	Husbands doing more female household tasks	...

Note: "..." indicates the concept was not measured.

questions would not be possible. This plan was, in turn, mandated by the economics of the large scale, multiple-site research design.

Based on these considerations a questionnaire booklet containing approximately 250 machine-readable, multiple-choice items was prepared. The questionnaire was administered by teachers both before they began the use of the FREESTYLE materials (pre-test) and after they completed the materials (post-test). The questionnaire was administered in four sittings which lasted from 20 to 40 minutes each. The teacher read each item to the class in an effort to reduce the impact of reading level on responses.

The second principle which guided development of the items was that a few, simple question formats must be used throughout the booklet. Most items followed one of a few basic prototypes. To measure attitudes the evaluative dimension used throughout was "very good idea" to "very bad idea." For example, two of the items measuring attitude toward girls involvement in mechanical activities are given in part A of Figure 6.2.

For interests, the dimensions used were "like it a lot" to "don't like it at all" (for pre-occupational activities) and "definitely consider" to "definitely NOT consider" (for adult occupations). In Part B of Figure 6.2, for example, are two items from the area of interest in pre-occupational activities. In part C are two items from the area of interest in adult occupations.

The measurement of beliefs required that a few beliefs be chosen for measurement from the enormous number of beliefs which could conceivably be associated with the attitudes and interests. Two sorts of beliefs which seemed to be particularly susceptible to change by the FREESTYLE materials were chosen. One was the proportion of children and adults who engage in various pursuits or the frequency with which they engage in them (see part D of Figure 6.2); the other was the proportion of children and adults in these pursuits who are competent at the pursuit (see part E of Figure 6.2).

The third principle for developing the measures was that whenever possible multiple items would be used to operationalize concepts. For example the measurement of interest in mechanical activities included five items: (1)

FIGURE 6.2

Illustrative Items from "My Interests and Activities" Questionnaire

A. Attitudes toward girls involvement in mechanical activities

How do you feel about GIRLS your age doing these things if they want to:

	Very good idea	Good idea	Bad idea	Very bad idea
fixing a broken bike............................	○	○	○	○
working with an adult on a car motor............	○	○	○	○
etc.				

B. Interest in pre-occupational activities

How much would you like to do each of these things if you had the chance?

	Like it a lot	Like it pretty much	Like it a little	Don't like it at all	Don't know what that is
fix a broken bike.......................	○	○	○	○	○
work with an adult on a car motor........	○	○	○	○	○
etc.					

C. Interest in adult occupations

It will be a long time before you choose an adult job. However, you probably know now that there are some jobs you would not consider doing and others that you would consider doing. What do you think about each of these jobs for yourself?

	Definitely consider	Probably consider	Probably NOT consider	Definitely NOT consider	I don't know what that job is
car mechanic............................	○	○	○	○	○
truck driver............................	○	○	○	○	○
etc.					

D. Beliefs about proportion of adults engaged in jobs

What do you think is true today? How many of the people who do each of these jobs are men and how many are women?

	Almost all are MEN	More than half are MEN	About half are men, half are women	More than half are WOMEN	Almost all are WOMEN
car mechanic............................	○	○	○	○	○
truck driver............................	○	○	○	○	○
etc.					

E. Beliefs about proportion of children who are good at doing things

How many GIRLS are good at:

	All	Most	Some	A few	None
fixing a broken bike.....................	○	○	○	○	○
fixing a car motor......................	○	○	○	○	○
etc.					

fix a broken bike, (2) build a model kit, (3) build a radio or something else that runs on electricity, (4) fix a leaky faucet and (5) work with an adult on a car motor. Multiple-item indices, of course, help reduce measurement error and thus increase reliability as compared to single-item measures. The "recipes" for combining the items into indices are found in the Glossary.

The fourth principle was that each question must have a very concrete referent. For example, the index of interest in mechanical activities focuses on such concrete activities as "fixing bikes" rather than "repairing things." The indices are built up from a collection of concrete examples, because it is believed that children think about their interests and attitudes at this very concrete level of abstraction.

The fifth principle was to include in the set of items some examples which were explicitly illustrated in FREESTYLE TV shows and others which were not. The index for interest in mechanical activities, for example, includes two items explicitly covered in the materials (viz., fix a leaky faucet and work with an adult on a car motor). The three other items were not explicitly covered. This procedure produced indices which could be subdivided to allow analyses either of the overall index or of the FREESTYLE subset.

The Independent Variables

As indicated in the introduction to this chapter, FREESTYLE's goal of having an impact upon fourth through sixth graders of both sexes and all races virtually dictated what the major independent variables would be. The assessment procedures for measuring these independent variables were quite straightforward, in contrast to the complex measurement procedures for the dependent variables described in the previous section. A Student Characteristics form was completed by teachers to provide the necessary demographic information on all students in each classroom. Instructions on proper completion of the form was provided in teacher training sessions held in each site.

The cover sheet of the Student Characteristics form contained information identifying the teacher, school building, and district by name. The form itself (a) listed the students in the teacher's classroom, (b) identified the classroom and each student by a unique identification number which matched the I.D. number on the student questionnaire, and (c) asked the teacher to complete, separately for each student, the sex, grade level, and racial/ethnic identification. Grade level was required for each student to accommodate the occasional multi-grade classrooms which were included in the study. The racial/ethnic identification codes used were consonant with those required by Federal guidelines; namely, White, Black, Hispanic, Asian or Pacific Islander, American Indian or Alaskan Native. A further division (of interest to the project) was made of the Hispanic group into Hispanic/Mexican American and Hispanic/other (Puerto Rican, Cuban, etc.). Teachers were told to consult student records as needed to complete this form accurately, but rarely was such consultation needed in actual practice.

Thus, the major independent variables of interest to the study -- student grade level, sex, and racial/ethnic identity -- were reliably assessed with minimal burden on the teacher via completion of the Student Characteristics form. At the same time, a careful and vitally important check on the accuracy of the student identification number was accomplished.

Chapter Seven

THE IMPACT OF VIEWING PLUS DISCUSSION

From the foregoing chapters it is clear that the FREESTYLE shows are a very attractive package, endorsed by teachers and students alike. Aside from audience satisfaction what impact does FREESTYLE have on its target audience? Are children changed as a result of experiencing the series? Do boys and girls view the world in less stereotyped terms after a FREESTYLE innoculation? This, after all, is what the TV Career Awareness Project is all about. To address this question the large number of outcome measures described in Chapter Six were analyzed, comparing changes in those who were exposed to FREESTYLE with those in the control group who saw none of the FREESTYLE materials. This chapter focuses on the children in School Full classrooms who experienced both viewing and extensive supplementary activity. Those who were in School View-Only classrooms are the subject of the next chapter.

Before we report the results, some discussion is needed of the analytic strategy and statistical conventions that were employed to answer the questions of effectiveness. The approach is summarized in the next paragraph and then explained in detail in the next section of this chapter -- "Analysis Strategy." The reader who does not want a detailed explication of this strategy may wish to skip the next section and resume at Part I of this chapter where the Goals of FREESTYLE are evaluated in a stepwise manner.

Succintly stated, the analyses were done separately within each site, using all of the control group children plus those experimental children in classrooms which implemented the FREESTYLE package extensively. The analysis strategy was to predict separately to three measures of every outcome -- the pre, post, and change score -- from the combined predictor set of treatment, sex, race and grade. The statistical technique is a form of multiple linear regression called Multiple Classification Analysis. The size of between-group differences or of pre-post shifts on any measure is judged with respect to the measure's standard deviation, with the threshold of a noteworthy difference being .20 standard deviation and a very large difference being .60. It was required that relationships replicate in one or more site before they are reported.

Analysis Strategy

As explained in Chapter Three, two sites were selected for each type of treatment: two for the test of School Full, two for School View-Only, and two for home viewing. Since samples of children were drawn separately in each site, the analyses are done separately within each site. But the pairing of sites does permit a kind of cross-site comparison that can extend the inferences beyond a single site. In this way the effects found in the School Full site of Long Beach can be compared with those in Milwaukee. In the case of the School Full treatment, comparisons can be made as well with the findings in Worcester and Kansas City since the School View-Only sites have a combination of School Full and School View-Only treatments implemented in them.

For School Full analyses the data from Long Beach are presented in the tables of this chapter. This site was chosen over Milwaukee as the primary site for two reasons. The experimental and control groups in Long Beach appeared to be slightly better matched; second, the Hispanic subgroup in Long Beach is more purely Mexican-American. Although the data from Long Beach are presented, the conclusions are drawn only when the Milwaukee data confirm the relationships seen in Long Beach. In a number of places in this chapter relationships found in Long Beach are rejected because of the failure to have them confirmed elsewhere.

Chapter Three gave details about the development of a measure of treatment implementation. Classrooms were divided into five groups based on their implementation score, where the score corresponded to how well the School Full treatment had been implemented in the classroom. A perfect implementation score was assigned for doing a preview activity for every 1/4-hour show, viewing the show, discussing it as a class, and engaging in a supplementary classroom activity related to the show's theme. Using this score 10 classrooms were dropped from the analyses in Long Beach on the assumption that it is unclear whether the students received enough of the intervention to warrant judging FREESTYLE on their responses. After elimination of the 10 classrooms from the Long Beach/Torrance site, 948 children were left for analyses. Their characteristics are shown below in Table 7.1.

Table 7.1
Characteristics of Long Beach Sample
After Eliminating Low Implementing Classrooms

Treatment		Sex		Grade		Race*	
n	%	n	%	n	%	n	%
Cont.=363	38	Girls=435	46	Four=310	33	White=649	69
Exp.=585	62	Boys=513	54	Five=237	25	Black=155	16
				Six=401	42	HisMex=144	15
948	100%	948	100%	948	100%	948	100%

*HisMex=Hispanic of Mexican origin

The analyses are conducted using the student as the unit of analysis. Recently Cronbach (1976) has argued that the most appropriate unit of analysis in studies such as this might be the classroom or even the school, since the intervention was delivered at this level. Our feeling was that FREESTYLE, while it was delivered similarly within each classroom, was processed differently by each individual within that class. We were not comfortable covering up that variation be aggregating to the classroom or school level.

The student outcome measures were discussed in some detail in the previous chapter. But more needs to be said about how they will be examined. There are three measures of interest for every outcome dimension: a pre-test score, a post-test score and a change score -- the post-test minus the pre-test. It is necessary to examine all three measures to understand the dynamics of FREESTYLE's effects. Each of these measures needs to be examined in relation to four different explanatory variables: treatment, gender, race, and grade. To accomplish this the analytic strategy of multiple linear regression is used to permit the prediction of each outcome measure from a combination of the four predictor variables. The primary analytic technique used in this report is a special form of multiple regression called Multiple Classification Analysis (MCA). MCA was chosen over other forms of regression because it treats predictor variables as nominal scales -- the scale which underlies three of the four predictor variables. MCA presents the average score for each subgroup on the outcome measure and yet provides an overall measure (termed Beta) of the effect of each variable statistically controlling for the other predictors. Even the subgroup estimates are adjusted to take into account differences which might exist in the composition of that subgroup on other predictors.[1] Like other forms of multiple regression MCA computes a multiple correlation coefficient, R, which provides an estimate of the effects of all of the predictors operating together. It may be helpful to think of MCA simply as a form of linear regression that has a good deal of extra freedom.[2] However, it shares with the other forms an assumption that the effects of the various predictor variables are combined <u>additively</u> -- i.e., it assumes that there are no interactions among the predictors. A search was made for all possible two-way interactions among the four predictors (e.g., treatment by sex), and this led to the conclusion that the effects are indeed

---

[1] An example of this type of adjustment might be useful here. If among the students in this study there was a 50-50 boy-girl split for whites and blacks, but among Mexicans 3/4 were boys, and if boys typically scored higher on a particular dimension than girls, then the unadjusted scores for Mexican Americans would be higher than they should be based on racial identification alone. There would be an artifact of sex here as well. Under this condition MCA would adjust downward the scores for Mexican Americans in a way that partials out the effects of sex and leaves only the unique effect of being a Mexican American. Although in theory such adjustments are important, in the vast majority of MCAs presented here the adjustments are trivial, owing to the good distribution of the sample across the various subgroups (e.g., there are equal proportions of boys and girls across all of the three racial subgroupings).

[2] A complete description of the MCA model and the corresponding computer program is provided by Andrews, et al., (1967).

additive. Occasionally, for some outcome measures there is an exception to this concerning a race-by-treatment interaction; this is highlighted in the data when it occurs.

What did we look for in these MCAs? There were two things; the first was the average movement of the experimental group relative to the control group as an indication that there were effects that could be attributed uniquely to FREESTYLE. The random assignment procedure by which classrooms were assigned to the experimental or control condition should have insured that the two groups were equivalent at the time of the pretest. Therefore, the beta for the treatment variable should be non-significant at the time of the pre-test, but significant at the post-test. The betas required for statistical significance at the .05 level are shown in the Table 7.2. The betas listed under the column "n=1000" would be appropriate if we had a simple random sample. As with most evaluation studies this sample was clustered. Typically this produces "design effects" which reduce the effective n for statistical purposes to something less than 1000. Exactly how much less is unknown. Our assumption is that a very conservative position is to assume an effective n no less than 400. For a two-category predictor such as treatment or sex, then, a beta of .13 is required before it can be said that FREESTYLE had a statistically significant effect.

To say that FREESTYLE made a statistically significant difference on some outcome dimension says nothing about the educational significance of the effect. With samples of children as large as 1000 small differences between groups are very often statistically significant. But in a study such as this, educational significance is more important than statistical significance. Yet this is very difficult to define when the measures being analyzed are scales with such relative anchors as "good idea" and "bad idea." Some yardstick is needed which indicates how big a difference is "big." In this study it is the size of a difference between groups expressed in standard deviation units. The conventions used in this study are an adaptation of a technique advocated by Cohen (1977). He proposes that the difference be calculated between the post-test means for the experimental and control groups and then divided by the pooled post-test standard deviation (SD). Using this method has the

Table 7.2

The Beta or Eta Required to be
Significantly Different from Zero

Number of Predictor Categories	Number of Cases		
	200	400	1000
Two (Treatment Group, Sex)	.182	.130	.085
Three (Grade, Race)	.212	.151	.095

SOURCE: Morgan, et al. (1976). Appendix D "Regressions with Categorical Predictors."

advantage of standardizing the measure of effects across different scales, and therefore different studies. These differences can then be compared to norms for little and big effects. At this point in time norms for effect size are somewhat arbitrary. Cohen himself proposes that .20SD be judged as a small effect, .50SD a medium effect, and .80SD a very large effect. Horst and Tallmadge (1976), based on their experience evaluating educational programs, suggest that a difference of one-third of a standard deviation can be considered "educationally significant." Indeed, this norm is advocated in the <u>Ideabook</u> issued by the Department of H.E.W. (Tallmadge, 1976). This sourcebook provides guidelines for what the Joint Dissemination Review Panel will consider acceptable evidence from evaluations for that body to endorse the product for future dissemination. Experience at the Institute for Social Research with two national studies of high school aged youth ("Youth in Transition" and "Monitoring the Future") suggests norms only slightly different from these. A difference of .20SD is the threshold of something interesting, .25SD a modest effect, .33SD a sizeable difference, and a difference in excess of .40SD a very large difference. These are the norms which are used in the present study.

A small modification of this approach increased its utility for the present study. The usual approach is to compare the post-test means of the experimental and control groups and divide by the pooled post-test standard deviation. However, the relevant question is how much of a change in the experimental group came about as a result of exposure to FREESTYLE. This suggests taking the difference between the pre- and post-test scores for just the experimental group and dividing by the pooled pre-test standard deviation. If there has been random assignment to the experimental and control groups, and if there indeed has been no significant pre to post shift on the part of the control group, this procedure will yield essentially the same results as Cohen's approach since the control group's score on the pre-test should be the same as the experimental group's which in turn should be the same as the control group at the time of the post-test. In addition, using the pooled pre-test standard deviation avoids the bias frequently introduced when the standard deviation for the experimental group shifts at the time of the post-test.

Using the pretest standard deviation permits making yet another comparison of interest in a study such as this which has differential goals for boys and girls. One way that sex-role stereotypes manifest themselves is that on measures of sex role beliefs or attitudes boys and girls are far apart; i.e., there is a gap between their views. A goal of FREESTYLE is to reduce this gap, so an evaluator would like to talk about the size of the gap at the time of the pre-test and again at the time of the post-test. For a given measure, one can take the difference between the group means for boys and girls and divide this by the standard deviation of the measure for the pooled sample of experimental boys and girls and come up with a measure of the gap which is standardized. Not only that, taking the difference at the time of the post-test and dividing by the pre-test standard deviation permits comparing the gap in the same metric. Indeed, this method permits comparing gaps at two points in time as well as shifts across time in a comparable metric -- a metric for which some norms exist for what is small and large.

An example may be useful here. Attitudes towards girls in athletics is measured on a four-point scale, ranging from one (it's a very bad idea) to four (it's a very good idea). At the time of the pre-test the overall mean on this scale for all respondents is 2.75 with an SD of 0.94 units. The average for girls is 3.08 and boys 2.47. Are the two groups far apart? A calculation of the difference in SD units -- (3.08-2.47)/.94 -- indicates a difference of .65SD, or two-thirds of a standard deviation. This is a very large difference. Do the boys change as a result of their FREESTYLE experience? Their average movement is from 2.47 to 2.93, a shift of .49SD -- again a very large difference.

There is one other complexity to keep in mind in judging the effects of FREESTYLE. The goals of FREESTYLE permit several different patterns of outcomes to be considered evidence of success. Three such patterns are shown in Figure 7.1. Pattern A shows the entire experimental group, both boys and girls, starting at an unacceptable point on some scale and being moved by their FREESTYLE experience to a more acceptable point on the scale. This is clearly evidence of success. For example, if both boys and girls believed that adult jobs such as mechanic or doctor were held only by men, then the hope would be that exposure to FREESTYLE would change this belief equally for both boys and girls. Pattern B is an example of an area where the target is only boys. The girls are already at the desirable end of the scale, and movement of just the boys would be considered evidence of success. However, in this case, the beta value for treatment group would not tell the entire story since the shift is only for one-half of the experimental group. Here the betas for both experimental group and gender must be examined. The last example of a positive effect of FREESTYLE is example C. Here there is no movement of the experimental group in the aggregate, because the boys' score increases about as much as the girls' score decreases. This is an example of reducing the gap between the two target groups. It would be a desirable effect particularly when the object is beliefs. Consider boys and girls estimating how many girls are capable of being good leaders. At the time of the pre-test the girls think that all girls make good leaders and boys think no girls make good leaders. FREESTYLE might moderate the extreme views of both groups, and in so doing bring the perceptions of two groups closer together. This can be judged a positive effect, because a shared view of reality will enhance girls' chances of achieving leadership positions.

Another reason for judging such a pattern as a positive effect is that interventions of this type have the potential to polarize one of the target groups. Guttentag and Bray (1978) found that adolescent boys and girls became more polarized after their sex-role intervention. A similar experience occurred in Germany with pre-school children. A special segment designed to reduce sex-role stereotypes was inserted into the German version of "Sesame Street." After viewing these segments the boys were more sexist (Kob, 1975). Experiences such as these lead us to judge positively a series which does not polarize the sexes, and instead reduces the gap between boys and girls. This pattern, however, can be detected only by examining the pattern for experimental boys and girls. While it is not a common occurrence, we do find a few examples of it in the results for FREESTYLE.

Figure 7.1
Patterns of Positive Effects

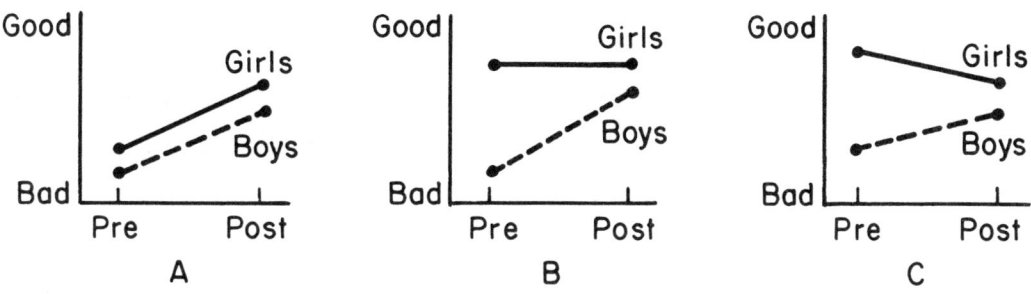

One final note should be made about educational significance. We are making judgments about the ability of FREESTYLE to change attitudes, beliefs, and interests. These are not behaviors, and they are not personality constructs; they are not measures of intelligence or scholastic achievement. At best they represent the orientations of children and perhaps their dispositions to behave in certain ways in a world that has had differing expectations for girls and boys. The authors feel that significant movement on such indicators is every bit as important as significant movement on measures of achievement, given the goals of the FREESTYLE series. But ultimately the readers of this report must judge FREESTYLE on the <u>kinds</u> of things it changed in children as well as how much it changed them.

PART I: CHILDHOOD ACTIVITIES

<u>Girls in mechanical activities</u>

<u>Attitudes</u>: Recall that for each outcome of interest, three MCAs were calculated, one for the pre-test measure, one for the post-test measure, and one for the difference score (post-test minus pre-test). Table 7.3 summarizes the three MCAs for the concept "attitude toward girls in mechanical activities." It provides an example of an area in which the series had a large effect, presumably as a result of children viewing the shows "Partners" and "Grease Monkey" and engaging in related classroom discussion and activities. The attitude measure is a composite index of items which ask how good an idea it is for girls to work with an adult on a car motor, fix a broken bike or build a radio (see the Glossary for a more precise definition of this measure). In Table 7.3 the first row shows the MCA for the pre-test measure. It is modestly predictable from the four independent measures (Multiple R = .235). The most powerful predictor of children's attitude toward girls in mechanics is their sex (beta = .183); the mean for girls is 2.67, while the mean for boys is 2.36, .40SD below the girls. (A score of 4.0 would be the most supportive attitude possible; 2.0 is a moderately negative attitude and 3.0 is moderately positive.) Grade in school -- a surrogate for age -- is somewhat important; sixth graders are a bit more supportive of this non-traditional behavior for girls than the two younger groups of fourth and fifth graders. Racial differences exist as well (beta = .126); Whites are the most supportive while Blacks and Hispanics express a more conservative attitude toward girls doing mechanical things. As expected, treatment group shows very little effect (beta = .06). The difference between the experimental and control groups is 0.10, only one-eighth of a standard deviation. Initially both groups have the same distribution of children's views on this issue, indicating that the assignment of students to experimental and control groups was successful.

Table 7.3

Predicting Attitude Toward Girls in Mechanical Activities (ATGMECH)

	Multiple R		Treatment	Sex	Grade	Race*
Pre Test Mean=2.50 S.D.=.84 n=978	.235	beta: means:	.060 Cont.=2.44 Exp.=2.54	.183 Girls=2.67 Boys=2.36	.107 4=2.41 5=2.45 6=2.61	.126 White=2.58 Black=2.37 HisMex=2.33
Post Test Mean=2.79 S.D.=.85 n=937	.381	beta: means:	.296 Cont.=2.46 Exp.=2.98	.167 Girls=2.94 Boys=2.65	.081 4=2.69 5=2.80 6=2.85	.196 White=2.90 Black=2.61 HisMex=2.49
Raw Gain Mean=.29 S.D.=.89 n=906	.242	beta: means:	.227 Cont.=.03 Exp.=.45	.005 Girls=.28 Boys=.29	.066 4=.29 5=.38 6=.23	.072 White=.33 Black=.23 HisMex=.17

Site: Long Beach   Experimental Groups: School Full and School Control

*HisMex=Hispanic of Mexican origin

To understand the effect of FREESTYLE, look now at the second and third rows. The second shows the prediction to the static post-test score while the third captures the dynamics of the shift by predicting to the difference score. The post-test is much more predictable than the pre-test (Multiple R = .381) due almost entirely to the increased power of treatment to explain variation in the measure. The control group did not change at all from September 1978 to January 1979, while the experimental group increased from 2.54 to 2.98, an impressive shift of one-half a standard deviation. This is summarized in the beta for treatment of .296, statistically significant and substantively important by almost any standard. Row two shows that sex retains its power to predict and row three shows why. Girls and boys increased equal amounts. So row two is useful to see how the participants in this experiment end up while row 3 shows the dynamics of the shift. In row three FREESTYLE's effect is captured almost entirely in the beta for treatment of .227, because the effects were fairly uniform for all of those who were exposed to FREESTYLE. Boys and girls shifted equal amounts. There were some small differences in the movement of the grade groups, but the pattern is not an interpretable one. There were also differential shifts for the racial groups. Whites were more likely to be affected by the message than Blacks and Hispanics. The beta of .072 does not capture this effect completely because Whites are 69 percent of the sample while Blacks and Hispanics each comprise 15 percent.

Considering that Whites started out more favorably disposed to girls in mechanical pursuits FREESTYLE has the effect of spreading out the groups even more than they were originally. Whites start out as the group most supportive of girls engaging in mechanical activities and show the biggest increase in supportive attitude. Blacks and Hispanics show less change, suggesting that these groups start out more resistant to the messages of FREESTYLE and are less likely to respond to its non-traditional message. This spreading out is captured in the beta values for race which increase from pre-test (.126) to post-test (.196). What the data cannot show is whether the smaller shift for minorities is due to cultural values or a failure of FREESTYLE to present role models sufficiently attractive to these minority groups. The assertive girl mechanic in "Grease Monkey" is White, as is the talented fixit girl in

"Partners." In none of the shows is a minority girl shown in a mechanical setting. Lest FREESTYLE be judged too harshly for this, two things should be pointed out. First, both minority groups shifted to a point as supportive of this non-traditional behavior as Whites were to start with. Second, FREESTYLE's impact in other domains (for example, attitudes toward girls acting independently) is to bring the racial groups to a more homogeneous viewpoint. We will return to this issue after considering the range of effects across the complete set of outcomes.

Note that the MCAs predicting to the post test and difference scores include both the unchanged control group and the much-changed experimental group. The mean scores for sex, grade, and race are based on this mixed sample and so underestimate the resulting level for the experimental group; e.g., experimental girls wound up with an average score of 3.14 and boys with a score of 2.84. These represent increases for both groups of one half of a standard deviation. The mean scores for just the experimental boys and girls are shown in Table 7.6.

In general, the first set of MCAs predicting to attitude change show that the series, when coupled with supporting activities, has the potential to produce very large changes in children's attitudes toward girls engaging in the non-traditional area of mechanics. But the picture is not yet complete. As discussed in Chapter Six, it is necessary to look as well at FREESTYLE's impact on related beliefs about girls as mechanics as well as on personal interest in mechanical pursuits.

<u>Beliefs</u> <u>about</u> <u>girls'</u> <u>mechanical</u> <u>ability</u>. What are the relevant beliefs underlying children's attitude toward girls in mechanics? The beliefs measured in this study were a set which exactly parallel the summary measure of attitude: how many girls <u>are</u> <u>good</u> <u>at</u> fixing a broken bike, fixing a car motor, or building a radio or something else that runs on electricity? Response to the three items were averaged in a single index of beliefs about girls in mechanics. The scale runs from 5.0 indicating "all" girls are good at these things to 1.0 "none." The results of the MCAs are shown below in Table 7.4.

Table 7.4

Predicting Beliefs About Girls in Mechanical Activities (BFGMECH)

	Multiple R		Treatment	Sex	Grade	Race
Pre Test Mean=2.20 S.D.=.82 n=973	.212	beta: means:	.051 Cont.=2.15 Exp.=2.24	.201 Girls=2.38 Boys=2.05	.024 4=2.22 5=2.17 6=2.21	.089 White=2.25 Black=2.06 HisMex=2.16
Post Test Mean=2.42 S.D.=.80 n=936	.272	beta: means:	.224 Cont.=2.19 Exp.=2.56	.134 Girls=2.54 Boys=2.32	.021 4=2.44 5=2.43 6=2.41	.117 White=2.49 Black=2.28 HisMex=2.30
Raw Gain Mean=.22 S.D.=.88 n=902	.170	beta: means:	.145 Cont.=.06 Exp.=.32	.065 Girls=.16 Boys=.28	.049 4=.22 5=.29 6=.18	.047 White=.25 Black=.19 HisMex=.14

Site: Long Beach   Experimental Groups: School Full and School Control

At the beginning of the study the average response to the index was 2.20, corresponding to the response, "a few" girls are good at these things. Again, sex is the strongest predictor of these beliefs (beta = .201), with girls averaging a response of 2.38, 40 percent of a standard deviation above the boys. Although there is a sizeable sex difference, both sexes are at the end of the scale which expresses the belief that only a few girls are good at mechanical endeavors. The racial groups are not as separated on this issue as they were on attitudes, although Black children seem least inclined to think that any girls are mechanically talented. The intervention is modestly effective in shifting this belief. The Multiple R for the gain score is .170 for predicting the shift, and the beta for treatment is .145. The movement of the experimental group is large -- .39SD. This is not quite as big a shift as the corresponding one for attitudes, but nonetheless quite large. Part of the reason the overall effect is smaller can be seen in the differential gain for the sexes. Boys shifted much more than girls; indeed experimental boys shifted .45SD with the result that their perceptions end up very close to where the girls began. The dynamics for boys and girls are illustrated in Figure 7.2. The greater effect on boys results in narrowing the gap between girls' and boys' beliefs. So the fact that the girls moved less than the boys can be interpreted as a positive result.

What are the implications of these findings for beliefs? Before answering this question consider the purpose that the project has in changing attitudes. Shifting children's attitudes toward girls in mechanics is being sought for two related reasons. For girls with mechanical interests it is hoped that the attitude will mediate behavior -- that as a result of feeling more positive about other girls engaging in mechanical activities they will themselves make the choice of engaging in mechanical pursuits should the opportunity present itself. A second reason for changing both boys' and girls' attitudes is to make all children more accepting of those girls who choose this non-traditional pursuit. If the peer group environment is supportive then it is more likely that the mechanically inclined females will actually engage in mechanical activities.

Figure 7.2
Girls and Mechanical Activities

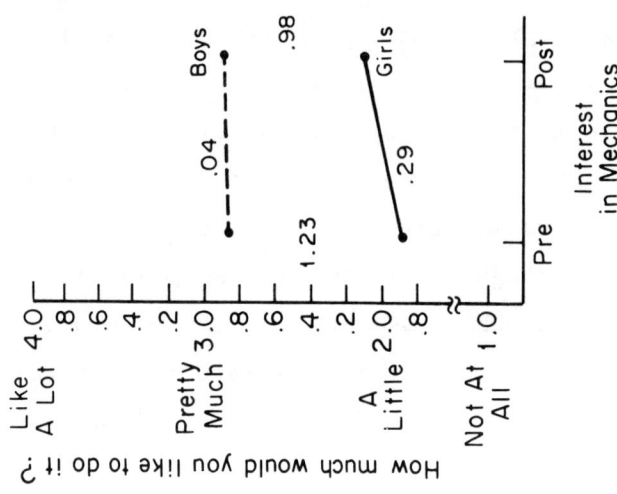
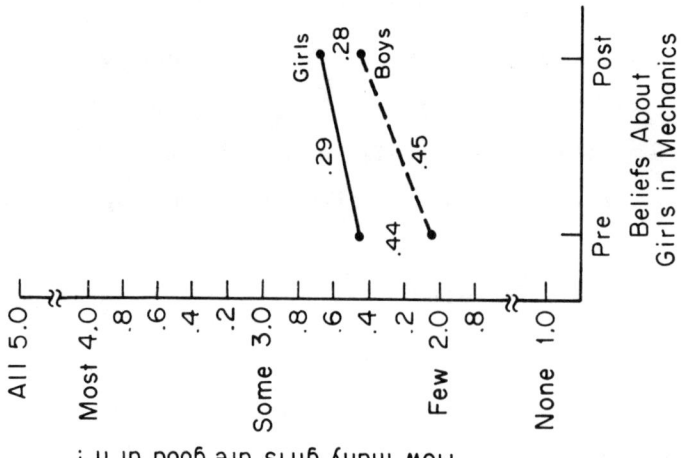
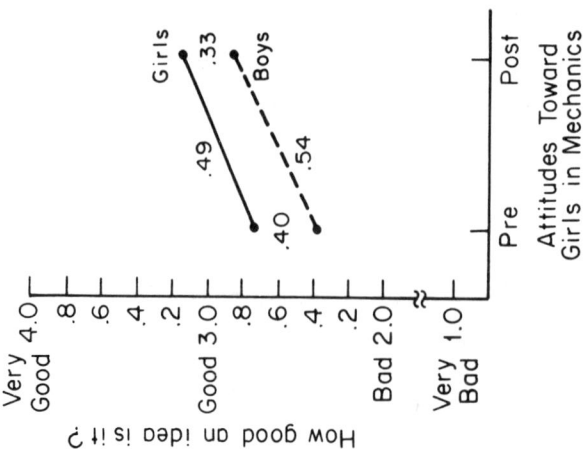

We have seen that FREESTYLE had a large impact on attitudes toward girls in mechanics. But the attitude was influenced through attractive TV role models and supportive classroom discussion. Will these attitudes persist after the intervention is long in the past? Attitude theory -- especially Fishbein's theory discussed in the previous chapter -- suggests that the attitudes are much more likely to persist if the underlying beliefs are supportive of the attitude. Note that the average post-test score for all those exposed to FREESTYLE is 2.56. This is half way between the scale points of "a few" and "some" girls indicating that the beliefs may not have been shifted sufficiently to support the new-found attitude. Since beliefs represent a perception of what is true of the world, it is unreasonable to expect FREESTYLE to "push" the limits of credibility. If indeed most girls are not good at mechanics, then children are not going to let television radically reorganize beliefs that have been built up over years of daily perceptions. The point is that the beliefs may not be sufficiently positive to support the new-found attitude beyond the end of the FREESTYLE experiment. A follow-up study in one of the seven test cities is scheduled for Fall 1979, eight months after the initial FREESTYLE intervention was completed. This additional data collection will provide the data on persistence of beliefs and attitudes which will take the above discussion out of the realm of speculation.

<u>Interest</u> <u>in</u> <u>mechanical</u> <u>activities</u>. The last type of outcome in the substantive domain of mechanics is personal interest in mechanical pursuits. For childhood activities this was measured by asking respondents how much they would personally like to do each of the following: fix a broken bike, build a model kit (plane, boat, etc.), build a radio, fix a leaky faucet, or work with an adult on a car motor. A response of 4.0 indicates they like doing all these things "a lot;" 1.0 indicates they don't like it at all. (See the Glossary for more details.) The summary measure is an average of the responses to these five activities. Table 7.5 shows the MCAs predicting to the summary measure. The results for the pre-test show that mechanical interests are highly predictable. The Multiple R is a very large .616, due almost exclusively to their strong association with gender. The beta for sex is .611. Boys average a score of 2.83 -- about the scale point "like it

pretty much;" girls are lower by more than one standard deviation, 1.85 "like it a little." This is typical of the type of differential boy/girl pattern which led the sponsor to fund the creation of FREESTYLE. This differential interest pattern is apparently independent of age and racial/ethnic identification.

Mechanical interests are strongly associated with sex-role identity in this culture. Is FREESTYLE able to break this pattern? It depends on the criterion that is used. In examining FREESTYLE's impact on attitudes and beliefs we looked for an overall shift of all children exposed to FREESTYLE and then looked at the various subgroups (sex, grade, race) to see if the effects were differential depending on group identity. Using this criterion we would conclude that FREESTYLE did very little to break the pattern; the experimental group increased by 0.11 points, a mere 14 percent of a standard deviation. All of this increased interest was for girls, but the gap between experimental boys and girls after FREESTYLE is still about a full standard deviation (1.23SD before the intervention and .98SD afterwards). If it is the overwhelming disposition of males to favor mechanical things which leads them later in life to choose courses and then jobs in the mechanical area, then FREESTYLE has not successfully changed the imbalance. This is not surprising. The TV shows were not well equipped to influence personal interests; much of this task was left to teachers who had to pick up on suggestions in the "School Guide" for expanding the interests of students through classroom activities. It is also probable that influencing personal interests requires much more time and reality testing than changing attitudes and beliefs. For example, it may require an opportunity to fix a broken bike and discovering that such an activity is rewarding.

Another perspective is that a different criterion might be justified for interests. The target for a change in attitudes and beliefs could appropriately be all boys or all girls, because these are associated with tolerance of an entire group for the expression of non-traditional interests by the _few_ who happen to be so inclined. If FREESTYLE could shift the interest pattern of a sizeable portion of the target group -- presumably those girls who are mechanically inclined but who hide this interest in the face of

Table 7.5

Predicting Interests in Mechanical Activities (INTMC)

	Multiple R		Treatment	Sex	Grade	Race
Pre Test Mean=2.38 S.D.=.80 n=948	.616	beta: means:	.041 Cont.=2.34 Exp.=2.41	.611 Girls=1.85 Boys=2.83	.060 4=2.34 5=2.47 6=2.36	.013 White=2.39 Black=2.39 HisMex=2.36
Post Test Mean=2.42 S.D.=.81 n=939	.579	beta: means:	.150 Cont.=2.26 Exp.=2.51	.548 Girls=1.94 Boys=2.83	.084 4=2.43 5=2.52 6=2.35	.060 White=2.42 Black=2.48 HisMex=2.32
Raw Gain Mean=0.05 S.D.=.64 n=879	.173	beta: means:	.124 Cont.=-.05 Exp.=.11	.094 Girls=.11 Boys=-.007	.072 4=.10 5=.07 6=-.005	.050 White=.06 Black=.08 HisMex=-.03

Site: Long Beach   Experimental Groups: School Full and School Control contrary sex-role norms -- then FREESTYLE could be considered successful in changing interests as well as attitudes. Indeed, 12 percent of the girls exposed to FREESTYLE did show a very large shift of one-half of a standard deviation.

However, the authors are still left with the nagging feeling that this argument may be weak in terms of the ultimate goal of FREESTYLE which is to increase non-traditional occupational selection by girls. The majority of 9-12 year old boys are interested in mechanics and we know that an overwhelming percentage of adults in mechanical occupations are male. If childhood interests were perfectly correlated with adult occupational choice, then it would take only a small proportion of boys having mechanical interests to produce a nearly all-male adult group in mechanical occupations. But this is not the case. Pre adolescent boys express a broad range of pre-occupational interests of which mechanics is only <u>one</u> category. As a result, at the time of occupational choice, a mixture of their interest hierarchy and market opportunities result in many with mechanical interests entering occupations which have little to do with mechanics. It is only the fact that an overwhelming number of boys have mechanical interests as children that there is a pool from which later a small percentage will pursue mechanical occupations. FREESTYLE, coupled with classroom activity can influence some girls to express a more positive interest, but its effect is probably not sufficient to influence later adult choices in any aggregate way among the girls who are exposed to it.

Equally important, if the interests of girls have not been shifted dramatically will the supportive attitudes of the experimental children persist? There is a causal chain to be considered here. It takes an interest in mechanics on the part of girls for them to engage in the activity -- let's say fixing bikes; and it takes many girls fixing bikes and coming to do it well to shift the belief that only a very few girls can do a good job at bike repair. Finally, it is a belief that many girls can do it well that supports an attitude which endorses the behavior. The chain then links back to interest.

Girls in Science

The goals for the FREESTYLE series emphasize science as much as they do mechanics. There are two shows -- "Cheers!" and "Hike" -- which focus on childhood scientific interests, although science is the secondary message in each. The present evaluation did not measure attitudes or beliefs about girls in scientific endeavors, but it does contain a measure of interest in science. The distinction between science and mechanics was seen to be this. Mechanical interest relates to using tools and objects to make something function. Scientific interest involves a curiosity about what makes things work. For example, a mechanically inclined person may enjoy building a radio while the scientifically inclined wants to know how the radio converted the voice from radio waves to audio waves. The two interests, mechanical and scientific, can exist in the same person, but an interest in one does not require an interest in the other. Indeed, the measures of mechanical and scientific interests used in this study are correlated only .33 (product-moment correlation).

The measure of scientific interest was difficult to construct, because so few behaviors of a 9-12 year old indicate unequivocally an underlying orientation to science. Mechanical interests have marvelously concrete examples which the pre-adolescent can readily recognize; for example fixing a broken bike or a leaky faucet. Scientific interests at this age level do not have this rich variety of readily recognized symbols. Nonetheless, several elementary science teachers considered interest in the following list of six activities as indicative of a scientific orientation. Among them are four activities modelled in FREESTYLE TV shows. The six are: raise goldfish; watch the stars and planets; make an insect collection; make a rock collection; read about rocks, insects, flowers or stars; and do a science fair project. (Exact wording of the items can be found in the glossary.)

What impact did FREESTYLE have on these interests? Rather than include all of the remaining MCA's in this chapter, only the highlights are shown in subsequent tables. Rows three and four of Table 7.6 show the data for mechanical and scientific interests. The first thing to notice is the initial scores of boys and girls. On mechanical interests boys are much more interested than girls, averaging an interest score of 2.85 -- well over a full standard deviation above the girls who are at 1.87. When it comes to scientific interest boys are still somewhat more interested than girls (2.95 vs 2.71), but the scale point for girls is very close to that of boys for mechanics. (In Milwaukee girls and boys had identical interest scores.) What this indicates is that FREESTYLE chose to concentrate on an activity which is not sex typed. The effects of FREESTYLE on the children is nil. Those involved showed no increased interest. The largest subgroup shift is for girls and this is only .06SD. Perhaps a combination of a lack of initial sex differences and the fact that scientific endeavor was not extensively developed in the shows explains these results. The experiment with goldfish in the show "Cheers!" was supposed to be secondary to the theme of being independent from peer pressure. In the show "Hike," rock collecting was the background for the theme of risk taking.

Girls in Athletics

Perhaps the strongest bastion of male exclusivism is athletics, especially contact sports. Although this has been challenged in recent years it is always news worthy when a girl tries out for Little League Baseball or Junior Football. Title IX has forced integration in the gym classes of most schools and in non-contact scholastic sports, but opportunities for girls and acceptance of their participation in most male sports is still small.

To measure the attitudes of 9-12 year olds toward girls engaging in athletics, they were asked how good an idea it is for girls to play either football or basketball on a team of both boys and girls. The football item corresponds to the sport highlighted in the show "Flag," where the character Denice becomes the star of the boy's flag football team. In the "Variety Special" there is a brief clip of girls challenging and beating some boys in a pickup game of basketball. The data are shown in row five of Table 7.6. In the pretest girls are very supportive of their own sex playing in these sports (Mean=3.08, "good idea"). Boys are not so sure; their attitudes are three-quarters of a standard deviation lower (2.47). One other difference of note is that sixth graders -- regardless of sex -- are a little more supportive than their younger counterparts, suggesting that age and experience by

Table 7.6

Summary Table of Effects of Intensive Exposure to FREESTYLE (Long Beach)
Part I: Childhood Interests

Index Name[6]	MCA Predicting Gain Score (Total Sample)[1]					Mean Scores for Experimental Group Only									
	Multiple R	betas				Total[2]			Girls[3]			Boys[4]			
		Treatment	Sex	Grade	Race	Mean pre	Mean post	S.D. Shift[5]	Mean pre	Mean post	S.D. Shift[5]	Mean pre	Mean post	S.D. Shift[5]	
ATGMECH	.243	.227	.005	.066	.072	2.54	2.98	.52	2.73	3.14	.49	2.38	2.84	.54	
BFGMECH	.170	.145	.065	.049	.047	2.23	2.55	.39	2.43	2.67	.29	2.07	2.44	.45	
INTMECH	.173	.124	.094	.072	.050	2.42	2.52	.13	1.87	2.10	.29	2.85	2.88	.04	
INTSCI	.077	.054	.036		.023	2.84	2.84	.00	2.71	2.75	.06	2.95	2.93	-.03	
ATGATH	.164	.163	.041	.068	.034	2.75	3.18	.46	3.08	3.47	.41	2.47	2.93	.49	
BFGATH	.126	.072	.045	.082	.044	2.83	3.06	.26	3.15	3.31	.18	2.55	2.84	.32	
INTATH	.192	.136	.116	.030	.066	2.98	3.18	.25	2.58	2.93	.44	3.31	3.40	.11	
ATBNRT	.212	.157	.132	.042	.063	3.00	3.27	.38	2.95	3.33	.54	3.03	3.22	.25	
BFBNRT	.205	.065	.171	.068	.669	3.07	3.20	.15	2.70	3.06	.41	3.39	3.31	-.09	
INTNRT	.158	.126	.035	.076	.054	2.77	2.90	.19	3.09	3.19	.15	2.50	2.65	.22	

[1-4] Approximate sample sizes are 1 950, 2 686, 3 314, 4 372. [5] Subgroup post score minus subgroup pre score divided by the standard deviation of the pre-test score of the entire Long Beach sample.
[6] KEY: ATG/ATB=attitudes toward girls/boys; BFG/BFB=beliefs about girls/boys; INT=interest in; MECH=mechanical activities; SCI=scientific activities; ATH=athletics; NRT=nurturant activities.

themselves contribute to more acceptance. The FREESTYLE experience has a modest effect in shifting these attitudes in the intended direction. The shift for the experimentals is quite large; the gain of .40 points corresponds to .46SD. Boys shifted slightly more than girls; but this is to be expected; not only were boys the target of the intervention, but the girls were already near the "ceiling" for this measure. An average post-test score of 3.47 for experimental girls is about the limit, although technically they could have an average score of 4.0. The most important thing to note is that the increase for boys results in a post-test score that is about as supportive as the girls started out to be. In Milwaukee the effects were much smaller and in Worcester the experimental group gain was offset by modest increases for the control group as well. The reason for these differences is not clear; but the Long Beach results show the potential is indeed there.

What about the beliefs about how many girls are good at football or basketball? These are also sex-typed to begin with. Girls think that "some" girls are good at these sports, but the boys' perception is less generous. Their score of 2.55 is a full one-half standard deviation below the girls. FREESTYLE is less successful in changing these beliefs than the corresponding attitudes. The Multiple R of .126 is quite small. However, the primary target group, boys, did increase a sizeable amount (.32SD).

Personal interest in athletics is also highly sex-typed. Athletic interest was measured by asking how much they would like to play not only football and basketball, but also dodgeball, soccer and baseball. Looking at the average liking for these five sports, boys show a very high interest. Their initial score of 3.31 is about at the ceiling for the measure. By contrast, girls are a full standard deviation below them at 2.58. This position is ideal for a FREESTYLE influence attempt and indeed FREESTYLE is quite successful. The average girls' interest shifts .44SD to a score of 2.93, equivalent to the scale point of "like it pretty much." This finding must be qualified somewhat, though. In none of the other sites were the girls as low on the athletic interest scale as Long Beach, although in every site there is some gap between boys and girls. In Worcester where the girls started out as high as the Long Beach girls ended up, FREESTYLE still increased girls' interest a little bit. But in Milwaukee where the boys' and girls' pretest scores were almost identical to those in Worcester, there was almost no movement at all among FREESTYLE participants. The finding is puzzling. But while FREESTYLE's effect in this dommain varied, the replication of the Long Beach findings in Worcester supports an interpretation that FREESTYLE has strong potential to increase girls' interest in athletics.

Taken as a whole the findings for attitudes, beliefs, and interests in athletics are the most encouraging yet for possible long term effects. Boys became more supportive of having girls play athletics and girls increased their interest in participating in athletics. This combination has a lot of potential for bringing about actual change in behavior.

Boys in Helping Activities

While athletics is the domain of males, nurturance is thought to be the domain of females. Indeed, among the 9-12 year olds in this study, this pattern is quite evident. The students were asked about their interests in a large number of nurturant activities:

- Take care of a younger child at the playground
- Help a younger child with math
- Teach a younger child how to play a game
- Sew a button on clothes or sew up a tear
- Help an adult fix meals for the family
- Help old people
- Help at a recreation center for handicapped people
- Take care of sick people
- Run errands for an elderly person

On the average girls showed much higher interest in these activities than boys (.87SD), confirming that nurturance is a female-typed activity -- not as extremely sex-typed as athletics and mechanics, but stereotyped nonetheless.[3] Accordingly, to have a series that is addressed to both boys and girls, the

---

[3]It is fascinating to find replication of a finding like this in three separate sites as geographically separated as Long Beach, Milwaukee, and Worcester. The average pre-test interest scores for the entire sample in each city are 2.77, 2.86, and 2.83 respectively with standard deviations of .68. For boys the interest scores were 2.50, 2.56, 2.49 and for girls 3.09, 3.14, and 3.18.

designers of FREESTYLE devoted two shows to increasing the acceptance of boys playing caring roles. In "Young and Old" Marcus and Walter discover what it takes to be helpful to older people. In "Helping Hand" Walter and Ramon become skillful tutors to a Mexican girl who is having difficulty with her English. Attitudes toward boys being nurturant was defined for the evaluation as attitudes toward boys doing the following: taking care of a younger child, helping a child with math, helping older people, and helping adults fix meals for the family. Initially, boys and girls are equally supportive of boys doing these things, with the average score being almost 3.0, "a good idea" (see row eight of Table 7.6). Virtually no differences occur by age or race either. Perhaps the "social desirability" of the items is so strong that few people can label these things as bad. Nonetheless, FREESTYLE had a strong effect, pushing the average even higher to 3.27, an upward shift of .38SD. The biggest shift was for girls who moved a full one-half standard deviation.

The girls' shift in attitude was associated with a corresponding shift in beliefs about how many boys are good at any of these nurturant activities (row 9, Table 7.6). Initially, girls thought somewhere between "a few" and "some" boys were skilled in this area (2.70) while boys thought much more highly of their own sex (3.39, or one full standard deviation above the girls). Girls were apparently impressed by what they saw and heard in FREESTYLE; by the end of the series they averaged 3.06 which is .41SD higher. Boys, meanwhile moderated their beliefs downward -- perhaps reflecting a more realistic appraisal.[4] It appears that both boys and girls start out quite accepting, on the surface, of boys engaging in helping roles. Girls are happy to see them do these things but don't feel many of them are very good at it. That is not surprising since boys are not very interested in doing these things (row 10, Table 7.6), and so it's likely that girls rarely see boys in these roles. But the TV images and the classroom discussion are strongly effective in shifting the girls' beliefs.

When it comes to personal interest, FREESTYLE and the related classroom activities do little to increase boys' interest in nurturant activities. Boys

---

[4]The Long Beach data shows that Blacks shifted an unusually large amount, but this was not confirmed in the Milwaukee data.

start out much less interested in helping activities than any other activities. Compare their interest score of 2.50 with that for science (2.95), mechanics (2.85), and athletics (3.31). And after FREESTYLE they are only .22SD higher at 2.65.

What are the implications of these findings for increasing nurturant behavior on the part of boys? We can only speculate. But compare nurturance with athletics. Girls participate less than boys in athletics, especially on boy/girl teams. This is associated not only with lower athletic interest scores for girls, but resistance from boys as well. Boys (and adults as well) can be thought of as gatekeepers. Sports such as football and basketball are dominated by boys' teams and it is up to boys to let girls join their teams. Although the attitudes of boys initially did not support having girls join their teams, FREESTYLE pushed the boys to a more supportive stance. FREESTYLE also increased girls' interest in sports. But the dynamics of nurturance may be of a different order. While nurturance may be the domain primarily of girls, neither boys nor girls are resistant to boys doing nurturant things. Although FREESTYLE did improve both the attitudes and beliefs of girls regarding boys entering their domain, this may not serve to increase the amount that boys will behave in nurturant ways. The barrier from girls was not there to begin with and boys' own interests were not moved much in a positive direction.

PART II: CHILDHOOD BEHAVIORAL SKILLS

The behavioral skills on which FREESTYLE focused were leadership, assertiveness, independence and risk-taking for girls. In evaluating FREESTYLE the choice was made to focus only on attitudes and beliefs regarding exercise of each skill. Each of the behavioral skills mentioned above was targeted toward girls, so there are measures of attitudes toward girls being leaders, being assertive, etc., and beliefs about how many girls are good at being leaders, etc. To enrich understanding, however, a set of measures were obtained for attitudes and beliefs about boys acting in these skill areas.

Girls in Leadership Roles

For this evaluation the activities chosen to represent leadership were these: being president of your class, being captain of your school's football team, being in charge of the class paper drive, and being editor of the school newspaper. The first of these is the leadership activity around which the plot of "Candidates" revolves and the last is a secondary theme for the two-part show "Scoop!" Attitudes toward girls engaging in these leadership roles are quite polarized. The data are shown in Table 7.7 and illustrated in Figure 7.3. Girls think it is a "good idea" (mean = 3.17), while boys are more than a full standard deviation lower at 2.25, "a bad idea." There are no differences by grade or race. To help get perspective on these attitudes it is helpful to look at the response to boys engaging in the same leadership activities. The top two graphs in Figure 7.3 display the two indexes. Look first at the pre-test measures. Girls are equally approving of both boy-leaders and girl-leaders. Not so the boys; they feel very positive about boy-leaders, but negative toward girls in this role. It is against this backdrop that FREESTYLE's effects must be assessed. After exposure to FREESTYLE girls are somewhat more supportive of either sex being leaders. Boys become more supportive of girls by a large amount, moving up .42SD from 2.25 to 2.58. While this shows strong effects for the boys it must be noted that their final position is still well below either sex's support for boy leaders. This may not provide a sufficiently supportive environment to stimulate a lot of girls to try out for leadership roles; but then again, only a few people are needed to fill all of the leadership roles available in any group.

What do children believe about the leadership ability of girls? This was assessed by asking children how many girls are good at doing each of the four elements of good leadership which were stressed in the show "Candidates." These include organizing things for the group to do, giving each group member a job they can do well, having good ideas about what the group should do, and listening to the ideas of other group members. Respondents were also asked how many boys are good at doing these things. The results are shown in the bottom half of Figure 7.3. At pre-test time boys and girls are far apart, each believing their own sex has more people talented in leadership skills.

Figure 7.3
Attitudes and Beliefs About Leadership

Attitudes Toward Girls and Boys in Leadership Roles

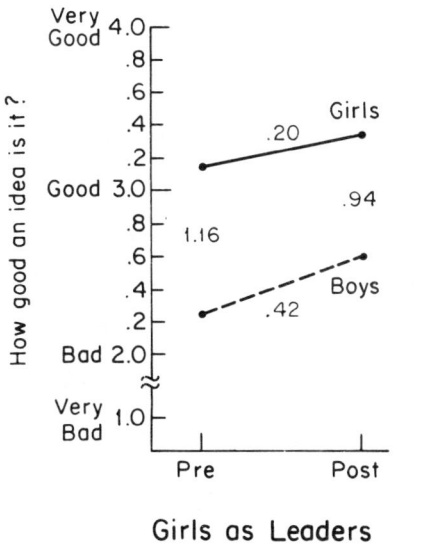

Girls as Leaders

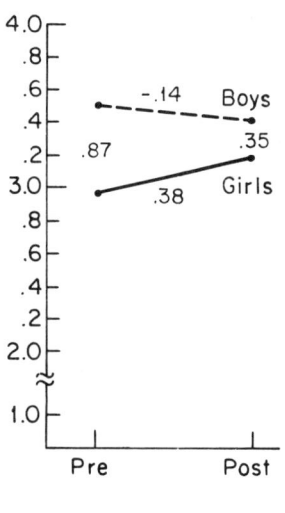

Boys as Leaders

Beliefs About Girls and Boys in Leadership Roles

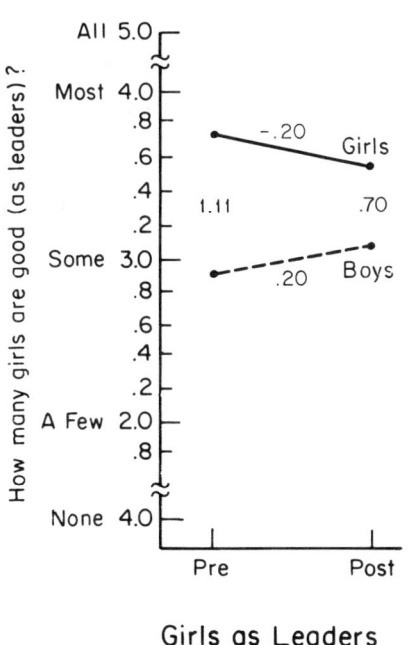

Girls as Leaders

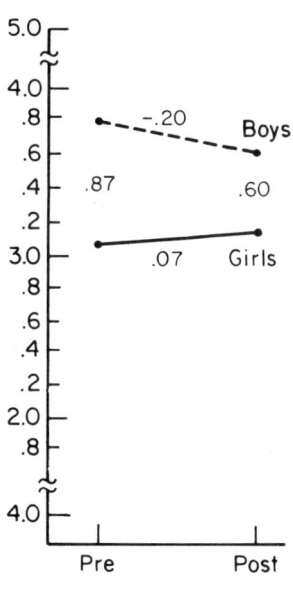

Boys as Leaders

Exposure to FREESTYLE has an interesting effect; it moves the two sexes in opposite directions. In estimating the number of girls with leadership skills, girls become less extreme, moving from "most girls" are good at these things toward the scale point "some girls." The tendency for boys is to move up from the point "some girls" toward "most girls."

Children's estimates of the number of boys who exhibit these leadership skills shows a similar but opposite picture. Boys moderate downward their estimate of the number of boys with these skills. Girls increase slightly their estimate of the number of boys. These equal and opposite effects for the two sexes contribute to homogenizing the beliefs of boys and girls, and do so in a way which contributes to the perception that there are equal numbers of boys and girls with these leadership qualities.

FREESTYLE makes the implicit assumption that the key to disarming boys' resistance to girl leaders is to convince them that girls can be just as competent as boys in the skills required to be a leader. Undoubtedly this is important but is it sufficient? What is at the root of boys' attitude? Is it a question of perceived competence or a more self-centered regard for the male prerogative? To address this question several additional items were presented to the children. What were their beliefs about how many girls "are too bossy when they lead a group" or "give all the good jobs to other girls in the group?" As an index these items were not strongly related to initial attitudes of boys toward girl leaders ($r=.17$), while beliefs about competence were strongly related ($r=.53$). Clearly FREESTYLE chose the appropriate beliefs for their target.

Girls Behaving Independently

Independence from peer pressure is a second behavioral skill which the FREESTYLE staff thought girls (and minorities) ought to practice more often. The FREESTYLE curriculum defines independence in this fashion:

1) Choosing an activity on the basis of one's own interest rather than what others want one to do.

2) Making decisions on the basis of one's own judgment even when some people disagree.

Table 7.7

Summary Table of Effects of Intensive Exposure to FREESTYLE (Long Beach)
Part II: Childhood Behavioral Skills

Index Name[6]	MCA Predicting Gain Score (Total Sample)[1]					Mean Scores for Experimental Group Only								
		betas				Total[2]			Girls[3]			Boys[4]		
	Mult-iple R	Treat-ment	Sex	Grade	Race	Mean pre	Mean post	S.D. Shift[5]	Mean pre	Mean post	S.D. Shift[5]	Mean pre	Mean post	S.D. Shift[5]
ATGLDR	.224	.175	.086	.024	.105	2.67	2.91	.31	3.17	3.33	.21	2.25	2.58	.42
BFGLDR[7]	.176	.084	.147	.019	.037	3.27	3.28	.01	3.72	3.57	-.20	2.90	3.05	.20
ATBLDR						3.27	3.32	.08	2.96	3.20	.38	3.51	3.42	-.14
BFBLDR[7]						3.44	3.38	-.07	3.05	3.11	07	3.78	3.61	-.20
ATGIND	.138	.126	.039	.066	.077	2.91	3.14	.33	2.96	3.25	.41	2.87	3.06	.27
BFGIND[8]	.122	.059	.014	.105	.004	3.28	3.31	.03	3.31	3.38	.07	3.24	3.27	.03
ATBIND						3.00	3.17	.25	3.11	3.30	.28	2.91	3.07	.23
BFBIND[8]						3.17	3.20	.03	3.19	3.19	.00	3.15	3.21	.06
ATGASRT	.194	.170	.045	.053	.078	2.24	2.47	.31	2.26	2.52	.35	2.23	2.42	.25
BFGASRT[9]	.141	.062	.009	.097	.083	3.24	3.24	.00	3.38	3.39	.02	3.12	3.11	-.02
ATBASRT						2.38	2.58	.26	2.26	2.56	.39	2.48	2.59	.14
BFBASRT[9]						3.52	3.51	-.01	3.31	3.40	.12	3.69	3.60	-.12
ATGRTK	.089	.004	.071	.048	.022	2.17	2.19	.03	2.21	2.19	.04	2.14	2.21	.12
BFGRTK[9]	.077	.001	.012	.055	.058	3.35	3.32	-.04	3.25	3.21	-.05	3.42	3.40	-.01
ATBRTK						2.24	2.28	.07	2.20	2.21	.02	2.27	2.34	.12
BFBRTK[9]						2.78	2.76	-.03	2.89	2.85	-.04	2.68	2.68	.00

[1-4] Approximate sample sizes are [1] 950, [2] 686, [3] 314, [4] 372.

[5] Subgroup post score minus subgroup pre score divided by the standard deviation of the pre-test score of the entire Long Beach sample.

[6] Index names: col. 1-2: ATtitude or BelieF; col. 3: Boy or Girl; col 4-8: LDR=leadership, IND=independence, ASRT=assertiveness, RTK=risk-taking.

[7] Scale: 1=none of them are good leaders; 5=all of them are good leaders.

[8] Scale: Act independently 1=never, 5=very often. In other sites there were no effects for independence.

[9] Scale: Behave assertively or act independent of peer pressure 1=none of them; 5=all of them.

The show which focuses on independence is "Cheers!" Penny and Ramon are two eighth graders interested in science, but they are also very talented and involved in other activities that are more traditional. Before the two can follow their science interests they must deal with peer pressure from others to choose more traditional pursuits. Penny must deal with the wishes of her mother and girlfriends who want her to try out for the cheerleading squad. Similarly, Ramon must deal with his soccer-playing friends who think he should try out for the team instead of devoting his time to a science fair project.

For the present study, beliefs about girls acting independently was measured by asking children how often girls their age actually did something they were really interested in when their friends thought only boys did it or when their parents wished they would do something else. Children were also asked about the frequency with which boys acted this way. Using these items there was a consensus that neither boys nor girls behave in an independent manner very often (rows 5-8, Table 7.7). This perception was shared by boys and girls. Independent behavior appears not to be stereotypic among 9-12 year olds. Not only that, as the data in Table 7.7 show, FREESTYLE had virtually no impact on this perception.

What about attitudes toward girls behaving independently? These start out quite positive (average score of 2.91 -- "good idea"), and opinions of both boys and girls are virtually identical. The same is true for opinions about boys behaving independently. The average score is almost the same, 3.00, with only a slight difference between the ratings by girls and boys. The effects of exposure to FREESTYLE are somewhat complicated; in brief it has the effect of increasing by a small amount the approval of all children toward girls acting independently. The complexity relates to the fact that the findings do not replicate from site to site. Table 7.7 shows the data for Long Beach. The overall effect looks moderately large. The Multiple R is .138 and the average shift for the FREESTYLE children is .33SD. But this comes not from uniform treatment effects (beta=.126) or from large single-sex effects (beta=.039). Rather it comes from a large shift by Mexican-Americans. They started out considerably lower than Blacks or Whites in their approval of girls behaving independently. But FREESTYLE changed this and brought their attitudes in close alignment with the other two groups. This would be quite noteworthy if it was replicated in Milwaukee. It was not. In Milwaukee Mexican-Americans started with attitudes identical with Whites; it was the Blacks who were less supportive. In this city the series had the effect of bringing the Blacks in line with the other two groups. This same phenomenon occurred in Worcester, although here there were no Mexican-Americans. Blacks started out much less supportive than Whites, but the series equalized this. It appears that the series has only modest overall effects, however the majority of children, both boys and girls, start out approving of the independent behavior anyway.

FREESTYLE's chief effect -- and the point is of interest -- is to influence groups who do not share the normative view to shift their position in line with the majority.

Girls Being Assertive

Another behavioral skill featured in the FREESTYLE series is assertiveness for girls. Two shows feature this theme, which is defined as standing up for what one wants or feels is right. In "Good Signs" a new student who is deaf is mainstreamed into a classroom. She is received with lack of compassion by most of the students. But Penny does not think this is right. She takes the initiative to read about deafness and befriends the deaf student. Finally she speaks out firmly to the rest of the class on behalf of her new friend. In "Grease Monkey" 13-year old Chris is very interested in automobiles and wants to get a job at a gas station. To secure the job she must assert herself and convince a crusty old station owner that she can do the job.

As with other behavioral skills, attitudes and beliefs about assertiveness are difficult to measure. There are no symbols which are readily recognized by 9-12 year olds as standing for the concept of assertiveness. To describe a person being assertive is difficult for two reasons. First the cues that distinquish an assertive person from one who is aggressive or "too pushy" are very subtle. Second, the judgment that a person is assertive comes from observing them in a number of situations, because assertiveness is a statement about a behavioral tendency, not a single event. For this study attitudes toward assertive girls was assessed by responses to these questions:

> You're on the playground and a little kid in second grade is being picked on by some kids in your grade. A girl you know thinks it's very unfair and wants to make the big kids stop. Someone else thinks she ought to go get the teacher instead. The girl says no, she will do it herself. How good an idea is it for her to try by herself to get the big kids to stop?

> Your school has a band. A girl you know plays the saxophone very well, but didn't get chosen to play because there were already enough saxophones in the band. She thinks this is unfair and thinks she should go to the teacher and prove that she's good enough to play. A friend says no, that she should just wait this year and try again next year. How good an idea is it for her to go see the teacher right now?

The response scale was the same as for all other attitude items: very good idea to very bad idea. Based on these items children expressed a more conservative attitude toward this behavior than most other behaviors (mean=2.24; see Rows 9-12, Table 7.7). There were virtually no differences in attitudes by sex, grade or race. This conservative attitude should not be surprising. Assertiveness has a time and a place; if someone is continually assertive they are likely to be perceived as aggressive to the point of being abrasive, so it is realistic to expect these children to be a little cautious about giving a general endorsement of these examples of assertiveness.

The same two questions were repeated with boys in the central role, and the response was quite similar: on the average the scale response was 2.38, slightly higher approval of boys being assertive than girls, due entirely to the response of boys. After exposure to FREESTYLE the Long Beach children show what appears to be a more accepting attitude toward assertive behavior in girls. The beta for treatment is .170. The girls shift up .35SD from 2.26 to 2.52 while the boys make a more modest increase of .25SD (2.23 to 2.42). However, this effect is not replicated in other sites. In Milwaukee children start with a more approving attitude (2.46) and are virtually at the same point after FREESTYLE (2.47). In Worcester the pre and post averages are 2.49 and 2.52. Note that the movement for Long Beach children was from a more conservative attitude than children in these other cities to a point that is comparable to them. It could be that this is another example of the kind of homogenizing effect that FREESTYLE can have for groups who are removed from the normative response.

Beliefs about girls being assertive was measured by asking how many girls your age: stand up for what they think is right, stop somebody from picking on younger kids, tell another kid when they think the other kid is wrong, demand to be treated fairly by grownups, demand to be treated fairly by other kids. Using these examples of assertiveness, children think "some" girls are assertive. After FREESTYLE their beliefs do not change. In sum, it appears that FREESTYLE had no perceptible influence on attitudes and beliefs about assertiveness, with the exception of the homogenizing effect.

Girls Taking Risks

Yet another behavioral skill stressed in FREESTYLE is reasonable risk-taking for girls. The show "Hike" was specifically designed to deal with risk-taking. The show's star, Tess, collects rocks. A school-sponsored geology hike to the mountains presents a good opportunity to add to her collection. However, she is afraid of mountains and does not want to go. Her brother convinces her that it represents a reasonable risk worth taking. Several developments in the plot help viewers make the distinction between reasonable and unreasonable risks. Elements of yet another show, "Grease Monkey" can certainly be construed as dealing with risk-taking, although the designers describe that show as dealing with assertiveness rather than risk-taking.

The measures used to assess risk-taking attitudes and beliefs can be found in the Glossary. (Attitudes toward girls taking risks; beliefs about girls taking risks.) The level of approval for risk-taking was the lowest of all behaviors. The average score of 2.17 is quite close to the scale point "bad idea." FREESTYLE had no effect at all in shifting these attitudes. Similarly for beliefs. It was believed before FREESTYLE that "some" girls took risks, and afterwards the perception was identical.

Why is FREESTYLE so ineffective in shifting concepts of independence and risk-taking? First it needs to be noted that each of these concepts is very complex. They are challenging to illustrate on TV, and probably also difficult to deal with in the classroom. In the Ann Arbor site there was a face to face interview with children after the series was over. In this site the children had both seen the show "Hike" and discussed it in class. Nonetheless, when asked about the show almost no one recalled any of the risk-taking elements. The central message for them was this: when you go on a hike, stay with the leader. It appears that at least some of the behavioral skills did not lend themselves to treatment in the fashion of FREESTYLE. Perhaps a number of related dramas extended over several weeks might be able to unravel better the essence of such complicated skills. Recall from Chapter Four that teachers who asked for additional shows wanted additional materials on behavioral skills more than any other content area.

Even if the shows and discussions had conveyed the message more aptly, it does not follow that the curriculum could affect attitudes and beliefs in these areas. Behavioral skills describe typical tendencies of people across a host of behavioral opportunities. The rationale for encouraging girls in these areas is that girls need to be more assertive or take more risks as children so that later in life they will make some -- maybe just one or two -- occupational and family choices that break sex-role barriers. To do this, girls need not become so assertive that they are viewed as outspoken or brash; neither do they need to become risk-taking daredevils. Suggesting to girls to take "just the right risk" may not be possible.

Moreover the data show that attitudes toward girls being assertive and taking risks are at the same level as attitudes toward boys behaving this way. Both sexes are also viewed as having about the same number of people who behave in this fashion. Since there are no sex differences to begin with the choice of including these attributes in the curriculum was probably a poor one.

PART III: ADULT WORK AND FAMILY ROLES

The purpose of the FREESTYLE intervention is to enhance the potential of youth to choose non-traditional occupations and family roles. One way of doing this is to encourage non-traditional behaviors in the current day-to-day lives of youngsters on the assumption that many of these behaviors will articulate to later choices. For example, if at age 11 a girl is able to pursue her non-traditional interest in mechanical things, then at age 18 she is more likely to feel comfortable choosing a non-traditional adult counterpart, such as auto mechanic or mechanical engineer. Another way to open up the potential of non-traditional adult choices is to influence the images of future potentiality. If a boy at 10 thinks all nurturant jobs are filled by women then he may close his mind to those avenues of fulfillment. Similarly, if a girl's only image of being a woman is that of a wife and mother she may close her eyes throughout adolescence to all opportunities to develop job skills that would serve her outside the home. Accordingly FREESTYLE made a concerted effort to present non-traditional images of adult work and family roles. The two-part show "SCOOP" has this topic as its primary focus. "Hey Mom" deals with a mother choosing to go to work as a machinist in a factory after many years of being a full time mother. In most of the remaining shows, non-traditional adults are always in the background. For example, Penny's mom owns a hardware store; Penny's science teacher is a Black male; Ramon's father, a Chicano, owns a construction firm, and so forth. To assess FREESTYLE's success in changing images of adulthood its impact is assessed in three areas corresponding to the belief-attitude-interest paradigm seen in the previous section. These include (1) children's perceptions of whether adult jobs and family roles are sex typed (beliefs), (2) children's approval of adults making non-traditional choices (attitudes), and (3) children's personal interest in considering non-traditional job choices for themselves.

Sex-typing of Adult Jobs

The children were presented with a list of jobs and told by their teacher (the administrator of the test) to "think about the kind of people who do the jobs, whether they are usually men or usually women." They rated each job on the following scale:

1) Almost all are men
2) More than half are men

3) About half are men, half are women
4) More than half are women
5) Almost all are women

The list of jobs had examples that were typically male and female. These included all the major adult jobs chosen by FREESTYLE designers for illustration in the series. By illustration is meant that the job was presented in the TV show with the non-traditional incumbent; e.g., a male is seen in the nurse role and a female owns a hardware store. The jobs are shown below. In parentheses after particular jobs are the notations "FL" standing for low emphasis in FREESTYLE and "FH" for high emphasis. If there is no notation then the job did not appear in the series, although it might have been discussed in the classroom.

Female Jobs: nurse (FL), secretary (FL), telephone operator, teacher of children who have problems with seeing or hearing (FH), occupational therapist (help sick or old people learn new skills) (FH).

Male Jobs: car mechanic (FH), truck driver (FL), machinist (makes parts for machines) (FH), pharmacist (gives out medicine in a drug store) (FL), owner of a hardware store (FH), city council member (someone elected to help run a city) (FH), geologist (scientist who studies rocks and minerals) (FH), worker in a factory who puts things together (like a car), sales person in a store who sells cars or TVs or refrigerators, owner of a restaurant, designer of electrical things like TVs, radios or calculators.

An index of each set of jobs was analyzed to look for FREESTYLE effects. To be judged effective, before seeing FREESTYLE male jobs would be seen as held predominantly by men, but after FREESTYLE, children should think a smaller proportion are men. The opposite should happen for female jobs. The data are shown in the first two rows of Table 7.8. Before FREESTYLE the two job sets are indeed perceived as quite different in terms of who holds them. "More than half" of those in female jobs are thought to be women and "more than half" of those in male jobs are believed to be men. Amazingly enough, these pre-test scores (3.81 for female jobs and 2.22 for male jobs were replicated exactly in Milwaukee and Worcester. This indicates that children are well aware of the realities of the job world and that this perception is widely shared throughout the country. From the data for the experimental group alone it appears that FREESTYLE has quite a large effect, shifting beliefs about both male and female jobs an average of .38SD toward the midpoint -- a response which corresponds to the belief that the composition of both male and female stereotyped jobs is split fifty-fifty between men and women. Even if such beliefs do not match realities, they are of the sort that facilitate FREESTYLE's goals -- create the image for children that jobs are not typed by the sex of those who hold them.

While the movement of the children is sizeable and in the right direction, the effects cannot all be attributed to FREESTYLE. Table 7.8 shows the data. (We will consider first the data for male jobs, then for female jobs: they are different.) For male jobs the beta for treatment is .062, low enough to indicate that the shift in beliefs is quite similar for the control group as well as the FREESTYLE participants. The average shift (not shown in the table) for the control group was .26SD and for the FREESTYLE group .39SD. This finding was replicated in Milwaukee and Worcester as well. One of two explanations are possible. The images of the gender of those in male jobs are shifting in our society at this time. Perhaps national media, such as TV, to which everyone has access was changing these stereotypes very rapidly during the same period that FREESTYLE was being viewed.

The other explanation is the possibility of reactivity of the instrument or questionnaire. By filling out the questionnaire at the time of the pre-test all respondents are sensitized to the issue of worker gender. During the ensuing months they are receptive to information on this topic and by the time of the post-test their beliefs have shifted. Social desirability provides yet another explanation. Having been sensitized to the issue of worker gender and other sex-role attitude issues, respondents become aware of the socially desirable response to this question and respond at the post-test in a way that they think teachers and researchers would like.

But the reactivity argument is difficult to maintain in the face of other data: The control group scores do <u>not</u> shift from pre to post for the majority of items in the questionnaire. Indeed the beliefs about female jobs <u>show a much smaller control group shift</u> and the items in the questionnaire immediately following these worker gender items -- attitudes toward more women in male jobs -- do not show <u>any</u> control group movement. Moreover, their

Table 7.8
Summary Table of Effects of Intensive Exposure to FREESTYLE (Long Beach)
Part III: Adult Job Roles

Index Name	MCA Predicting Gain Score (Total Sample)[1]						Mean Scores for Experimental Group Only									
	Multiple R	betas					Total[2]			Girls[3]			Boys[4]		
		Treatment	Sex	Grade	Race		Mean pre	Mean post	S.D. Shift[5]	Mean pre	Mean post	S.D. Shift[5]	Mean pre	Mean post	S.D. Shift[5]
Sex of those in Male Jobs[6]	.100	.062	.028	.077	.039		2.22	2.37	.39	2.31	2.46	.39	2.15	2.30	.39
Sex of those in Female Jobs[6]	.145	.134	.014	.045	.017		3.81	3.62	-.37	3.81	3.64	-.33	3.81	3.62	-.37
Att. toward more women in Male Jobs	.192	.164	.088	.043	.019		2.62	2.91	.44	2.87	3.08	.32	2.40	2.76	.55
Att. toward more men in Female Jobs (excl. nurses)	.114	.104	.004	.030	.028		2.99	3.17	.23	3.12	3.29	.22	2.89	3.08	.25
Female Jobs (inc. nurses)							2.60	3.01	.59	2.77	3.17	.58	2.46	2.87	.59

Approximate sample sizes are 1 950, 2 686, 3 314, 4 372.

[5] Subgroup post score minus subgroup pre score divided by the standard deviation of the pre-test score for the entire Long Beach sample.

[6] Scale: 5=almost all are women; 3=half are men, half are women; 1=almost all are men. Desirable movement is from an extreme position, 1 or 5, toward the midpoint, 3. are good at.

subject matter -- attitudes toward more men and women entering non-traditional occupations -- should be much more susceptible to post-test distortion for reasons of social desirability. Clearly there are no data in this study which can explain convincingly the phenomenon. The authors feel that the most plausible explanation is the first one -- that in the broader society beliefs and realities regarding women entering male jobs were shifting at the same time FREESTYLE was making its debut. If this is true then FREESTYLE's unique contribution in this specific category is quite small.

Significantly, FREESTYLE's contribution to shifting beliefs about the sex of those in female jobs was not compromised in the same way. Table 7.8 shows a beta of .134 for treatment corresponding to shifts of only .10SD for the control group (not shown in the table) and .37SD for the experimentals. If, as argued, the issue that has been prominent in the broader society is women entering traditionally male jobs and not the reverse, then it takes a targeted intervention with FREESTYLE's goals to bring about this second types of change -- beliefs about the sex of those in female jobs.

Attitudes Toward Men and Women Entering Non-traditional Jobs

Do the FREESTYLE children approve of non-traditional shifts in the labor force? To find out, some of the most sex-typed jobs from the belief list were presented in a different format. "What do you think it would be like if things were different than they are today? How would you feel if more women were..." This introduction was followed by a list of jobs; the children indicated for each one whether they thought it was a good or a bad idea if more women entered the occupation. The list included "car mechanics, truck drivers, machinists (makes parts for machines), owner of a hardware store and geologists (scientists who study rocks and minerals)." A similar question asked about men entering traditionally female jobs; the job list included "nurses, teachers of children who have problems with seeing or hearing, and occupational therapists (help sick or old people learn new skills)." A single index was created for each set, corresponding to attitudes toward women entering male jobs and men entering female jobs. The results are shown in rows 3-5 of Table 7.8.

Boys and girls started out quite separated on the issue of women entering male jobs. Girls were fairly approving (2.87) while boys were .71SD below them (2.40). FREESTYLE had quite strong effects. Boys moved up the scale a full one-half standard deviation to a point that was almost as approving as the girls started out to be. Girls also became more approving, moving up one-third standard deviation. On the question of men entering female jobs (last two rows) a similar picture emerged. Again the boys were much more conservative than the girls to begin with. FREESTYLE moved each group by .59SD (last row) retaining the gap between boys and girls, but the boys moved to a point on the scale that was slightly more approving than the girls started out to be.

The last two rows of Table 7.8 show the results for two indexes of attitudes toward men entering female jobs. One includes the job of "nurse" and the other does not. This occupation is about the most female stereotyped jobs there is. The data show that much of the movement in attitudes toward men entering female jobs comes from FREESTYLE's ability to influence values regarding this one job. This is truly quite remarkable since "nurse" may well stand as one of the primary symbols of female jobs. If boys can come to affirm that male nurses are a "good idea," many other female jobs in the helping area may open up as well.

Adult Family Roles

Raising a family is difficult work. There are many tasks which need to be accomplished ranging from child care to "breadwinning." Throughout history the tasks have been divided between the husband and wife. In western culture the most common division has invested the nurturing responsibilities with the wife and the breadwinning with the husband. In this century this pattern has been shifting somewhat to accommodate to both economic realities and female aspirations. Most importantly the whole thrust of the women's movement, and a clear implication of FREESTYLE's message, is that rigid role definitions in which a woman is identified with home and child care operates to inhibit the potential of both men and women. For women it reduces the possibility of their aspiring to fulfillment in the non-domestic labor force. For men it inhibits their consideration of more nurturant job roles. It has even been argued that it inhibits their playing an active role in nurturing their own children. Regardless of the issue of fulfillment it is clear that it is difficult for women to work outside the home and continue to be responsible for all of the domestic chores that traditionally are assigned to the wife. Accordingly, the FREESTYLE curriculum holds that children should become more open to the possibilities of non-traditional divisions of labor in families.

For this evaluation the major domestic chores were identified and assigned to their traditional adult role. Male tasks were:

- Take care of things around the house (paint the house, fix leaky faucets, and so forth)
- Take care of the car (keep it clean, have the oil changed, and so forth)

Female tasks included:

- Do the grocery shopping, cook the meals, do the dishes, and so forth
- Do the housecleaning (dust, vacuum, scrub the floors, clean the bathroom, and so forth)
- Take care of the children

For measures of beliefs children were asked for each male task how much of it was done by wives today ("all of it" to "none of it"); and for each of the female tasks how much was done by husbands. The attitude measures presented the same tasks with the questions for each: how much _should_ the task be done by wives or husbands? Initial analysis of the item responses indicated that the children think differently about duties inside the house and earning money outside the home. Accordingly the discussion to follow will treat these separately.

Do children see household tasks clearly divided into separate domains for husbands and wives? The answer, in short, is yes. The data for this discussion appear in Table 7.9. When asked how much the male tasks are done by wives, the average response is between "a little" and "some" (row 1 in Table 7.9). There are some small differences in this perception by sex; girls are more likely to say wives do more male tasks. There are also some small racial differences. Blacks and Hispanics say wives do more of the male jobs.

Attitudes toward wives doing male tasks (row 2) are initially at about the same level as beliefs. (Remember, the same scale is used in this domain for both beliefs and attitudes. One time it is used to describe the way things are -- beliefs; the other time it is used to describe the way things should be -- attitudes.) Boys and girls are pretty much in agreement on this. But the racial groups are separated as they were on beliefs with Blacks and Hispanics saying more male tasks should be done by wives.

Exposure to FREESTYLE is associated with moderately large shifts. Both boys and girls shift their beliefs and attitudes in favor of wives doing male household chores, but, as with women entering male jobs, the control group shifted as well.

Something interesting happens to the racial groups here. For both beliefs and attitudes Whites, who started out below Blacks and Hispanics, shift more than the other groups with the effect of once again homogenizing the groups. At the time of the post-test there were virtually no differences among racial groups.

With respect to females having the opportunity to choose a career outside the home, the more crucial domain is beliefs and attitudes regarding husbands doing female chores. Table 7.9 (row 3) shows that the initial scores were about the same as for the wives questions. Both boys and girls believe that husbands do somewhere between "a little" and "some" of the female tasks. Again there are racial differences, but this time it is Blacks who see husbands doing more of the female chores than the other two groups.

FREESTYLE shifts these beliefs, although girls are more likely to think husbands help out more often. Both boys and girls become more supportive of husbands sharing, with boys shifting .40SD to a point quite close to the girls.

Earning Money to Support the Family

It is one thing to approve of a husband helping with nurturant tasks at home. This would facilitate a family arrangement in which the wife might be able to free herself of enough domestic responsibilities to work outside the

Table 7.9
Summary Table of Effects of Intensive Exposure to FREESTYLE (Long Beach)
Part IV: Adult Family Roles

Index Name	MCA Predicting Gain Score (Total Sample)[1]					Mean Scores for Experimental Group Only								
	Multiple R	betas				Total[2]			Girls[3]			Boys[4]		
		Treatment	Sex	Grade	Race	Mean pre	Mean post	S.D. Shift[5]	Mean pre	Mean post	S.D. Shift[5]	Mean pre	Mean post	S.D. Shift[5]
Wives don't do male chores[6]	.110	.074	.015	.035	.077	3.61	3.37	-.26	3.48	3.22	-.28	3.73	3.50	-.24
Wives should not do male chores[7]	.114	.079	.061	.045	.048	3.61	3.28	-.33	3.57	3.16	-.41	3.64	3.38	-.26
Husbands don't do female chores[6]	.161	.129	.041	.047	.066	3.51	3.27	-.29	3.54	3.22	-.39	3.49	3.31	-.22
Husbands should not do female chores[7]	.170	.151	.019	.042	.062	3.37	3.04	-.36	3.24	2.94	-.33	3.48	3.12	-.40
Husbands earn all income[8]	.114	.031	.078	.079	.025	4.31	4.22	-.10	4.22	4.20	-.02	4.37	4.24	-.15
Husbands should earn all income[9]	.078	.066	.003	.039	.014	4.24	4.11	-.13	4.25	4.07	-.19	4.24	4.14	-.10
Wives earn no income[10]	.118	.086	.027	.044	.061	2.66	2.65	-.01	2.46	2.48	.02	2.83	2.80	-.03
Wives should earn no income[11]	.127	.072	.020	.083	.058	2.87	2.76	-.09	2.68	2.61	-.06	3.02	2.90	-.12

NOTE: for all scales desirable movement is negative, toward 1.

Approximate sample sizes are [1] 950, [2] 686, [3] 314, [4] 372.

[5] Subgroup post score minus subgroup pre score divided by the standard deviation of the pre-test score for the entire LB sample.

[6] Scale: 5=wives/husbands do none of it, 1=do all of it; [7] Scale: 5= wives/husbands should do none of it, 1=should do all of it; [8] Scale: 5=husband earns all of it; [9] Scale: 5=husband should earn all of it; [10] Scale: 5=wives earn none of it; [11] Scale: 5=wives should earn none of it.

home. But it is yet another thing to respond to the issue of the wife leaving home to earn money to help support the family. Rows 5-8 of Table 7.9 show the data. Recall that these data are based on responses to single items which asked children how much "working to earn money to support the family" is done by husbands vs. wives. Consider just husbands working to earn money. Not surprisingly, husbands are thought to do between "most" and "all" of this task, and there is a very small tendency for boys to think husbands do a little more of the breadwinning. There are no race differences. FREESTYLE did not affect these beliefs at all. A similar picture appears for attitudes. Children who hold the opinion that husbands should earn most of the money show very little change after exposure to FREESTYLE.

Turning to wives earning money, the initial picture is quite different although FREESTYLE again has very little effect. At the beginning the estimate of how much of the breadwinning wives do is estimated to be close to the scale point "some." Boys and girls are somewhat different in their estimates; girls estimate wives do a little more breadwinning. The standard deviation for the overall estimate is quite large (1.21), indicating that opinions vary substantially on the issue. Racial identity is the only factor in this study which is associated with this variability. Blacks estimate between "some" and "most" wives, while whites estimate only "some" wives. These beliefs were virtually unchanged by FREESTYLE except that the Blacks and Whites drew closer together in perceptions. The picture for attitudes is very similar.

Despite a concerted effort on FREESTYLE's part to show non-traditional occupational attainment by women, children seem very rarely to have gotten a message that the basic division of labor in breadwinning is -- or should be -- any different than they already perceive.

Interest in Non-traditional Adult Roles

Finally, let's take a look at FREESTYLE's impact on children's own interest in non-traditional adult jobs. The FREESTYLE curriculum explicitly stated that children engaging in the program should afterwards express increased interest in "exploring" non-traditional occupations. For this study children were presented with a list of 36 occupations and asked for each whether they would "consider doing" it. The scale options included definitely, probably, probably not, and definitely not. The jobs in the list were carefully chosen to include a sampling of traditional male and female jobs, as well as jobs that did and did not get illustrated in FREESTYLE. In addition, using the occupational coding scheme of John Holland, jobs were selected in each of the six domains identified by him as covering the spectrum of job types in the labor force. Given the age of the children, jobs with difficult names were described as well as labelled. In order to address the issue raised by the FREESTYLE curriculum the jobs can be divided into two categories, male and female. In the list below an "F" in parentheses after the occupation indicates the job was extensively illustrated in FREESTYLE.

> Male jobs. Car mechanic (F), truck driver, electrician, carpenter, worker in a factory who puts things together (like a car or other machine), machinist (makes parts for machines) (F), boss in a factory, professional athlete, coach (F), reporter (writes stories for a newspaper), photographer (takes pictures for a newspaper), pharmacist (gives out medicine in a drug store), geologist (scientist who studies rocks and minerals) (F), designer of electrical things like TVs, radios, or calculators, scientist who studies how the weather works, scientist who studies how plants and animals grow, designer of airplanes or rockets, owner of a hardware store (F), owner of a business which makes things like shoes, toys or furniture, manager of a motel or hotel, owner of a restaurant, owner of a company which builds houses, sales person in a store who sells cars or televisions or refrigerators, city council member (someone elected to run a city (F), someone who sorts mail in the post office.

> Female jobs. Nurse, school teacher (f), librarian, dental assistant (clean people's teeth or help dentist fix their teeth), occupational therapist (help sick or old people learn new skills) (F), teacher of children who have problems with seeing or hearing (F), homemaker -- a father or mother who stays home and cares for the children, cooks meals and cleans the house (F), secretary, bookkeeper (keep records of money spent and received by a business), check-out clerk at a grocery or discount store, telephone operator.

The children's expressions of interest in these occupations are summarized in several ways. One is the average interest expressed across all male occupations and across all female occupations. The other is the total number of occupations in which interest is expressed, where to be interested in a job means the respondent indicated they would either "consider" or "definitely consider" it. This total can be broken down into the number that are male jobs vs. female jobs. This count of endorsed occupations is especially useful for assessing the FREESTYLE curriculum goal: "given a list of careers for females, an increased number of girls will select non-traditional occupations they would like to explore."

The data are summarized in Table 7.10. The first two rows show the average interest in male and female occupations. In a sample of children evenly split between boys and girls the average interest in male and female occupations is identical. But this comes about because of the sharp contrast between boys' and girls' interests. Boys average considerably higher than girls in interest in male jobs: 2.50 vs. 2.15 -- a half standard deviation difference. The opposite is true for female jobs, with girls' interest averaging 2.75 and boys a full standard deviation lower at 1.92. This is clear evidence that at the time of pre-adolescence children's occupational interests follow a sex-typed pattern. This can be seen in another way elsewhere in Table 7.10. Out of a list of 36 occupations these children on the average show interest in 15 of them. Of these, girls prefer male jobs by a ratio of approximately 1.5:1, while boys prefer male jobs by a ratio of 4:1.

What effect does FREESTYLE have on this pattern? Looking at male jobs first the results of the MCAs are not large; the beta for treatment is only .110 and girls change only a little more than boys. The overall movement for the experimental group is a modest .24SD, with the largest movement being that of girls. Their increase of .30SD brings them close to the average pre-test interest of boys. This increase corresponds to girls showing an interest in about one and one-half more male jobs on the average. FREESTYLE appears to have had a modest effect in increasing interest in non-traditional careers, but this conclusion must be balanced by the finding that there was also a small increase in the number of traditional female jobs selected as well.

For boys the opposite is true. Their average interest in female occupations increases .26SD, but for boys this increase results in an average that is still at the "would not consider" point on the scale. It does correspond to an increase in the selection of female jobs of roughly one, i.e., from 3 female jobs before FREESTYLE to 3.8 jobs afterwards. With the

Table 7.10

Part V: Adult Occupations

	MCA Predicting Gain Score (Total Sample)[1]					Mean Scores for Experimental Group Only											
		betas				Total[2]			Girls[3]			Boys[4]					
Index Name	Mult-iple R	Treat-ment	Sex	Grade	Race	Mean pre	Mean post	S.D. Shift[5]	Mean pre	Mean post	S.D. Shift[5]	Mean pre	Mean post	S.D. Shift[5]
Interest in Male Occup.	.161	.110	.006	.041	.108	2.34	2.52	.24	2.15	2.37	.30	2.50	2.64	.19
Interest in Fem. Occup.	.173	.129	.039	.059	.077	2.30	2.46	.20	2.75	2.84	.11	1.92	2.13	.26
No. of Occup. Endorsed	.148	.121	.008	.069	.056	15.1	17.5	.27	15.1	17.5	.27	15.1	17.5	.27
No. of Male Occup. Endorsed						10.6	12.1	.22	8.6	10.3	.27	12.3	13.6	.19
Male Occ. as Pct. of total Endorsed						70%	69%		57%	59%		82%	78%	
No. of female Occup. Endorsed						4.61	5.37	.22	6.6	7.2	.18	3.0	3.8	.24
Fem. Occ. as Pct. of Total						30%	31%		43%	41%		18%	22%	

boys as with the girls there is a countervailing increase in the selection of male jobs. Apparently FREESTYLE has the effect of stimulating a modest increase in overall interest in occupations and, to a small extent, this happens in a way which suggests that sex typing of jobs is reduced.

A check was made to see if there was a separate pattern of response for just those occupations heavily portrayed in the FREESTYLE shows. There was not. Similarly, occupations which were highlighted in FREESTYLE by having Blacks or Hispanics playing the roles were examined for differential effects among minority participants. There was none.

Apparently, as with interests in childhood activities, a program such as FREESTYLE can have only limited affects on the interest pattern of 9-12 year olds.

SUMMARY

This chapter has provided a detailed description of the sex-role orientations of children prior to FREESTYLE and documented the ability of FREESTYLE to intervene in these orientations when used in a classroom with teacher-led discussion and supplementary activities. The effects of FREESTYLE are summarized in Table 7.11. Overall, the program is capable of producing very large changes in the beliefs and attitudes of 9-12 year olds. In the test cities boys and girls alike became more supportive of non-traditional sex-role behavior, both of their own and of the opposite sex. This was true with respect to girls in mixed-sex athletics, mechanical pursuits and leadership roles; and for boys in helping roles. It was largely true with respect to non-traditional choices in adult job and family roles as well. The series was notably unsuccessful in affecting beliefs and attitudes in three areas: independence from peer pressure, assertiveness, and risk-taking for girls. These topics are probably too complex to be dealt with in a short dramatic series which has only one or two 1/2-hour shows for each topic. While FREESTYLE was successful in changing some perceptions of appropriate family roles for wives and husbands, it was not sufficient to break down the image of the wife as the primary domestic partner and the husband as the breadwinner.

Table 7.11

Summary of FREESTYLE Effects

	Beliefs About	Attitudes Toward	Interest In
Childhood Pre-occupational Activities	••• Boys in Helping Roles • Girls in Athletics ••• Girls doing Mechanics ---	••• Boys in Helping Roles ••• Girls in Athletics ••• Girls doing Mechanics ---	(helping) ••• Athletics[3] •• Mechanics (science)
Childhood Behavioral Skills	•• Girls as Leaders (girls being independent) (girls being assertive) (girls taking risks)	•• Girls as Leaders • Girls being Independent[2] • Girls being Assertive[2] (girls taking risks)	--- --- --- ---
Adult Work and Family Roles	(extent "male" jobs are done only by men)[1] •• Extent "Female" Jobs are Done Only by Women (extent "male" household tasks done only by husbands)[1] •• Extent "Female" Household Tasks Done Only by Wives (extent wives earn money) (extent husbands earn money)	••• More Women in "Male" Jobs •• More Men in "Female" Jobs (wives doing more male household tasks)[1] •• Husbands Doing More Female Household Tasks (extent wives should earn money) (extent husbands should earn money)	("male jobs) ("female" jobs) --- --- ---

KEY: ---=the concept was not measured
Size of effect: •••=large ••=medium •=small ( )=no effect
[1] Positive shift for control group invalidates an otherwise sizeable shift for the treatment group.
[2] "Homogenizing" effect only.
[3] Positive effects in only one site.

FREESTYLE was much less successful in changing interest patterns in non-sexist ways. Girls came to express increased interest in athletics and mechanical activities, but not scientific activities or adult occupations typically held by men. Boys did not expand their interests to include helping activities or those adult occupations typically held by women. A TV series of this type and length aimed at 9-12 year olds should probably not have occupational interest patterns among its targets. While expanding interest in childhood activities is more appropriate, the pattern of strong and weak effects highlights the importance of choosing the activities carefully.

Overall, FREESTYLE is capable of reducing sex-role stereotypes and expanding "career awareness" when used in a classroom setting with teacher-led discussion and activities. We turn in the next chapter to effects derived from mere viewing of the television shows.

Chapter 8

THE IMPACT OF MERE VIEWING

It was shown in the previous chapter that FREESTYLE can be very effective in producing change when the shows are viewed and discussed in a classroom setting -- the so-called School Full treatment. But FREESTYLE was designed as well as a series of TV shows that would be viewed just like any other dramatic children's series without the advantages of organized classroom discussion. In this chapter the effects of "just viewing" are examined first for viewing in the captive environment of the classroom (School View-Only treatment) and then in the less structured environment of the home.

PART I: VIEWING IN THE CLASSROOM

The School View-Only treatment condition was described in detail in Chapter Three. In brief, past research indicates the great difficulty of studying home viewing behavior; it is difficult to induce high levels of viewing, and the quantity and quality of viewing is hard to monitor. To circumvent these difficulties, the simulation capabilities of the "product validation" notion were applied in the following way: the effect of mere viewing was studied in the captive setting of the school, with special provision to insure that the programs were not discussed by the teacher. Teachers in this arrangement were asked to have the class view each quarter-hour show. To discourage class discussion, broadcast times were set up so that each show ended just before a recess period. The research project's success in implementing this experimental condition is described in Chapter Three. The data presented here are based on those classrooms that viewed at least 24 of the 26 1/4-hour shows and did not discuss any of the shows.

The primary analysis site for School View-Only is Worcester, MA, with North Kansas City, MO as the replicate. In Worcester, schools were assigned randomly to three conditions: control, School View-Only, and School Full. This permits comparisons -- within one site -- of the relative strength of View-Only and Full conditions. The data presented in this chapter are from Worcester, with interpretations modified only if they were not replicated in North Kansas City.

A description of Worcester can be found in the appendix. Characteristics of the Worcester children in this study are summarized in Table 8.1: of the 1064 students, 25 percent are in the control group, 35 percent in the View-Only group, and 40 percent in the School Full group. There are equal proportions of boys and girls, and of fourth, fifth and sixth graders. The sample is almost entirely White, reflecting the character of the city itself. Throughout this chapter comparisons will be made between the View-Only and School Full groups. The latter group will be referred to by the acronym SCFULL.

Table 8.1
Characteristics of the Worcester
Sample After Eliminating
Low Implementing Classrooms

Treatment[1]		Sex		Grade		Race	
n	%	n	%	n	%	n	%
Control = 268	25	Girls = 518	49	Four = 368	35	White = 1030	97
View-Only = 375	35	Boys = 546	51	Five = 347	33	Black = 33	3
View-Plus = 421	40			Six = 349	33	Other = 1	*
1064	100	1064	100	1064	100	1064	100

[1]View only="School View-Only" treatment group; View-Plus=School Full treatment group

An assumption underlying this part of the investigation is that mere viewing should result in effects quite similar to the SCFULL treatment, but attenuated in their strength. Although the dynamics might be somewhat different in the absence of group discussion, it was expected that mere viewing would not show effects in areas in which SCFULL treatment had shown none. Accordingly, evidence of impact was sought among those outcomes which were shown in the previous chapter to be domains in which FREESTYLE could be effective when used intensively in the classroom. These are the indices which appear in Table 8.2.

In the previous chapter the indicator of strength of effect was the experimental group's raw gain score divided by the standard deviation of the pretest score. It was argued that this was an appropriate measure as long as the control group did not show any shift from pre to post. If the controls showed a similar shift, the measure of effect was discounted, although not by an exact amount. In this chapter a similar strategy is employed, but here the raw gain of the control group is subtracted from the raw gain of both the View-Only and SCFULL groups as a way to discount change that cannot be attributed uniquely to FREESTYLE. These "net" gains are then divided by the standard deviation of the pretest score for the combined control and experimental groups. To compare the effect of View-Only relative to SCFULL, a third calculation is made. View-only is expressed as a percent of the SCFULL effect. An example may be useful here. Consider the first row of Table 8.2. In the area of attitudes towards girls in mechanics, the View-Only group shifted their attitudes in a more approving direction by .33SD (SD = Standard Deviation). The attitudes of the SCFULL group showed a positive shift of .43SD. Dividing the View-Only effect by that for School Full yields a figure of .77, suggesting that mere viewing can produce 77 percent of the effect of SCFULL. Judging the effects of mere viewing, then, will be made on the basis of the absolute effect for mere viewing and the effect relative to the effects possible with viewing plus discussion. One other technical note. In the previous chapter, effects of less than .20SD were considered inconsequential. Accordingly, if the SCFULL effect is less than this figure, the percentage is not calculated.

Table 8.2
Effects of "School View Only" as a Percent of "School Full" Effect
(Worcester)

	Total			Girls			Boys		
	School View SD Increase	School Full SD Increase	View as percent of Full	School View SD Increase	School Full SD Increase	View as percent of Full	School View SD Increase	School Full SD Increase	View as percent of Full
Attitude toward girls in mechanics	.39	.51	77	.52	.59	88	.26	.43	61
Beliefs about girls in mechanics	.23	.33	70	.37	.49	76	.08	.16	--
Interest in mechanics	.30	.31	96	.46	.51	91	.16	.13	--
Attitude toward girls in athletics	.00	.26	00	.04	.24	17	-.01	.26	16
Interest in athletics	.08	.12	--	.11	.16	--	.05	.09	--
Attitude toward boys in helping activities	.22	.55	40	.18	.70	25	.27	.40	68
Beliefs about boys in helping activities	.02	.35	06	.05	.47	11	-.01	.24	04
Attitude toward girls as leaders	.12	.23	55	.02	.11	--	.23	.33	70
Beliefs about girls as leaders	.13	.17	--	.13	.05	--	.13	.27	48
Beliefs that only women hold female jobs	-.23	-.26	86	-.06	-.23	25	-.42	-.30	138
Attitude toward more women in male jobs	.06	.23	27	.06	.24	25	.06	.20	31
Attitude toward more men in female jobs	.18	.43	41	.34	.55	62	.05	.34	15
Belief that husband does female home tasks	.26	.32	81	.31	.31	100	.21	.35	61
Attitude toward husband doing female home tasks	.18	.29	62	.32	.39	83	.04	.18	--
Belief that wife does male home tasks	.33	.38	86	.23	.29	78	.40	.40	100
Attitude toward wife doing male home tasks	.14	.29	50	.18	.45	39	.12	.13	--

KEY: AT=attitude toward; BF=beliefs about; INT=interest in; "--"=SD increase is less than .20
NOTE: "SD Increase" is calculated by (1) subtracting the average pre-post raw gain of the control group from that of the experimental group and dividing by the standard deviation of the pre-test measure for the total sample.

Girls in mechanical activities. It was in this domain that FREESTYLE showed some of its strongest effects under the SCFULL condition in Long Beach and Milwaukee. A similar thing happened for SCFULL children in Worcester; attitudes toward girls engaging in mechanical activities became much more supportive (See Table 8.2). For the combined group of boys and girls, SCFULL showed an increase of .51SD and mere viewing .39SD, or 77 percent as much effect. In absolute terms, for girls the size of the effect is very large -- .52SD; for boys it is only a modest effect -- .25SD. In relative terms mere viewing was almost as effective as SCFULL for the girls, but much less so for the boys -- 88 percent of the SCFULL effect for girls vs. 61 percent for the boys. It is quite likely that boys represent the more difficult target group for the message and so it is reasonable that they would be harder to persuade with just the television shows alone.

Beliefs about how many girls are good at mechanical activities changed only for girls. After FREESTYLE all Worcester girls increased their estimate of how many girls are good at mechanical endeavors. View-only girls increased .37SD and SCFULL girls .49SD; both effects are quite large. But the boys held on to their negative assessment, both in SCFULL and View-Only conditions.

Increasing interest in mechanical activities was targeted only for girls. This area showed a very strong effect for mere viewing. In Worcester the effect was in excess of 90 percent. However, these findings were not corroborated in the replicate site, North Kansas City. Although the pre-test interest scores were virtually identical in the two sites, in North Kansas City only the SCFULL girls showed heightened mechanical interest (Table 8.3).

Table 8.3
Girls Increase in Interest
in Mechanical Activities

	Worcester	N. Kansas City
SCVIEW	.38SD	.08SD
SCFULL	.42SD	.39SD

In the mechanical activities domain, then, it appears that viewing has the potential for inducing much of the same change as SCFULL among girls, the primary target group. For boys in these two sites SCFULL was able to produce only one appreciable change -- attitude toward girls engaging in mechanical activities; mere viewing yielded a little over half of this effect.

Girls in athletics. Consider first attitudes toward girls playing athletics. It was noted in the previous chapter that in Worcester, at the same time FREESTYLE was on the air, these attitudes were shifting for the control group as well. In spite of this, in Worcester the SCFULL children -- both boys and girls -- showed enough additional change to show a moderate unique effect. But not in the View-Only group -- their responses were no different than the control group.

Girls' interest in athletics did not change for either SCFULL or View-Only groups; but again pre-conditions account for this. Recall from the previous chapter that girls in Long Beach began the experiment with lower levels of interest in athletics than girls in any other site, especially Worcester. While FREESTYLE increased the athletic interest of Long Beach girls by a very large amount, their post-test interest scores were about the same level as the Worcester pre-test scores, suggesting that Worcester girls were not in need of change on this dimension.

In short, in the domain of girls in athletics mere viewing showed no effect, although the "need" in Worcester did not provide much opportunity either.

Boys in nurturing activities. The SCFULL treatment had a strong positive effect on girls' perceptions regarding boys in helping roles. Their attitudes and beliefs shifted .70SD and .47SD respectively. But the effects of mere viewing did not meet the minimum level for educational significance. In North Kansas City it was somewhat different; mere viewing shifted girls' attitudes almost as much as SCFULL, but it did not shift their beliefs.

The attitude of boy participants toward nurturant boys shifted .40SD in SCFULL classrooms, and mere viewing yielded 68 percent of this effect. For boys' beliefs about whether boys are good at nurturing, viewing had no effect.

The domain of boys in nurturing activities provided eight tests of viewing effects (attitudes and beliefs for boys and girls in Worcester and North Kansas City). In only two of the eight tests did mere viewing produce an appreciable portion of the effects of the SCFULL treatment. Both of these instances were shifts in attitudes, not beliefs.

Girls in leadership roles. In the SCFULL condition FREESTYLE increased substantially boys' support (attitudes) for girl leaders (.33SD). As in Long Beach, this movement was all at the negative end of the scale. Thus the .33SD movement for boys represents a shift from 1.95 to 2.28 on a scale where 2.0 is a "bad idea" and 3.0 is a "good idea." The effect of mere viewing is 70 percent of SCFULL. In North Kansas City the effect for SCFULL boys was higher (.58SD), and the View-Only condition was associated with 85 percent of this effect. In the area of attitudes toward girls as leaders mere viewing fares well in relative terms, but in absolute terms the effects of neither condition are impressive.

It was noted in the Long Beach and Milwaukee data that beliefs about girls as leaders has an interesting and contrasting pattern for the two sexes. Before FREESTYLE girls thought most girls are good leaders while boys believed the opposite. The effects in Long Beach of viewing and discussion was to make girls' beliefs less positive (perhaps more realistic) and boys' beliefs more positive, thus closing the gap between boys and girls' beliefs. The positive movement of boys and the gap closing were interpreted as positive effects for FREESTYLE. In both Worcester and North Kansas City the SCFULL effects occurred only for boys and these were quite modest -- .27SD. The View-Only treatment captured 48 percent of this effect in Worcester yielding a non-significant shift of .13SD. In North Kansas City mere viewing showed no effects for boys.

In sum when it comes to girls as leaders, mere viewing does not appear to have been adequate to the task.

Women and men in non-traditional jobs. Children's beliefs about whether some jobs are held only by men or women can affect boys' and girls' sense of which jobs are appropriate aspirational goals. As noted earlier, FREESTYLE's unique contribution lay not in convincing children that more women can be found in male jobs today, but rather that a lot of men are now being found in traditionally female jobs. In Worcester boys who saw FREESTYLE came increasingly to think female jobs (nurse, secretary) were likely to be held by men as well as women. Interestingly, the effects of mere viewing were even stronger than SCFULL (.42SD vs. .30SD).

When it comes to shifting attitudes toward men and women entering non-traditional jobs, the effects are associated mostly with SCFULL. In SCFULL boys and girls became modestly more supportive of more women entering male jobs and much more supportive of men entering female jobs. View-only shifted only one of these four sets of attitudes. This was girls' attitudes toward men entering female occupations. This is a much less important accomplishment than convincing boys that it is acceptable for their own sex to enter female jobs. In North Kansas City the pattern was similar.

Overall, mere viewing makes a modest contribution in this area although not sufficient to achieve the broader goals of the series.

<u>Husbands</u> <u>and</u> <u>wives</u> <u>in</u> <u>non-traditional</u> <u>family</u> <u>roles</u>. FREESTYLE's designers assumed that non-traditional job attainment, in particular women working outside the home, requires a redistribution of family roles: men being willing to share in the child care and cooking and perhaps women in some of the home maintenance. The SCFULL treatment affected beliefs in this regard; both boys and girls came increasingly to think that husbands sometimes do the child care and cooking. Girls even became more approving of it, but not the boys -- the group that would actually be required to take on this new role.

Mere viewing showed a mixed pattern of results. Both attitudes and beliefs of girls moved almost as much just from watching. But not so for the boys. The beliefs of View-Only boys shifted only to the threshold level of effect and their attitudes did not shift at all.

When it came to wives doing the husband's household tasks the effects on beliefs were more equivalent for viewing and SCFULL, but not for attitudes. Mere viewing did not shift the attitudes appreciably.

Table 8.4

Summary of FREESTYLE Effects on 9-12 Year Olds For Classroom View-Only Condition

	Girls	Beliefs About	Boys	Girls	Attitude Toward	Boys	Girls	Interest In	Boys
Childhood Pre-occupational Activities	no	Boys in Helping Roles	no	•••	Boys in Helping Roles[3]	•	inap	Helping	no
	no	Girls in Athletics	no	no	Girls in Athletics	no	no	Athletics	no
	••	Girls doing Mechanics	no	•••	Girls doing Mechanics	•	•	Mechanics[3]	inap
		---			---		no	Science	inap
Childhood Behavioral Skills	no	Girls as Leaders	no	no	Girls as Leaders	•[3]		---	
	•	Girls being Independent	no	•	Girls being Independent[2]	no		---	
	••	Girls being Assertive	no	no	Girls being Assertive[2]	no		---	
	no	Girls taking Risks	no	no	Girls taking Risks	no		---	
Adult Work and Family Roles	no	Extent "Male" Jobs are Done Only by Men[1]	no	no	More Women in "Male" Jobs	no	no	"Male" Jobs	no
	no	Extent "Female" Jobs are Done Only by Women	•••	•	More Men in "Female" Jobs	no	no	"Female" Jobs	no
	•	Extent "Male" Household Tasks are Done by Husbands	•••	no	Wives Doing More Male Household Tasks	no		---	
	••	Extent "Female" Household Tasks are Done by Wives	•	•	Husbands Doing More Female Household Tasks	no		---	
	no	Extent Wives Earn Money	no	no	Extent Wives Should Earn Money	no		---	
	no	Extent Husbands Earn Money to Support Family	no	no	Extent Husbands Should Earn Money to Support Fam.	no		---	

KEY: ---=the concept was not measured
Size of effect: •••=large ••=medium •=small no=no effect

[1] Positive shift for control group invalidates an otherwise sizeable shift for the treatment group.
[2] "Homogenizing" effect only in SCFULL sites; cannot be measured in view-only sites.
[3] Positive effects in only one site.

In this domain it appears that mere viewing is more effective shifting beliefs than attitudes. Distinguishing among target audiences, it appears that viewing is more likely to have an effect on an audience that is receptive to its messages. Thus, for example, View-Only girls shifted as much as SCFULL when it came to letting husbands do a wife's chores, but not so View-Only boys. It required the additional input of class discussion, perhaps in a mixed sex setting, to move the boys.

Summary. The effects of mere viewing are summarized in Table 8.4, using "bullets" again to show the size of effect. Reviewing the effects, two conclusions seem warranted. Viewing by itself is capable in some instances of delivering an effect almost as large as viewing accompanied by extensive classroom discussion. The factors which determine whether mere viewing will fare as well as SCFULL are unclear, although it seems that it occurs most often for the simpler communication tasks -- i.e., where the audience is receptive to the message to begin with, such as convincing girls that people of their own sex make good leaders.

The second conclusion is that the complex integrated set of goals which comprise the FREESTYLE package cannot be delivered effectively by a strategy of mere viewing. While viewing does not have negative effects and indeed children like the shows enough that they would be happy to simply watch FREESTYLE -- the percentage of educational goals that could be achieved in this way is undoubtedly too small by anyone's standard. The amount of teacher mediation and class discussion needed to yield the more desirable levels of effect of SCFULL is unknown at this time, but it may require just a little input, focused around certain shows, to heighten the effect.

Yet another perspective could find mere viewing cost effective. The research design used to evaluate FREESTYLE looked for effects after insuring that all subjects had watched all shows. If one looks at the areas where mere viewing seemed to fare best: girls in mechanics, boys in nurturance, and non-traditional adult family roles, these effects might be secured through the viewing of just six of the 13 shows:

"Grease Monkey" and "Partners" for girls in mechanics.

"Young and Old" and "Helping Hand" for boys in helping activities.

"Scoop" Parts I and II for changing adult roles.

This would represent just three hours of viewing time -- a very small investment.

PART II: VIEWING AT HOME

The usual place for unmediated viewing to occur is in the home, not the school. However, home-viewing is not as intense a learning environment. Many activities compete for viewing time, restricting the total number of shows viewed in a 13-part series. When viewing does occur it is likely to be less attentive than in the School View-Only condition because of distractions in the home environment. It was for these reasons that the effects of mere viewing were investigated in the school environment.

But FREESTYLE was designed largely for home viewing. Can it draw sufficient audiences to conceive of delivering the FREESTYLE messages directly to the home instead of the school? It is a well-accepted fact that PBS offerings do not draw the audiences of the commercial networks. Indeed, individual FREESTYLE shows drew only a 2.2 share of the viewing households in November and December of 1978 -- high by PBS standards for children's programming, but not very impressive if someone wants to reach large segments of the population with its messages.

FREESTYLE's designers had no marketing plan to induce larger numbers of households to view. They did produce a home calendar with the avowed purpose of helping parents introduce their children to FREESTYLE and its messages. It was never made clear how this was to be distributed or how parents would be attracted to use the calendar.

In the absence of any plan to increase home viewership, the evaluation study chose a plan which it judged was at least feasible, and which had the potential of increasing home viewership enough to study it. The plan was based on using the community's dominant educational agency -- the public schools -- to endorse the series for students and their parents, and to have

Table 8.5

Characteristics of the Home Site Samples

Treatment			Sex			Grade			Race		
	n	%		n	%		n	%		n	%

Saginaw

control =	99	28	Girls =	182	52	Four =	189	54	White =	266	76
view =	252	72	Boys =	169	48	Five =	41	12	Black =	62	18
						Six =	121	34	Mex =	19	5
									Other =	4	1
	351	100		351	100		351	100		351	100

Covina

control =	112	26	Girls =	211	49	Four =	227	53	White =	315	74
view =	315	74	Boys =	216	51	Six =	200	47	Black =	4	1
									Mex =	97	23
									Other =	11	2
	427	100		427	100		427	100		427	100

the classroom teacher remind children weekly to watch the shows. If the series can be categorized as career education, and the upper elementary curriculum is too crowded for this material, it is perhaps a viable alternative to have the schools call on home television to extend the educational reach of the schools beyond their own walls. One variation on this would be to get children to watch the shows by themselves, another would be to get parents to "co-view" with their children to enhance the possibility of parent mediation of the educational messages.

As described earlier, two districts -- Saginaw, MI and Covina, CA were enlisted in this effort. The demographics of the sample in the home sites are shown in Table 8.5. In each district ten schools were selected to participate, with two participating classrooms in each. Letters signed by each school's principal were sent home to the parents. The letter asked the parent to encourage the child to watch FREESTYLE. In some cases the parent was asked to encourage the child -- but also to watch FREESTYLE with their child. Each week the classroom teacher reminded the class on Friday to watch the home broadcast. On Monday the students completed the classroom home viewing chart which indicated whether they viewed and whether it was alone or with a parent. Using these data it was clear that parent co-viewing -- supposedly a separate treatment -- occurred as frequently in both types of experimental conditions, leading to the conclusion that <u>experimentally</u> there was only one treatment: viewing.

Show-by-show viewing behavior, based on the combined samples of Saginaw and Covina, are displayed in Figure 8.1. On the average, 32 percent of those asked to view watched any one show, resulting in a high of 42 percent for the show "Flag" and a low of 21 percent for "Hey Mom!" It is hard to know what factors account for this variation. The two shows with the lowest viewing were broadcast quite close to Christmas -- a time when children are not in the classroom and seasonal activities and network specials provide competition for the activity of viewing FREESTYLE. Overall, the average viewing rate of one in three is interpreted by the present researchers as quite high -- indicating that schools could achieve reasonable levels of home viewing with minimal effort.

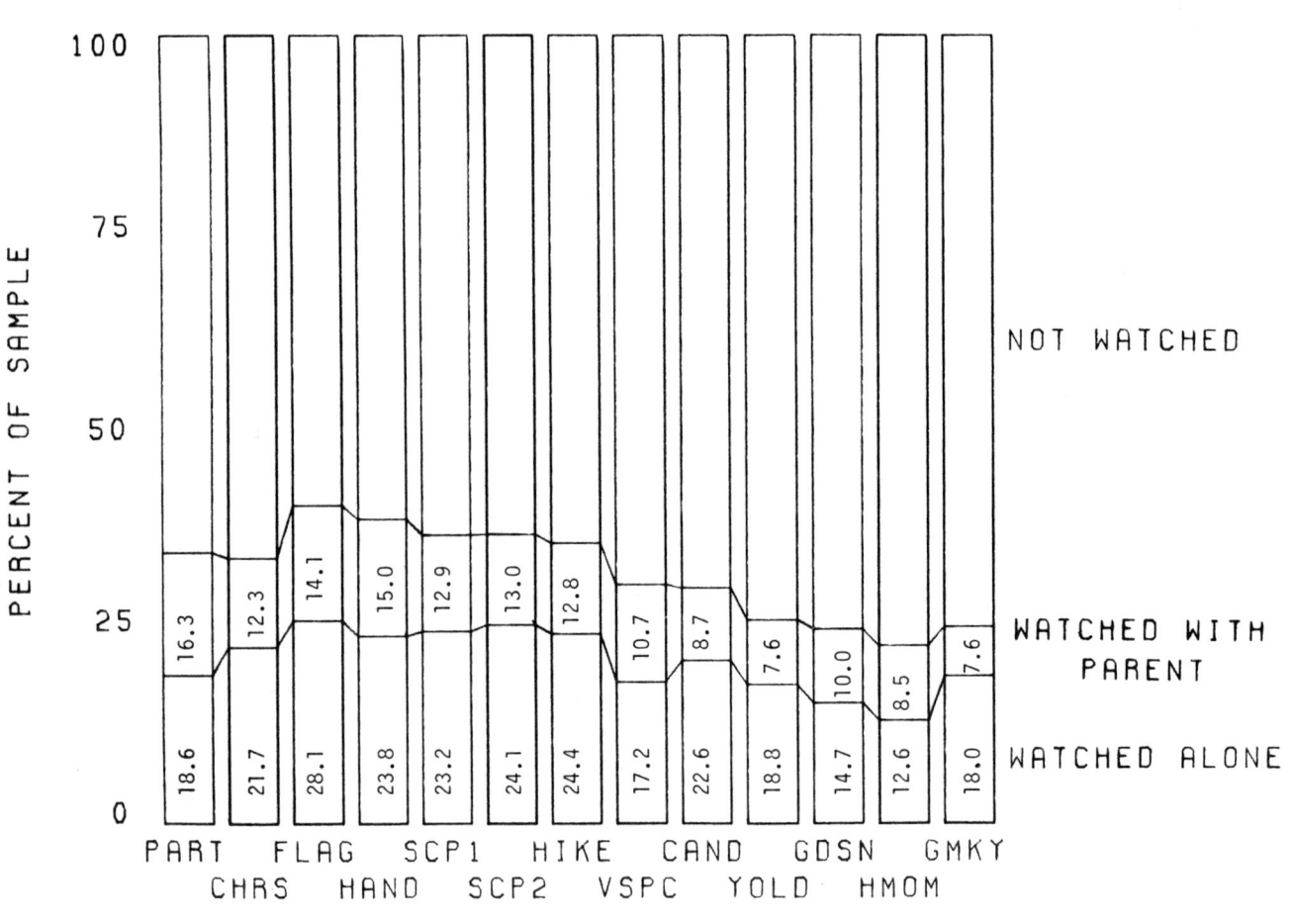

Figure 8.1

SHOW-BY-SHOW VIEWING BEHAVIOR IN HOME SITES

Table 8.6
Series Viewing Behavior Among
Those Asked to View

Total Number of Shows Watched	Percent Viewing		
	Saginaw n=232	Covina n=315	Combined n=547
0	15	38	28
1-3	33	27	29
4-6	23	15	18
7-9	15	11	13
10-13	14	10	12
	100	100	100
Average	4.6	3.2	3.8

Bearing in mind that FREESTYLE's messages are spread throughout an integrated 13-part series, what is the viewing behavior across the series? This is shown in Table 8.6. On the average, children watched only four out of the 13 shows. It is not known how many shows would be necessary to transmit the key messages of FREESTYLE. But if we allow a very liberal criterion -- a minimum of seven shows -- exactly one-quarter of the students meet that criterion.

A search for effects was made comparing the control group with those who met the criterion of viewing at least seven shows. But the analyses were compromised by sample sizes of only 40 in each of the eight cells, where an example of a cell is control group girls in Saginaw, or viewing girls in Covina. The small numbers were associated with experimental and control groups being non-equivalent on most of the pre-test measures, and there are no acceptable statistical methods to adjust away these differences. There were suggestions in the data that home viewing had some positive effects. For example, Covina and Saginaw boy viewers improved their attitudes toward girls in mechanical activities and Covina boys became more accepting of girls in athletics. But the patterns were not consistent enough to make a convincing case for the size of effects possible with home viewing. We are forced instead to look at the effects associated with the classroom view-only condition and infer that these are possible with home viewing.

What are the implications of this viewing behavior for delivering FREESTYLE through the home? If the criterion is change on the educational outcomes, and it has already been shown that intensive viewing of at least 12 of the 13 shows produces minimal effects, then home-based delivery of FREESTYLE is not sufficient. However, if it can be shown that some of the desirable effects are associated with a smaller set of shows, and particular emphasis is placed on promoting these, then it may indeed be cost effective to encourage home viewing. This much is clear; viewers like the series, and no harmful effects have been detected such as widening the gap between boys and girls on sex role issues. This being the case, FREESTYLE probably represents a quantum-sized increment of quality and educational potential over what is available for 9-12 year olds now, and it is therefore worthwhile to promote the series for home use, although how many seasons it could run with just the current set of shows is not clear.

Chapter 9

SUMMARY AND CONCLUSIONS

Four years ago the National Institute of Education invested four million dollars in the creation of a large scale television intervention to reduce sex-role stereotypes among 9-12 year olds. The FREESTYLE series represents one of the largest projects in purposive television programming with predominantly <u>affective</u> as opposed to cognitive goals. This evaluation is an assessment of the success of that product in achieving its goals. It is, to a great extent, a success story, although such a judgment represents a particular interpretation of the data. Readers are invited to examine the data and come to their own conclusion.

In 1975 NIE identified a societal problem in sex equity. At a time when the composition of the American labor force was approaching 50 percent female, the majority of women were still reaching the working years with little or no expectation or training for careers outside the home. The Career Awareness Division of NIE saw a partial remedy for this problem in a television intervention aimed at 9-12 year olds. Called the TV Career Awareness Project, the product would be a carefully articulated package designed to influence the attitudes and behaviors of this age group in a way that would reduce sex-role stereotypes and expand the "career awareness" of children, especially girls, in non-traditional ways. The task was to be accomplished by focusing on non-traditional possibilities in the 9-12 year old's own world, an approach that would distinguish it from more typical career education programs that focus on adult occupations. Its purpose would be to have children relate non-traditional childhood interests to educational, and ultimately to occupational choices. For example the girl who as a 10 year old FREESTYLE viewer came to pursue a hidden interest in mechanics would later make a non-traditional course selection such as auto shop in high school and after school a non-traditional choice of auto mechanic or mechanical engineer.

The quality and importance of the FREESTYLE television product can be judged on several grounds -- of which this evaluation emphasizes: (1) its success in the marketplace and (2) its potential to bring about intended changes in children.

Test of the marketplace

Four indicators of the project's success in the marketplace were examined: acceptance by the Public Broadcasting Service, TV station carriage, Nielsen ratings, and the ratings of test groups of teachers and students in 7 cities around the country. The Public Broadcasting System (PBS) responded very favorably when KCET-TV offered them FREESTYLE. During its initial season the network chose to feed each weekly episode several times during the week: for home broadcast it fed the 1/2-hour version to affiliate stations twice a week, with and without captions for the hearing impaired; for school broadcast it fed the show as two 1/4-hours. Eighty-seven percent of the 265 PBS affiliates selected the show for broadcast in their coverage area making FREESTYLE available to approximately three-quarters of America's households. In the Nielsen ratings it earned an average share of 2.2 which translates to more than 1.5 million households tuning to any one episode. In comparing these ratings to ones for other PBS children's programs FREESTYLE did quite well (see Chapter Five for more details).

The evaluation was conducted in seven sites spread across the U.S. involving 268 classroom teachers and over 7000 9-12 year-old children. In 142 classrooms teachers used the series and supporting materials very intensively for a full semester. Based on this experience 71 percent recommended it "strongly" or "very strongly" to other teachers at their grade level. Twenty-four percent recommended it, but with "some reservations." Only four percent had "serious reservations" and just one teacher did "not recommend it at all." In the evaluators' opinion it is hard to imagine a new curricular product being received with more uniformly positive recommendations.

There had been much concern prior to the first season of FREESTYLE that the adoption of FREESTYLE in grades 4-6 would be extremely unlikely, since the upper elementary curriculum is already very crowded. The evaluators were also told this when seeking volunteer school districts. There were sufficient volunteer teachers in every site however. In point of fact, of the teachers who spent over two hours a week using the series, 72 percent were of the opinion that their schools' priorities permitted this much time, or more. Only three teachers indicated that they could not include FREESTYLE in the curriculum under normal conditions (i.e., exclusive of their participation in an evaluation process).

The teachers reported a supportive attitude from other teachers in the building, and from principals, central administration, the school board and parents of school-aged children. There was no evidence that any groups in the test cities would be opposed to the FREESTYLE message.

While FREESTYLE was designed for 4th through 6th grade classrooms, teachers saw the value of it in junior high as well. FREESTYLE was clearly supported for use in grade four, although teachers point to variation in the maturity of fourth graders. Adoption at this grade level should be more carefully weighed than at higher grades.

Teachers felt FREESTYLE fit best into the area of career education, where the topics are part of the curriculum. Otherwise, FREESTYLE fits "pretty well" into social studies and language arts. One teacher noted "good extension into language arts particularly -- ideas pop up in other areas such as film [and] books, where they see situations of bias or prejudice in job situations." Many teachers felt FREESTYLE did not "fit perfectly" into the usual curricular areas; over half indicated they sometimes felt they needed to "steal time" from other curricular areas to teach FREESTYLE.

The School Guide received high marks as an aid for teachers. The student magazine was rated slightly lower. Designed as a supplementary component, the indication is that the magazine fills a need for many, but not all, teachers. Its value probably relates to the teachers' style of teaching and the degree to which they feel such supplementary help is necessary. Many teachers felt that the students were very enthused by it, and, for this reason alone, saw it as a valuable adjunct.

FREESTYLE was innovative in being produced in both 1/2 and 1/4-hour versions. The 1/2-hour format is a clear requirement for prime time home broadcast, while the 1/4-hours are more suitable for instructional use in the classroom. Two-thirds of the test teachers preferred the 1/4-hour mode for classroom use -- and this seems to justify the added expense and difficulty of designing programs to fit both formats.

Some of the most impressive evidence of support for FREESTYLE emerged when teachers who had used the series extensively for a full semester were asked about the ideal span of time for using FREESTYLE. Nine percent indicated a few months longer than one semester and 36 percent said a full year. Asked about the adequacy of 13 shows, 39 percent said they would like more shows. Most teachers view FREESTYLE as a well-done worthwhile addition to the curriculum, and there is a very sizeable demand to have more of this product. (See Chapter Four for more details on teacher reactions to FREESTYLE.)

Children liked watching the series "a lot" (80 percent). Compared to other TV shows, they found watching FREESTYLE "more fun" (72 percent); compared to other things they did in class watching FREESTYLE was "more fun" (91 percent) and discussions surrounding the shows were "more interesting" (81 percent).

Clearly the KCET-TV Consortium created an attractive product, appreciated by broadcasters, enthusiastically approved by teachers and enjoyed by the primary target audience -- 9-12 year olds. But we need to see gaining this acceptance -- however gratifying it may be -- as only the means to the end of reducing sex-role stereotypes and increasing career awareness.

Educational effectiveness with intensive viewing and classroom discussion

FREESTYLE's educational effectiveness was tested under an evaluation design called a product validation (Chapter Three). This meant that the package was used intensively for a full semester in 142 classrooms. Using a pre-post measurement design, changes in children exposed to FREESTYLE were compared with children in other classrooms who were not exposed at all to FREESTYLE.

FREESTYLE's educational goals called for changes in children's <u>attitudes toward</u>, and <u>beliefs about</u>, various non-traditional behaviors ranging from young girls engaging in mechanical endeavors to adult men sharing in the traditionally more feminine family responsibilities such as child care. In addition, FREESTYLE hoped to change the <u>interest</u> pattern of its audience so that it might include in its options a broader range of sex-atypical choices. For example, boys would include more nurturing activities and girls more athletic and mechanical endeavors (See Chapter Six). As suggested in the examples, the three types of outcomes -- attitudes, beliefs and interests -- were matched with three content domains: (1) childhood pre-occupational activities (mechanical, scientific, athletic, and helping activities), (2) childhood behavioral skills (leadership, independence, risk-taking and assertiveness), and (3) adult job and family roles.

The pattern of results are understandably difficult to represent in a concise form. Chapter Seven provides a thoroughgoing look at these complex results; Table 9.1 summarizes them by the device of assigning bullets to each content area, with the number of bullets corresponding to size of effect.

It may be helpful to point to two things before summarizing the results. First, "beliefs" in this research refer not to values, but to perceptions about reality. As an example, beliefs about girls in athletics refers to perceptions of children about how many girls are good at playing football, basketball, etc. As such it is a form of knowledge measure but one without an accepted criterion of accuracy. This definition gives rise to related <u>attitudes</u> as the product of the belief and the value which one places on it. The attitude which relates to the above example of belief is: how good an idea is it for girls to play football, basketball, and other sports dominated by males?

A second point concerns the perspectives of project goals and target audiences. FREESTYLE's intention is to influence children's beliefs and attitudes about the behaviors of <u>other</u> boys and girls. Thus, it is hoped that

Table 9.1
Summary of FREESTYLE Effects on 9-12 Year Olds
Under Conditions of Intensive Classroom Use

	Beliefs About	Attitudes Toward	Interest In
Childhood Pre-occupational Activities	•••Boys in Helping Roles •Girls in Athletics •••Girls doing Mechanics ---	•••Boys in Helping Roles •••Girls in Athletics •••Girls doing Mechanics ---	(helping) •••Athletics[3] ••Mechanics (science)
Childhood Behavioral Skills	••Girls as Leaders (girls being independent) (girls being assertive) (girls taking risks)	•••Girls as Leaders •Girls being Independent[2] •Girls being Assertive[2] (girls taking risks)	--- --- --- ---
Adult Work and Family Roles	(extent "male" jobs are done only by men)[1] •Extent "Female" Jobs are Done Only by Women (extent "male" household tasks done only by husbands)[1] •Extent "Female" Household Tasks Done Only by Wives (extent wives earn money) (extent husbands earn money)	•••More Women in "Male" Jobs ••More Men in "Female" Jobs (wives doing more male household tasks)[1] •Husbands Doing More Female Household Tasks (extent wives should earn money) (extent husbands should earn money)	("male jobs") ("female" jobs) --- --- --- ---

KEY: ---=the concept was not measured
Size of effect: •••=large ••=medium •=small ( )=no effect

[1]Positive shift for control group invalidates an otherwise sizeable shift for the treatment group.
[2]"Homogenizing" effect only.
[3]Positive effects in only one site.

both boy and girl viewers will become more accepting of their female peers engaging in mechanical pursuits such as fixing a bike or leaky faucet. But FREESTYLE wants to enhance personal interest for only one sex; in the case of mechanical pursuits it is only for girls.

Childhood pre-occupational activities

Some of FREESTYLE's strongest effects were in the area of girls engaging in mechanical activities. Boys and girls' beliefs and attitudes were quite disparate before FREESTYLE, with boys disapproving and girls approving. FREESTYLE shifted both beliefs and attitudes in a positive direction by a very large amount: i.e., children, especially boys, became more accepting of girls engaging in mechanical activities. Their belief about whether any girls are good at mechanics increased from just "a few girls" to a point close to "some" girls. FREESTYLE's impact can be judged not only by its movement of viewers in general, but also by the fact that it did so differentially for boys and girls such that the gap between them decreased. Thus, boys and girls who were separated in their beliefs and attitudes before FREESTYLE afterwards narrowed this gap. Given evidence in other studies (for example the sex stereotyping component in the German version of Sesame Street) of the potential to widen the gap between boys and girls, the evaluators chose to value highly evidence that FREESTYLE can narrow the gap.

Girls' interests in mechanical activities did increase as a result of FREESTYLE; the size of the shift was judged to be a little more than modest. Girls interest in science -- also a target for change -- did not increase. But then again, and the point is important, interest in science -- as opposed to mechanics -- did not appear to be very stereotyped to begin with: boys are only a little more interested than girls. If interest in science was adequately operationalized by the researchers, this finding may have implications for the commonly held notions about sex differences in science. It may be that the real gap is related not to the investigative aspects of science, but rather the mechanical/engineering aspects.

In the area of girls in athletics, the FREESTYLE audience became much more accepting of girls participating in football and basketball. Girl viewers who heretofore had not been very interested in athletics, expressed increased interest.

The last domain of childhood activities is boys in helping roles. Boys and girls alike became far more accepting of boys doing such things as caring for younger children, helping around the house, and assisting sick and old people. Girls and boys both became more supportive of this behavior, and girls exchanged their belief that few boys were any good at nurturant activities for a belief that some boys may be skillful at them. Boys, however, showed virtually no increased interest in engaging in helping activities. Although the ground may have been prepared for boys, much more intervention would be needed to change the interest repertoire of the target group.

Overall in the domain of childhood pre-occupational activities, FREESTYLE fared quite well in changing beliefs and attitudes in the intended direction, but it was less successful shifting interests.

Childhood behavioral skills

FREESTYLE's second target area is behavioral skills -- in particular girls' skills -- in leadership, independence from peer pressure, assertiveness, and reasonable risk-taking. These represent complex concepts, difficult in many cases for adults to define. Effects were measured in the area of viewer beliefs and attitudes regarding girls and boys behaving independently, taking risks, etc. FREESTYLE was successful in narrowing the gap between the sexes in the domain of leadership. Prior to exposure to the show, boys tended to think that girls do not make good leaders, while girls thought that all girls have leadership qualities. After FREESTYLE, the girls moderated their assessment downwards, perhaps reflecting a more realistic and less defensive posture. Meanwhile the boys' assessment went up, indicating they had come to think that some girls do indeed have leadership qualities.

With the two qualifications detailed below, FREESTYLE seems to have had no effect on beliefs and attitudes regarding the other behavioral skills. The reasons for this are not entirely clear, however these two things can be noted. Interviews with some 300 children suggest that the concepts were simply too subtle to be decoded from the shows or understood by the target audience. Second, the sex differences presumed to exist by the designers, were small or non-existent, reducing their appropriateness as targets for the TV shows.

The two exceptions concern a phenomenon termed in this report "homogenizing." Beliefs and attitudes about girls behaving independently were the same among both boy and girl viewers. The only difference related to race. In Long Beach, before FREESTYLE, Mexican-Americans were less approving of independent behavior in females than either Whites or Blacks. After FREESTYLE their attitudes were the same as the other two races. In Milwaukee the same phenomenon occurred, but with a different group. Here Blacks were much less approving to begin with than Whites or Hispanics. After FREESTYLE the Blacks responded as the other two groups. How much of this can be attributed to the shows or to the group discussion which surrounded them is not apparent from this research.

The second exception again concerns an example of homogenizing -- this time across sites. The content area is assertiveness in girls. Before FREESTYLE the Long Beach children, both boys and girls, were less approving of this behavior in girls than were children in other sites. FREESTYLE changed the response of Long Beach children, but the level of their approval was approximately the same as children in other sites before the intervention. Correspondingly, children in the other sites did not change their attitudes.

These two examples of homogenizing are suggestive that FREESTYLE's effects are dependent on where children are to start with, and that where children can be "moved to" is somewhat dependent on norms shared throughout society.

<u>Adult</u> <u>work</u> <u>and</u> <u>family</u> <u>roles</u> is the third and last domain in which FREESTYLE sought to change children's sex-role orientations. The series was fairly successful in shifting beliefs and attitudes regarding adult job roles, but not in shifting interests. Throughout the shows the designers highlighted men and women in non-traditional jobs (a woman as owner of a hardware store, a man as a nurse, etc.) hoping to show the adult job world as less stereotyped. If they were successful in this, children before viewing FREESTYLE would see

masculine jobs (mechanic, truck driver, engineer) as filled almost entirely by men and would be disapproving if women entered such jobs. Afterwards they would see these same jobs filled sometimes by men and sometimes by women, and would be more approving of women entering these occupations. FREESTYLE appeared to be successful in changing the image of traditionally "male" jobs, but the control group as well came to see the male job world in less stereotypic terms during the same time. This reduced considerably the ability to say that FREESTYLE effected anything unique. The most plausible explanation for what occurred is that during the same time period the media highlighted women as telephone installers, detectives, etc. In other words, it, too, was shifting images. However, while the control group changed their perception of what was happening in the world, they did not become more approving of it: only the FREESTYLE children did.

The other non-traditional combination is men entering traditionally female jobs such as nurse and secretary. Here only the FREESTYLE participants changed their beliefs -- coming to think that some nurses and secretaries are men. Correspondingly, they were more approving by a large amount -- especially the boys -- of men entering these occupations. It may perhaps be a tribute to FREESTYLE that the program could with only two short vignettes on male nurses change perceptions with respect to the job of nurse. In the U.S. nurse is virtually synonymous with woman.

The impact on beliefs and attitudes was not paralleled by changes in adult job interests. The children were presented a list of 36 occupations, some of them traditionally female and some male. Before the show the girls' list of preferences showed 57 percent male choices; afterwards 59 percent. The list for boys was 82 percent male before FREESTYLE and 78 percent afterwards. While these percentage shifts are quite small, the length of boys and girls' lists was longer after FREESTYLE, suggesting that FREESTYLE did expand the number of possibilities which children consider, but not in a way which reduces sex stereotypes. After FREESTYLE girls typically had 1.7 more male jobs on their list and boys 0.8 more female jobs on their list. Since both sexes had longer lists overall, the percentage figures did not shift very much.

Adult family roles refers to the division of labor between a husband and wife in a family with children. If women are to enter jobs outside the home and yet participate in marriage and rearing a family, some redistribution of family roles is typically needed. FREESTYLE had modest to large effects on perceptions about which person -- husband or wife -- does and should do tasks such as child care, cooking, and home repair. In all cases the shifts were in the direction of children seeing the typically male and female household tasks being completed by the non-traditional partner and feeling that this was all right. In the case of earning money outside the home to support the family, this was seen as the responsibility primarily of the husband. FREESTYLE had no impact on this perception.

In sum, when implemented under conditions of heavy viewing and extensive classroom discussion FREESTYLE showed the capability of changing a large number of beliefs and attitudes regarding sex appropriate childhood behavior, and adult job and family roles. It was less successful influencing the children's own interests in non-traditional endeavors. With the exception of girls in leadership roles it was noticeably ineffective in changing beliefs and attitudes regarding childhood behavioral skills. Most of these skills are apparently too complex to be dealt with in any single television show and supporting classroom activities. This should be instructive to future production in the "affective" area. Designers and producers must understand in considerable depth how the viewing audience perceives the issues, as well as the dynamics by which beliefs and attitudes are held in place by the target audience. Failure to understand this in FREESTYLE resulted in an expenditure of resources for a few shows that were ineffectively designed and targeted. These funds might have been better diverted from attempts to include a number of behavioral skills within a single show to multiple episode elaborations of a single behavioral skill.

While instances of FREESTYLE's failures to produce change could be amplified here, the evaluators feel that the project's successes are the more appropriate focus. Where the topics were aptly chosen and developed, FREESTYLE was able to produce larger effects -- at least short term -- than any other documented television intervention. It accomplished this by occasionally moving the entire audience in a desirable direction; at other times by shifting groups separately such as to narrow the gaps between boys and girls, or between a deviating subgroup and the majority.

Educational impact: mere viewing

These accomplishments are the product of viewing supplemented with classroom discussion and activity. What about viewing alone? How much of these effects can be accomplished simply by watching the 13 shows? The effect of "mere viewing" was tested in two environments. One was in the school classroom where the teacher could insure that the students watched every show, but did not discuss them afterwards. The other was at home where it was more difficult to secure consistent viewing (Chapter 8).

The effect of intensive viewing was judged by comparing the size of effect for mere viewing with the size of effect for viewing supplemented by classroom discussion. The comparisons were made in sites where classrooms had been randomly assigned to one viewing condition or the other.

A survey of the effects of mere viewing seems to warrant two conclusions Viewing by itself is capable in some instances of delivering an effect almost as large as viewing accompanied by extensive classroom discussion. The factors which determine whether mere viewing will fare as well as School Full are unclear, although it seems that it occurs most often for simpler communication tasks, where the audience is receptive to the message to begin with; for example convincing girls that people of their own sex make good leaders.

Second, the complex integrated set of goals which comprise the FREESTYLE package cannot be delivered effectively by a strategy of mere viewing. Such a strategy does not have negative effects and indeed children like the shows by themselves enough that students would be happy to simply watch FREESTYLE. But the percentage of educational goals which could be achieved in this way is very small. How much teacher mediation and class discussion is needed to yield the more desirable levels of effect of School Full is an unknown at this time, but it may require very little, focussed around certain shows, to heighten the effect.

A perspective that could make mere viewing cost effective is the following: The research design used to evaluate FREESTYLE looked for effects after insuring that all subjects had watched all shows. Looking at the areas where mere viewing seemed to fare best: girls in mechanics, boys in nurturance, and non-traditional adult family roles, these effects might be secured through the viewing of just six of the 13 shows:

--"Grease Monkey" and "Partners" for girls in mechanics.

--"Young and Old" and "Helping Hand" for boys in helping activities.

--"Scoop" Parts I and II for changing adult roles.

This would represent just three hours of viewing time -- a very small investment.

When home viewing was encouraged by a single communication to parents and weekly reminders by teachers, children's viewing rate was very high by PBS standards. For any one show 32 percent of those encouraged watched; and 25 percent watched at least seven of the 13 shows. However, FREESTYLE's messages are spread throughout an integrated 13-part series. If the criterion for home use of FREESTYLE is change on the educational outcomes, it has already been shown that intensive viewing of at least 12 of the 13 shows produces only modest effects. Home-based delivery of FREESTYLE to accomplish these educational goals is not sufficient. However, if it can be shown that some of the desirable effects are associated with just a subset of the 13 shows, and viewing of these shows were heavily promoted, then it may indeed be cost effective to encourage home viewing. This much is clear. Viewers like the series and no harmful effects have been detected such as widening the gap between boys and girls on sex role issues. FREESTYLE for home viewing probably represents an increment of quality and educational potential over what is available on television for 9-12 year olds now. It is therefore worthwhile promoting for home use. How many seasons it could run with just the current set of shows is not clear.

Concluding thoughts

FREESTYLE represents a powerful tool for influencing the career awareness of children in ways that can reduce the influence of sex-role stereotypes. But, the project's full potential can be realized only with if it is delivered in the context of a classroom, where a sympathetic teacher can help interpret and facilitate discussion of the show's messages.

This conclusion was reached by studying FREESTYLE's impact under ideal conditions. The "product validation" method is limited in that it does not provide answers to the questions surrounding delivery of FREESTYLE under conditions of normal diffusion and adoption. The very success of the series raises two issues. One concerns the continued availability of existing programs, the other the creation of new programs.

It is not inconceivable that FREESTYLE will be "retired" as a series before large numbers of people see it. Existing contracts call for PBS to feed FREESTYLE to its affiliates a maximum of four times in three years, and for stations to broadcast the series the same number of times. At the end of Fall, 1979, PBS will have fed the series three of the four times. Stations may have additional broadcast times because they did not broadcast one of the live feeds from PBS, but this is of little use unless they have taped the show for future broadcast. KCET -- the producing station -- will need to "buy out" local rights for four of the shows if it wants to broadcast the series in the Winter of 1980. To alter this state of affairs would require a national buyout of rights that would probably cost in the neighborhood of a quarter million dollars.

Schools can use tapes of the series until October of 1983, _if_ they were sufficiently interested and aware to have made the tapes during one of the four series broadcasts. (The tapes cannot be rented from a library; however, they can be purchased from L.A. County Schools for about $450.) It is likely that a large part of the school market for FREESTYLE will not become aware of its existence until it is too late for them to receive it.

To negotiate additional broadcast rights would require both people and money. None of the members of the consortium that produced FREESTYLE is in the position to act on this; and the sponsor, the National Institute of Education, does not see such activities as falling in their domain as a Research and Development organization. As of the fall of 1979 teacher guides are in short supply with no plans for additional printings. Some state ITV networks will cope with this problem by re-printing the guides, but this does not meet the needs of a majority of school districts. There is a clearcut danger that a four million dollar investment of tax dollars will have a very short half-life.

A second issue relating to dissemination concerns TV shows not yet produced. The NIE sponsorship of FREESTYLE led to the creation of 13 half-hour shows -- no small contribution from a Research and Development organization. The data from this evaluation indicate that among teachers who do adopt FREESTYLE and use it intensively, 39 percent would use more shows if they were available; and fully 36 percent said they would use FREESTYLE for a full year instead of its current one-semester length. Arguments might be made on the other side, that the existing repertoire is adequate (with some shows redone or replaced). The point is that the system that created FREESTYLE is now "out of business," and nobody has the responsibility for considering such alternatives. The NIE division which sponsored FREESTYLE no longer exists: the production consortium which produced it has dissolved and its members moved on to other things. The blueprint which led to the creation of FREESTYLE -- NIE's Request for Proposal -- was unusually comprehensive; it even had stipulations on buy-out rights (although some of this was lost in later negotiations). But it did not require that a "home" be found for the products.

The FREESTYLE experiment involved the creation of educational television by a temporary system, a consortium of agencies brought together for a single purpose, and dissolved upon completion of its task. In creating the initial product the consortium model works well, but in promoting the product and caring for future use it is a weak model. In this respect, it is in sharp contrast to the models of the Children's Television Workshop or the Agency for Instructional Television -- where a parent organization takes responsibility for continued nurturance after each of its products is born. Those who would use the FREESTYLE model should consider the potential problem of creating an orphan unless linkages are set up with an adopting parent.

Since completing this research another project was undertaken to explore the persistence of FREESTYLE effects nine months after the original intervention. The results are quite encouraging; they are described in the next chapter.

Chapter Ten

THE PERSISTENCE OF EFFECTS: AN EPILOGUE

Four months after the FREESTYLE experiment was completed, the first analyses of the data became available. They indicated that FREESTYLE was indeed capable of bringing about large changes in the sex-role orientation of 9-12 year olds. Was this based on the transitory feelings of children who had been temporarily "hyped" by an attractive media intervention, or would these changes disappear after children had a chance to check some of their new ideas against the realities of the broader social fabric? The original research proposal in 1976 had suggested that the research design include a follow-up study if the immediate post-viewing results warranted it; but such a prospect was remote enough at that point in time that funds were not sought for such an effort. With positive effects in hand three years later, The National Institute of Education was approached to fund a follow-up study in one site, preferably Long Beach, California. This site had the best demographic distribution, and the effects were slightly larger in this city than any other. Unfortunately, there were not enough funds available to conduct a study of 1000 children in a site so remote from the home offices of the research team. However, the available funds were sufficient to cover a third data collection from perhaps 600 children but only if travel and other costs could be eliminated. This fact dictated that if a follow-up study were to be conducted it would have to be in Ann Arbor, the home city of the research staff. It was not an ideal site for two reasons. Although there is a broad demographic distribution both in the city and in the student sample, there are no Hispanics and there is perhaps some restriction on the range of social and ethnic diversity. Second, the Ann Arbor children had been asked to complete only part of the pre- and post-questionnaire; thus some of the measures would not be available for the students in this site. Nonetheless, a persistence study in Ann Arbor was preferable to none at all.

The major goal of the persistence study, simply put, was to see if the effects associated with a four-month intervention could be found to persist after a nine-month period during which there was no continued intervention. Clearly, between February, 1979 (the end of the FREESTYLE experiment) and November, 1979 (the third data collection point) many things could have happened which would have augmented the FREESTYLE intervention. Children would have had the same teacher from February until June and during this time the teacher could have done a number of things to extend the original intervention. But summer vacation would have intervened and in the fall children would have been passed on to other teachers as the new school year began. Of course the students who were sixth graders during the experiment had moved to totally new buildings, not just to new teachers. In a few cases, some of the teachers who were in the original experiment were the new teachers for the previous fourth and fifth grade students, but this was true for less than 20 percent of the students. By and large it could be said with considerable certainty that the period between the original post-test in February, 1979, and the "post-post" test in November, 1979 was a time when FREESTYLE was not an integral part of the educational environment of these children.

The next few sections of this chapter describe the procedures used to collect the follow-up data and describe the characteristics of the resulting sample. This description is brief but detailed at some points. It is important because it provides the reader with material to judge the generalizability of the findings presented later.

Data Collection Procedures

During a three-week period in the fall of 1979, follow up data were collected from students in nine Ann Arbor elementary schools and four junior high schools. The questionnaire used was identical to the one used for the original pre-test and post-test. The data collections followed an organizational meeting in each of the schools attended by a member of the FREESTYLE staff, the building principal, and several classroom teachers. Dates were established for the administration of the follow-up data collections, and procedures were designed in such a way as to minimize any disruption of the teachers' ongoing instructional activities. Several elementary teachers who had earlier experience with FREESTYLE pooled their students, with one teacher administering the questionnaire to the students of interest to the research staff while the other teacher assumed responsibility for the remaining students. In yet other elementary classrooms, and in all junior high schools, the questionnaire was administered by members of the FREESTYLE staff, assisted by school personnel. Due to budgetary constraints there were no follow up administrations for students who were absent on the day the questionnaire was administered.

Panel attrition

These procedures worked reasonably well, at least when examined from the perspective of making contact with the majority of the students who participated in the experiment during the preceding school year. Questionnaires were completed by 459 students; this number represents 78 percent of the 589 "target" students who had completed both the pre and post questionnaires.[1] Contacts were more successful with students who, in the preceding year, had been in the fourth or fifth grades than with students in the sixth grade. This was due largely to the problems encountered when a student moves from one building to another. It was also more difficult to secure individual students at the junior high level, especially when the school's administrators and teachers had not been involved in the previous year's FREESTYLE experiment. While the response rate was high, the question should be asked: is there any systematic bias among those who chose to continue in the study?

The first avenue to explore is the demographic distribution in the retained and original samples. Table 10.1 displays the absolute and relative frequencies of the sample of available respondents in three ways; in the first row are the distributions of the original group of 687 respondents by sex, grade, treatment, and race. In the second row are similar data for the 589

---

[1] Twenty two of these cases had to be dropped from subsequent analyses due to problems with invalid or mismatched identification numbers.

Table 10.1

Demographic Characteristics of the Ann Arbor Sample Across Time

		Sex		Grade[1]			Treatment		Race		
Sample	Total	Male	Female	Four	Five	Six	Exper.	Control	Black	White	Other[2]
T1	687	368 53.6	319 46.4	263 38.3	118 17.2	306 44.5	550 80.1	137 19.9	181 26.9	456 67.9	50 5.2
T1-T2	589	306 52.0	283 48.0	229 38.9	96 16.3	264 44.8	477 81.0	112 19.0	148 25.2	412 70.2	29 4.6
T1-T2-T3	437	224 51.3	213 48.7	194 44.4	75 17.2	168 38.4	345 78.9	92 21.1	106 24.4	308 70.8	23 4.8

[1]Grade level at T1

[2]"Other" is a combination of other races plus a few missing data cases

respondents who provided complete data for both pre (T1) and post (T2) administrations of the questionnaire. In the third row are the data describing the 437 respondents who completed questionnaires at all three points in time (T1-T2-T3). In general, there are no large shifts evident in the demographic characteristics of these three samples. The most noteworthy exception is the grade level composition of the T1-T2-T3 sample. There are proportionately more fourth and fifth graders because of the higher losses of sixth graders who were now in junior high schools.

To further explore the issue of panel mortality, the 550 T1 experimental students and the 137 T1 control students were divided into two subgroups; those who "persisted" in the study at all three points in time and all others who did not. It can be seen in Table 10.1 that 345 or 63 percent of the experimentals persisted, and 92 or 67 percent of the controls did so. The pre-test data for persisters and others were then compared to see if the two groups differed. These comparisons were performed for a set of thirteen FREESTYLE belief and attitude indexes. None of the comparisons even approached the .05 level of statistical significance for the experimentals,[2] suggesting that for experimentals, a student's initial score is not an important predictor of whether or not (s)he will persist in the study. However, this was not the case for control students; four of the thirteen mean differences attained or exceeded the .05 level of significance, and six of the thirteen differences were significant at or beyond the .10 level. Bayesian posterior probabilities were calculated to examine the hypothesis that, for control students, persistence is positively related to initial scores. In each of the six instances just described, and in two additional instances as well, this hypothesis was confirmed at or beyond the .90 probability level. In short, the control students who provided questionnaire data at all three points in time are a biased subset of the initial 137 control students with which we began the study.

---

[2] As a matter of fact, none of the mean differences were significant at the .10 level either, and only one of the thirteen differences was significant even at the .20 level.

Thus, panel mortality is seen to be a source of considerable bias within the control students, but not a major problem for the experimentals. For purposes of the present analyses this problem was resolved by adopting an analytic strategy based exclusively upon the experimental students. It should be noted, however, that the dependent variables of interest in the persistence study are ones for which the control group in Ann Arbor and other sites had shown no movement between the initial pre and post test. It is reasonable to assume that the controls showed no movement between Time 2 and Time 3 as well.

Before describing the analytic strategy and presenting the results, there is one additional issue which should be mentioned. What should be done with the experimental students from classrooms in which the FREESTYLE experiment was not completely implemented? When the implementation scores[3] were examined, five experimental classrooms had unacceptably low scores, and were therefore dropped from analyses of treatment effects. This further reduces the total number of available T1-T2-T3 experimental students from 345 to 280. However, the resulting sample is remarkably similar in many respects to the initial T1 sample, as can be seen in Table 10.2. They are identical in gender composition and differ only slightly in their racial composition from the total initial sample of 687 students. Only in the area of grade level do these two groups differ more than a trivial amount. Therefore, except for analyses in which grade level is important, the reader can be reasonably comfortable about the internal validity of the findings. Data presented later comparing the T1 attitude and belief scores of Ann Arbor and Long Beach children are quite encouraging for the external validity of the findings as well.

An Analysis Strategy for Measuring Persistence

In the original study only two measurement points had to be considered in analyzing effects. As explained in Chapter Seven, a two-step strategy was used. First a form of multiple regression was used to predict the outcomes of interest using as predictors the variables of treatment group, sex, grade, and

---

[3]A detailed discussion of implementation scores and their use in this study can be found in Chapter 3.

Table 10.2

Demographic Composition of Experimental
Persisters from High Implementing Classrooms
Compared With Original T1 Sample

Sample	Total	Sex		Grade[1]			Race		
		Male	Female	Four	Five	Six	Black	White	Other[2]
T1 all students	687	368	319	263	118	306	181	456	50
	100%	53.6	46.4	38.3	17.2	44.5	26.9	67.9	5.2
T1-T2-T3 Experimentals only	280	150	130	130	60	90	72	190	18
	100%	53.6	46.4	46.4	21.4	32.1	25.7	67.9	6.4

[1] Grade level at T1

[2] "Other" is a combination of other races plus a few missing data cases.

race. When this analysis indicated that there were effects attributable only to involvement in FREESTYLE, then another type of analysis was invoked to describe the size of the effect. The control group was eliminated and the experimental group was examined. The pre-post raw gain was divided by the pre-test standard deviation (SD) and judged for size against a yardstick which ranged from .20SD ("barely important") to .65SD ("an extremely large effect"). Extending that same model to the persistence data, the difference between the post (T2) and post-post (T3) score is divided by the pre-test SD. Since we are interested in comparing the effects of FREESTYLE (the difference between the pre-test and post-test score) with the effects of a non-FREESTYLE environment (the difference between post and post-post scores), this method assures that scores being compared will be expressed in a comparable metric.

An example may be useful here. Look at Figure 10.1 which describes attitudes toward girls engaging in mechanical activities. (As with all of these figures, the raw data can be found in Appendix J.) The left hand portion of Figure 10.1 shows the results for Long Beach experimental children.

In Chapter Seven Long Beach children comprised the primary sample for analysis of effects of viewing supplemented by classroom discussion. The numbers that lie on the pre-post lines are the pre-post shift for boys and girls each expressed as a proportion of the pre-test SD for the boys and girls combined. The FREESTYLE experience shifted girls' attitudes .48SD and boys' attitudes .53SD. The numbers between the boys and girls' data points at each point in time are the between-group differences expressed again in pre-test SD units. Thus, at the time of the pre-test, boys and girls' outlook were separated by .41SD -- a very sizeable difference. This gap narrowed a small amount by the time of the post-test to .35SD.

Now look at the Ann Arbor portion of the figure. The comparable data for the Ann Arbor experimental group is shown above the "pre" and "post" points on the horizontal axis. In addition, there are T3 data points above the "post-post" point. The figure shows that in Ann Arbor the girls' attitudes increased by .46SD during FREESTYLE and that they increased an additional .01SD in the nine month period subsequent to the intervention.

Presenting the data for both the Long Beach and Ann Arbor samples permits comparisons between the two sites, both of the initial scores and the immediate effects. In general such comparisons will show that the Ann Arbor sample prior to FREESTYLE is very similar to Long Beach, and the pre-post effects are very similar in both sites. Thus, although persistence of effects was tested only in Ann Arbor, this cross-site comparison increases our confidence that the dynamics are representative of what might have happened in other sites as well.

The Persistence of Effects

It was noted earlier that not all of the paper-and-pencil measures used in the other six sites were collected in Ann Arbor. In particular, most of the behavioral skill measures and the personal interest measures were not available. Fortunately, all of the content areas in which FREESTYLE had large effects were included. This includes measures of beliefs and attitudes regarding: girls in athletics, mechanics, and leadership roles as well as boys in helping and leadership roles. In addition, there are beliefs and attitudes about the gender composition of the adult labor force.

Girls in mechanical activities. The attitude measure for this concept is a composite index of several items which ask how good an idea it is for girls to do such things as work with an adult on a car motor, fix a broken bike, and build a radio or something else that runs on electricity (see the Glossary for a more precise definition). Figure 10.1 presents the data. FREESTYLE was very persuasive with both boys and girls, as shown by the increase in their post-test scores of .46SD and .47SD. Data in Chapter Seven show that this is an area in which there was no corresponding movement for the control group so we can conclude that it is entirely the FREESTYLE intervention that accounts for this shift in attitude. The persistence data for the girl respondents indicate that there is no decay during the subsequent nine months. Their support for girls engaging in mechanical activities persists -- exactly what the designers of FREESTYLE hoped for. For boy respondents the effect decays somewhat (-.14SD). This decay corresponds to 30 percent of the initial effect (.14/.47). Another way of looking at it is to say that the net gain for boys from the FREESTYLE intervention is .33SD (.47SD - .14SD) over a 13 month period. Based on the criteria mentioned earlier, this would still be a sizeable effect to attribute to an intervention such as this. Table 10.3 presents for all of the outcomes both cross-time SD shifts and the decay as a percent of initial effect.

On the negative side it can be pointed out that the trend line for boys is having the effect of widening the gap between boys and girls' attitudes, and this could eventually play a role in inhibiting girls from expressing an interest in mechanical activities. The authors feel that a balanced judgment would be this. In the domain of girls and mechanics, FREESTYLE had impressively large initial effects and much of this effect persisted across time -- even over a period of nine months. However, enduring change may require additional exposure to the issues at several points in time. The repetition is not currently a part of the FREESTYLE package and perhaps should be.

Figure 10.1

The Persistence of Attitudes and Beliefs
About Girls in Mechanical Activities

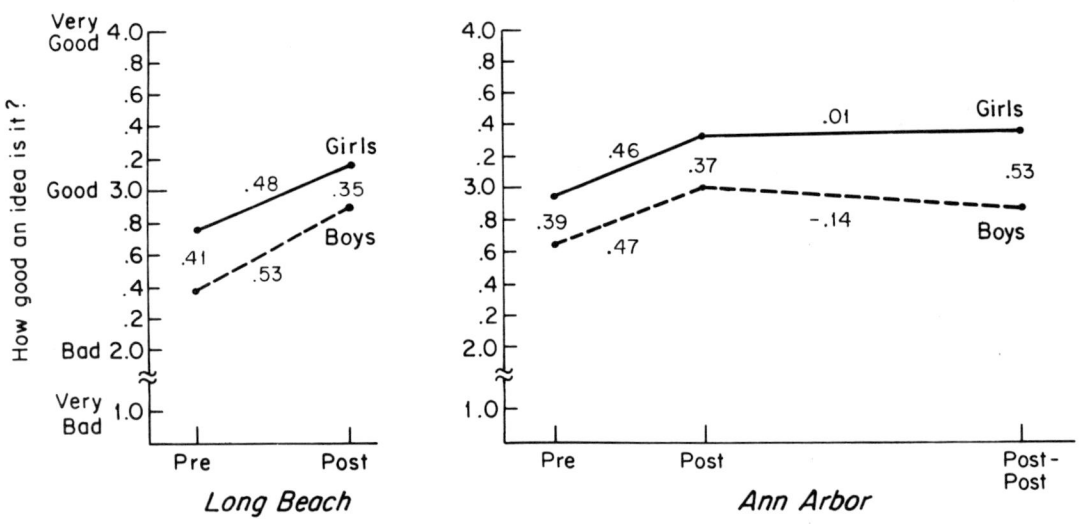

Attitudes Toward Girls in Mechanics

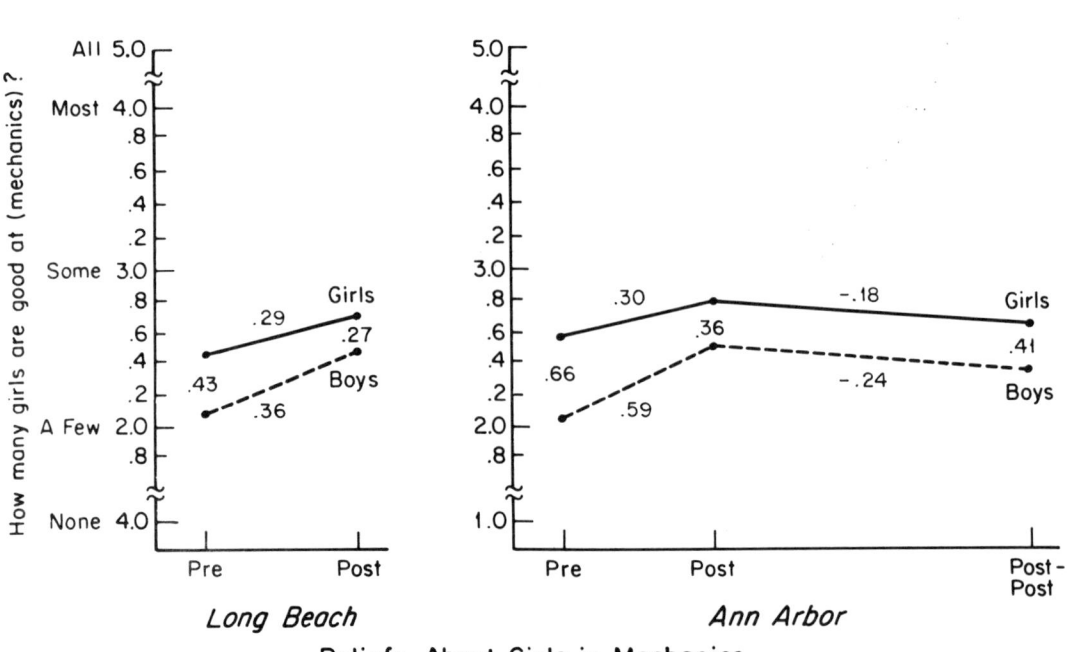

Beliefs About Girls in Mechanics

Table 10.3

Cross-Time Shifts in Ann Arbor Experimental Persisters[1]

Outcome	Total T1 Mean (a)	Total T1 SD (b)	Girls T1 Mean (c)	Girls T2-T1 b (d)	Girls T3-T2 b (e)	Girls e/d as pct (f)*	Boys T1 Mean (g)	Boys T2-T1 b (h)	Boys T3-T2 b (i)	Boys i/h as pct (j)*
Childhood Activities										
1. Att twd girls in mech	2.78	.78	2.94	.46	.01	+02	2.64	.47	-.14	-30
2. Belief about girls in mech	2.26	.78	2.53	.30	-.18	-60	2.03	.59	-.24	-41
3. Att twd girls in ath	3.01	.87	3.43	.21	-.07	-33	2.65	.51	-.12	-24
4. Belief about girls in ath	2.86	.81	3.20	.19	-.07	-37	2.57	.59	-.25	-42
5. Att twd boys helping	3.25	.61	3.25	.43	-.13	-30	3.26	.46	-.41	-89
6. Belief about boys helping	3.10	.79	2.81	.61	-.51	-84	3.36	.01	-.08	a
Behavioral Skills										
7. Att twd girls as ldrs	2.67	.80	3.21	.25	-.06	-24	2.20	.60	-.21	-35
8. Belief about girls as ldrs	3.40	.84	3.83	-.04	-.13	a	3.03	.35	-.35	-100
9. Att twd boys as ldrs	3.16	.70	2.84	.60	-.11	-18	3.44	-.03	-.01	a
10. Belief about boys as ldrs	3.45	.83	3.14	.33	-.36	-109	3.71	-.03	-.08	a
Adult Job Roles										
11. Belief about sex of those in fem jobs	3.78	.48	3.81	-.44	.04	-09[b]	3.75	-.25	.02	-08[b]
12. Att. twd more men in fem jobs	2.78	.61	2.80	.85	-.34	-40	2.76	.58	-.29	-50
13. Belief about sex of those in male jobs	2.22	.38	2.31	.32	-.18	+56	2.15	.45	-.13	+22
14. Att twd more women in male jobs	2.62	.66	2.87	.34	-.16	-47	2.40	.68	-.25	-37

[1] Children in high implementing classrooms who provided data at all three points in time. n=280.

[a] Initial effect too small to calculate decay as a percentage

[b] Scale is reversed; negative shift indicates a positive effect

*This column presents decay as a percent of initial effect.

Beliefs about whether girls are good at mechanical pursuits were strongly influenced by the original FREESTYLE intervention (bottom of Figure 10.1). Girls increased their estimate of the number of girls with mechanical skills by .30SD, and boys increased their estimate by a very large .59SD. For each of these groups there was a 40 percent decay over the nine months subsequent to FREESTYLE. This suggests that FREESTYLE and the accompanying classroom activities presented a view of girls that was larger than life. Perhaps the image of Chris successfully repairing the car in the show "Grease Monkey" was very vivid in children's minds at the time of the post-test. Subsequently, the children's experience suggested that Chris was too atypical. However, while the beliefs undergo a readjustment, girls and boys' perceptions are closer together at the time of the final data collection and this is a desirable effect.

Girls in athletics. To measure the attitudes of 9-12 year olds toward girls in athletics, participants were asked how good an idea it is for girls to play either football or basketball on a team of both boys and girls. In Long Beach, FREESTYLE had a very strong effect on these attitudes, as is shown in the top of Figure 10.2. Long Beach girls were moved more than Ann Arbor girls, but in Long Beach the scores were much lower to begin with (3.08 for Long Beach girls vs. 3.43 for Ann Arbor girls). Both Long Beach and Ann Arbor girls at post-test time were very high in approval (3.47 for Long Beach and 3.61 for Ann Arbor). There was some decay of these attitudes -- a decline of one-third of the initial effect for girls and one-fourth of the initial effect for boys.

What about the beliefs about how many girls are good at football or basketball? FREESTYLE had convinced boys to think there were at least "some" girls capable in these endeavors. It was even more effective at this in Ann Arbor than Long Beach. This effect decayed considerably; the initial effect of .59SD for boys was followed by a -.25SD decline. This decline is 42 percent of the original effect.

Boys in helping activities. In this area an example of almost total decay can be seen. At the time of the pre-test girls and boys were both supportive of boys doing such things as taking care of a younger child,

Figure 10.2

The Persistence of Attitudes and Beliefs
About Girls in Athletics

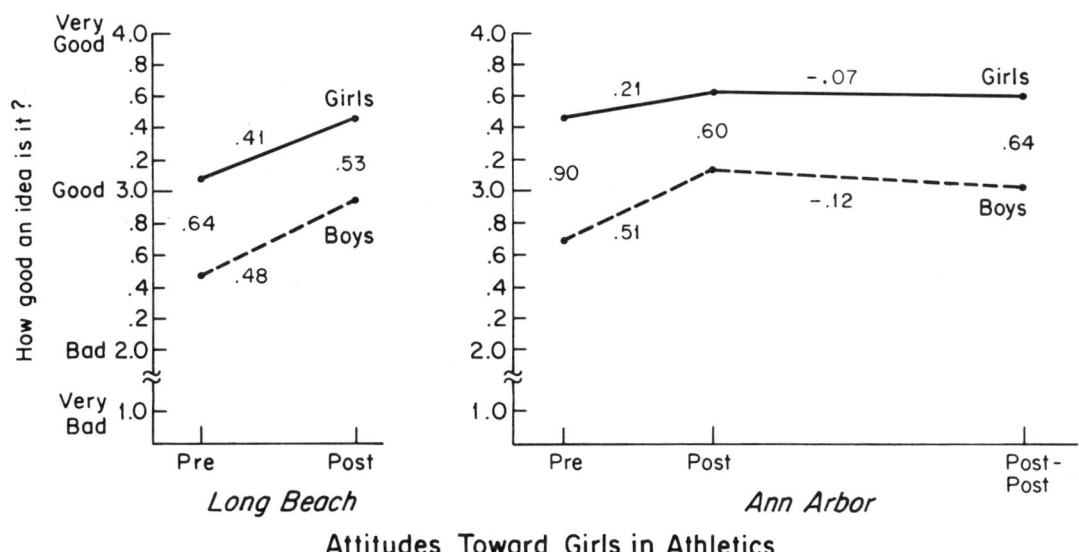

Attitudes Toward Girls in Athletics

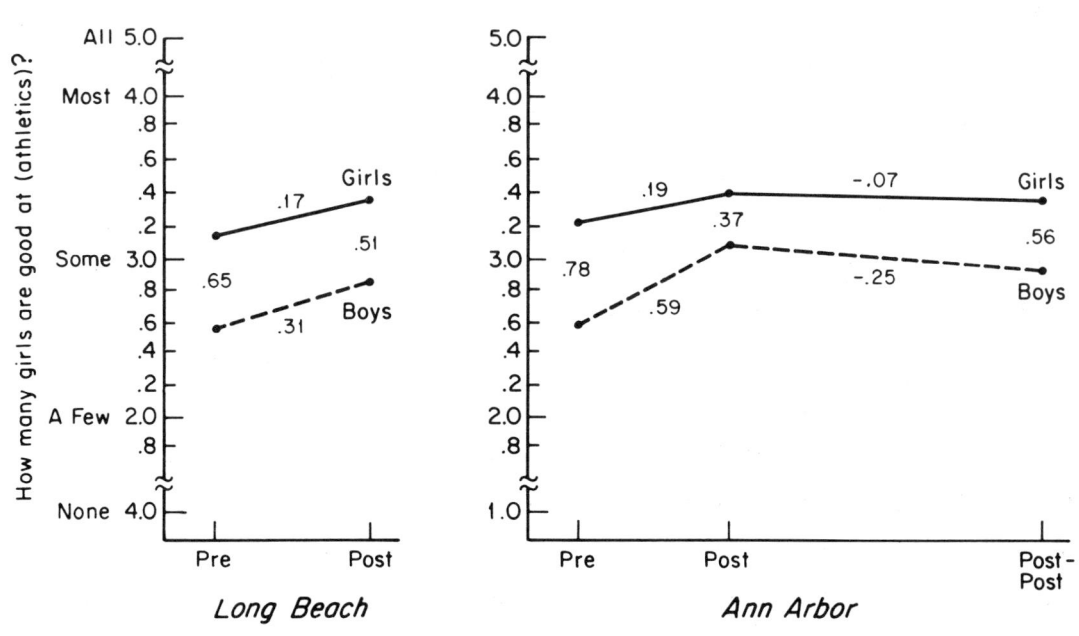

Beliefs About Girls in Athletics

helping a child with math, helping older people, and helping adults fix meals for the family. Despite the high level of initial support, FREESTYLE enhanced these attitudes by .46SD for boys and .43SD for girls (Figure 10.3). But for the boys there was a decay of 89 percent of the original effect. However, given the high level of support to begin with (3.26 on a 4.0 scale), this decay may not have any implications for boys' behaviors.

Beliefs about how many boys are good at these helping activities were very high initially for boys (3.36, corresponding to an estimate between "some" and "most" boys). FREESTYLE reinforced this estimate and it stayed fairly constant for boys at all three points in time. Girls estimated at the pre-test that many fewer boys were capable in this domain, but were strongly impressed by FREESTYLE and the classroom activities. Their post-test estimates were quite close to those of the boys. But in the period following FREESTYLE they reconsidered their estimates, with a decay of 84 percent of the original effect.

Thus far the level of decay has ranged quite broadly -- from no decay at all to 89 percent. But typically it was within the range of one-quarter to two-fifths of the original effect.

<u>Girls</u> <u>and</u> <u>boys</u> <u>in</u> <u>leadership</u> <u>roles</u>. In this domain, FREESTYLE wanted to make the idea of girls in leadership roles more acceptable. As Figure 10.4 shows girls were quite supportive of this before FREESTYLE. Nonetheless, the series was able to augment this supportive attitude by .25SD and this new level of support (3.41) persisted for the ensuing nine months. Figure 10.4 also shows the comparable data for attitudes toward boys being leaders. FREESTYLE was not trying to alter attitudes and beliefs in regard to boy leaders, but the data are informative. Male respondents started out very supportive of boy leaders (3.44) and their attitude shifted only slightly across the 13 months. So girls and boys reached the same level of high positive support for leaders of their own sex. But what about those of the opposite sex? After FREESTYLE the girls were much more supportive of boys as leaders (.60SD); in fact their attitudes toward boy leaders became almost as supportive as those toward girl leaders, and this attitude decayed only 18 percent after FREESTYLE. Boys, on the other hand, started out quite negative

189

Figure 10.3

The Persistence of Attitudes and Beliefs
About Boys in Helping Activities

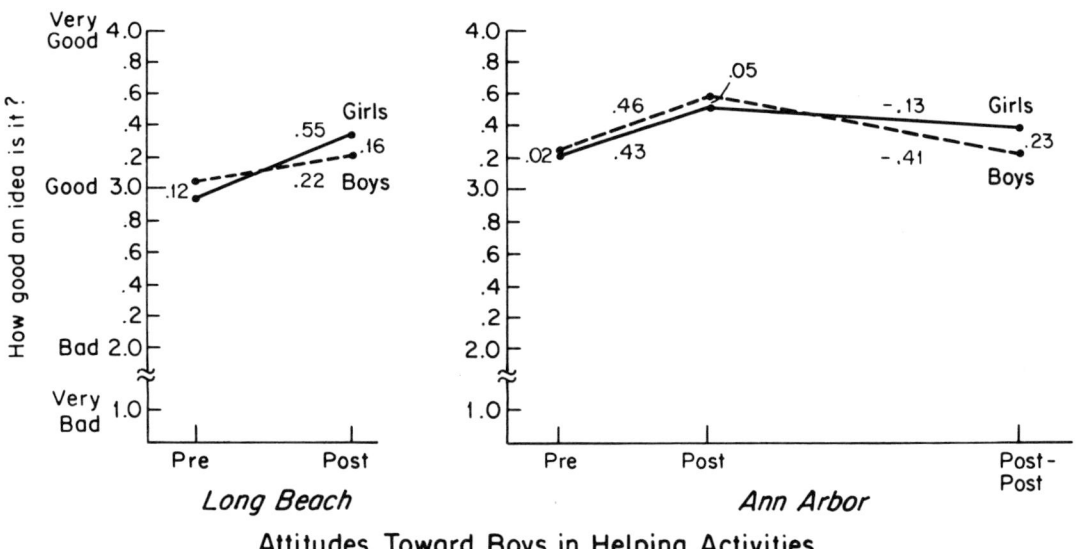

Attitudes Toward Boys in Helping Activities

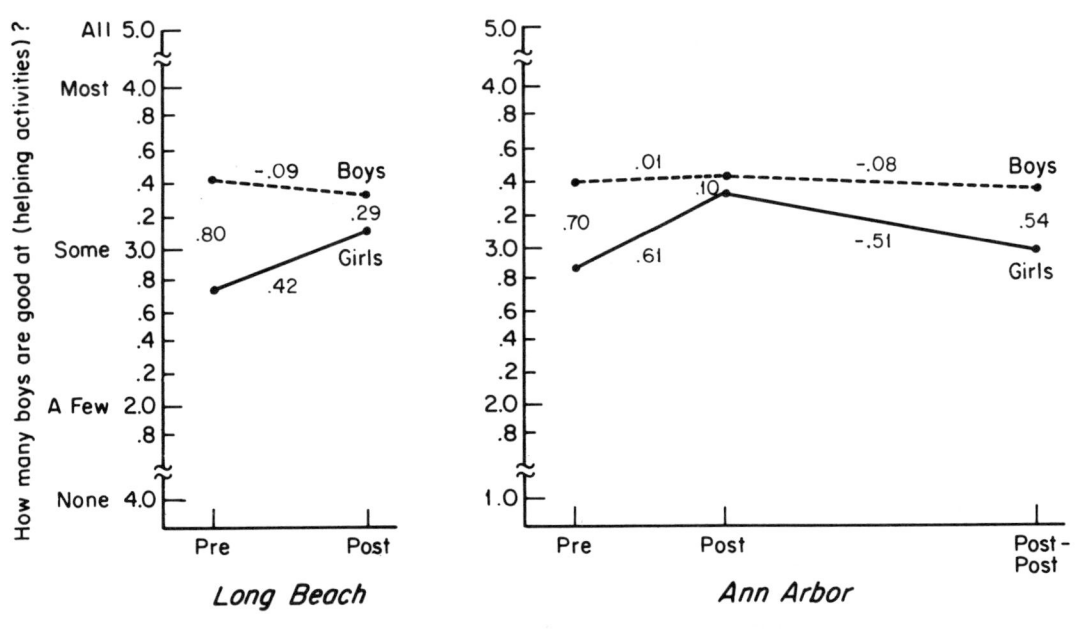

Beliefs About Boys in Helping Activities

190

Figure 10.4

The Persistence of Attitudes
Toward Boys and Girls in Leadership Roles

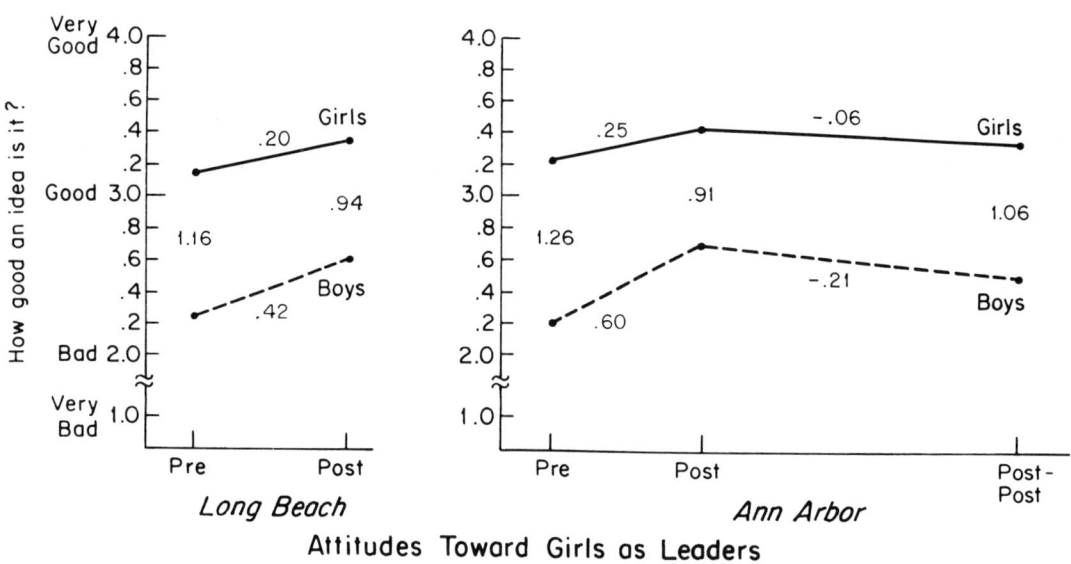

Attitudes Toward Girls as Leaders

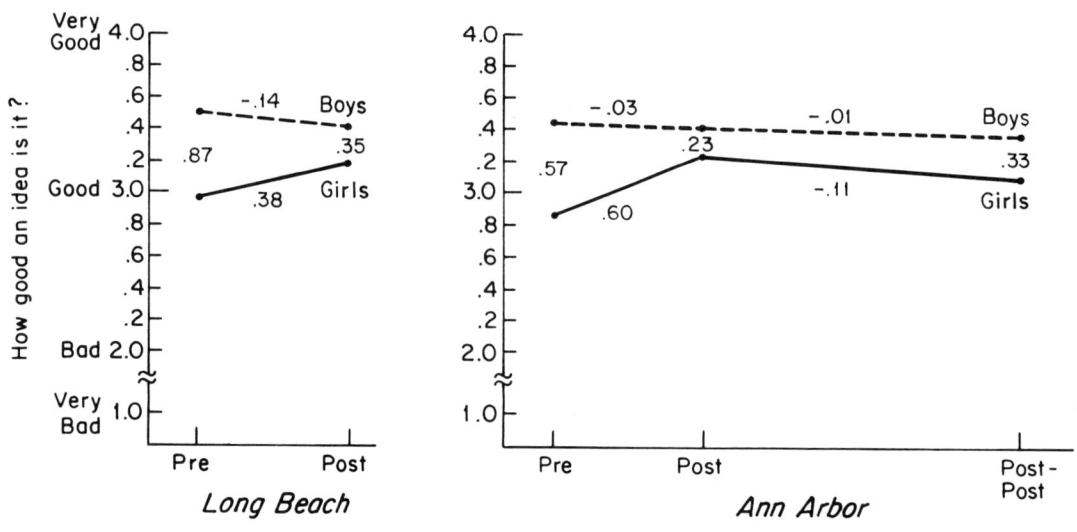

Attitudes Toward Boys as Leaders

Figure 10.5

The Persistence of Beliefs
About Boys and Girls in Leadership Roles

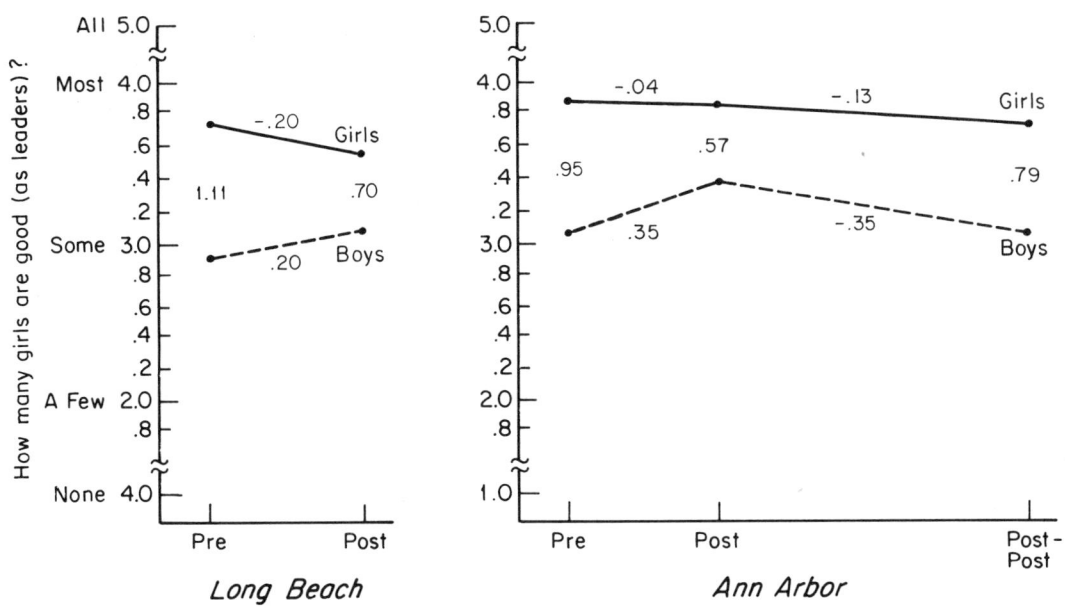

Beliefs About Girls as Leaders

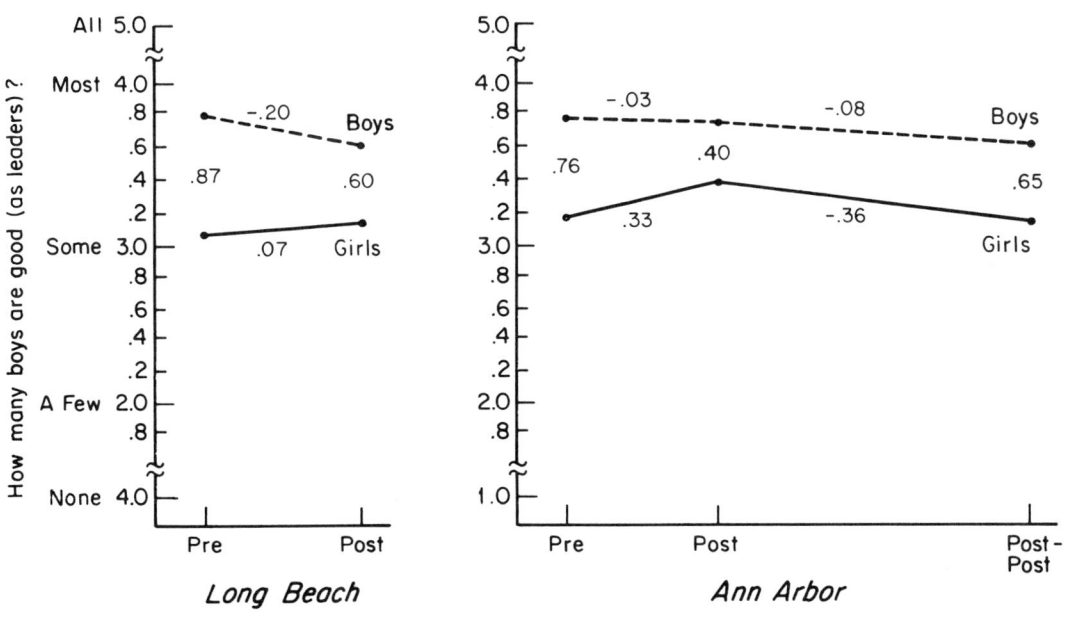

Beliefs About Boys as Leaders

toward girl leaders (2.20, or a "bad" idea). After FREESTYLE their attitudes shifted .60SD also, but it was to a level much lower than girls' attitudes; furthermore the attitude decayed 35 percent.

Two conclusions seem warranted from these data. FREESTYLE increased the general level of support for leaders of either sex, although the boys still had a long way to go to be convinced that girl leaders are a good thing. FREESTYLE accomplished the easier communication task of convincing girls that girl-leaders are a good idea, and influenced boys to a large extent, but not to the extent that sexism in peer leadership roles would likely be eliminated by the time of the next classroom election. The second conclusion is that these effects persisted to a remarkable degree. The level of decay for shifted attitudes in the domain of leadership ranges from 18 percent to 35 percent.

When it comes to beliefs about how many boys and girls are good at leadership tasks, each sex defends its own group. Figure 10.5 shows the data. Girls think "most" girls are good at being leaders and this belief is constant across all three points in time. Similarly for boys' beliefs about boy leaders. Before FREESTYLE each sex thought that only "some" of the other sex were good leaders, but FREESTYLE increased this estimate by about one-third SD. But in the ensuing nine months all of this effect disappeared. So FREESTYLE did nothing in the area of beliefs about leadership that would increase the likelihood of more girls being chosen as leaders.

Adult job roles. FREESTYLE hoped to change the child's image of the adult occupational world. In particular its designers wanted to change the stereotype that some jobs are only for women and others only for men. It was noted in Chapter Seven that FREESTYLE was partially successful in this regard. The children were asked to estimate the number of men and women in each of a list of jobs. Estimates for the "male" jobs (mechanic, hotel manager, doctor, etc.) shifted dramatically across the FREESTYLE intervention period; the movement was from the "more than half are men" point on the scale toward the "half men, half women" point (see Figure 10.6). But it was discovered that the control group shifted as well so the effect could not be attributed uniquely to FREESTYLE.

A similar picture of movement occurred for estimates of the composition of "female" jobs (nurse, secretary, etc.). But here the effect was unique to FREESTYLE -- the control group did not shift at all. Figure 10.6 shows that this latter effect persisted perfectly across the nine month period subsequent to FREESTYLE.

Figure 10.6

The Persistence of Beliefs
About the Sex of Those in Male and Female Jobs

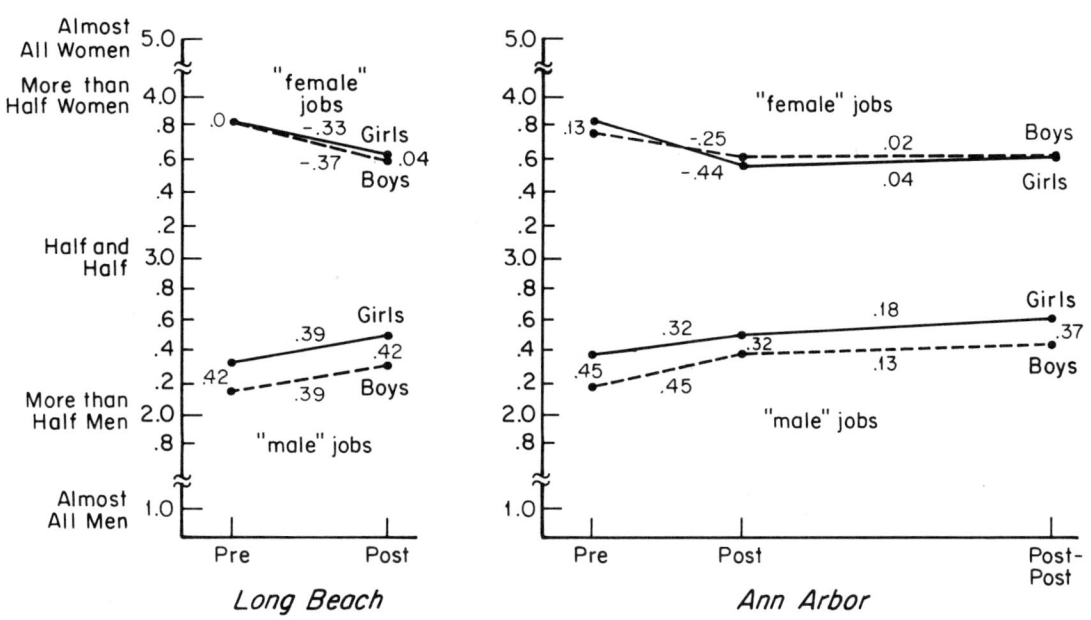

Beliefs About the Sex of Those in Male and Female Jobs

NOTE: Scale on vertical axis is really two scales. As a result large effects (e.g. .44SD) appear in the figure to be unusually "flat."

The lack of decay for these beliefs leads to the speculation that decay is much less likely if there is minimal exposure to the relevant concepts

Figure 10.7

The Persistence of Attitudes
Toward Decreased Sex Typing of Adult Jobs

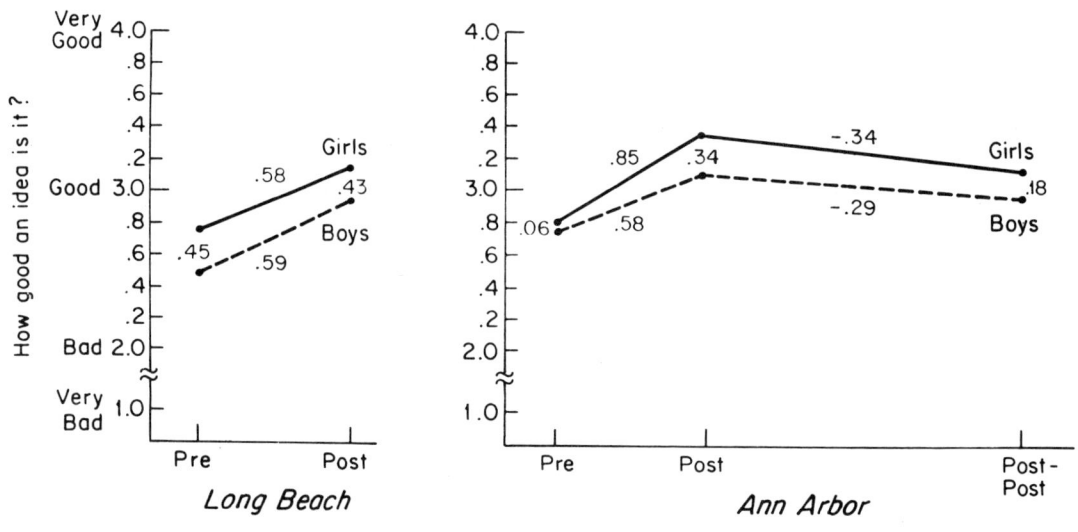

Attitudes Toward More Men in Female Jobs

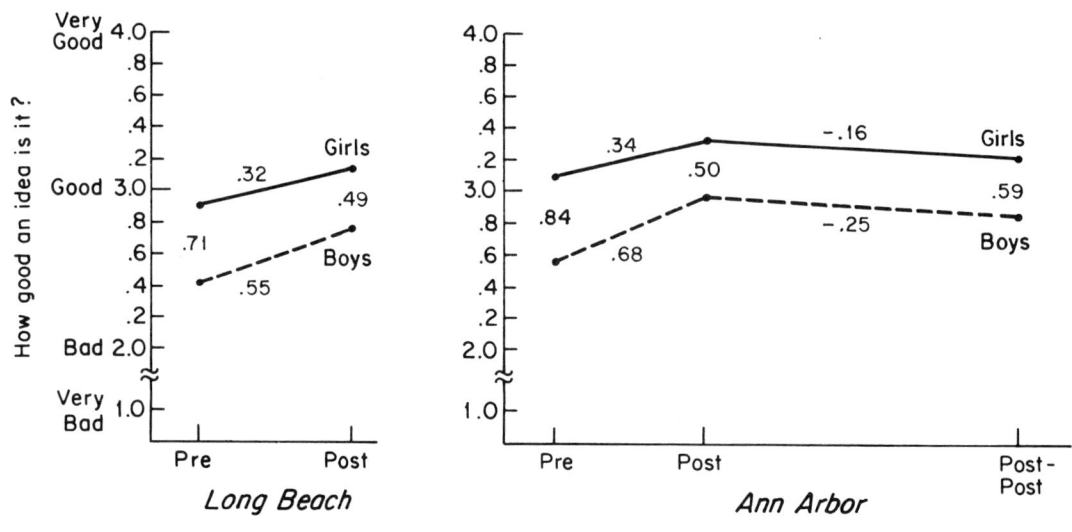

Attitudes Toward More Women in Male Jobs

during the post-intervention period. Children would undoubtedly have had more opportunities to engage the concepts of girls in athletics and mechanical activities than they would men in the job roles of nurse or secretary.

However, the attitudes toward how good an idea it is to increase the proportion of men in "female" jobs and women in "male" jobs showed quite a bit of decay. Figure 10.7 displays the data. FREESTYLE had an unusually large effect on attitudes toward more men entering "female" jobs -- .85SD for girl respondents and .58SD for boys. But the decay for these two groups was 40 and 50 percent respectively. In one sense this decay is quite large; but the net effect across all three points in time is still quite high for girls (.51SD) and modest for boys (.29SD). Although it should be noted that boys are the more important target for the intervention, their attitude after decay is still at the "good idea" level. Attitudes toward more women entering "male" jobs were also influenced by FREESTYLE. Girls increased .34SD and boys .68SD. The decay for girls reduced their net effect below the threshold of importance. But the 37 percent decay for boys still left them with a very large net effect of .43SD.

Conclusion

The data on the persistence of effects show a most encouraging picture for effects secured through a combination of TV viewing and classroom activities. Recall that the initial large effects were secured by a 13-week intervention. Each week the 9-12 year olds were exposed to about 30 minutes of viewing and 1 1/2 - 2 hours of classroom discussion and activities. The post-intervention period without FREESTYLE was nine months long. Examining those outcome areas (attitudes and beliefs) for which there were large initial effects, these observations can be made. There are some areas for which there is no decay at all, and a few others for which there is almost total decay. But, the typical decay observed was in the range of 25-40 percent of the original effect. In most cases this is a small enough decay to leave a residual net effect that is quite large and educationally significant. It appears from the FREESTYLE experience that prosocial television for children on a timely topic, when reinforced by classroom activities, is capable of inducing large changes in the attitude and beliefs of children and that the method "innoculates" them fairly well for at least nine months against a return to pre-intervention orientations.

The examples of total decay point to the importance of careful selection of the topic and its treatment in the intervention package. The examples of partial decay argue strongly for incorporating "booster shots" into program designs. Granted, it is a Herculean task just to create and "sell" a self-contained package with an intervention that has a discrete start and stop point. But the ultimate goal of such interventions is persistent change and this goal might be better served by a non-traditional design that cycles children through several interventions spaced over two or three school years. While this presents a challenge to program designers, it might be welcomed in school districts. In Chapter Four it was noted that over one-third of the teachers in the study wanted additional television shows in order to extend their classroom use of FREESTYLE. A sequel package of FREESTYLE materials might indeed be very welcome.

Appendix A

GLOSSARY

The glossary contains definitions of the major indices used in this study. An index consists of two or more items which have been averaged or summed to create a composite measure. In general, several items were selected to represent a domain. Examples of domains are: interest in athletics, beliefs about boys being nurturant, and attitudes towards girls being leaders. Where it was appropriate, the items were chosen so that some of them were illustrated specifically in FREESTYLE shows while others were not. By creating one index consisting of just the FREESTYLE-specific items and another with all of the items it is possible to tease our the extent to which FREESTYLE learnings were generalized in children's minds.

The names of each of the indices in the glossary are followed by parenthetical expressions containing one or more acronyms which title different versions of the index. If the acronym has an "F" suffix, it indicates that a separate index of FREESTYLE items exists for that domain.

For each index, there is an abbreviated description of the scale used for the items which make up the index. The complete version of each of the scales is given below.

Interests:

   A) Like it a lot; Like it pretty much; Like it a little; Don't like it at all; Don't know what that is

   B) Definitely consider; Probably consider; Probably NOT consider; Definitely NOT consider

Attitudes:

   C) Very good idea; Good idea; Bad idea; Very bad idea

Beliefs:

   D) All; Most; Some; A few; None

   E) Almost all are MEN; More than half are MEN; About half are men, half are women; More than half are WOMEN; Almost all are WOMEN

   F) All of it; Most; Some; A little; None of it

   G) All of them; Most; Some; A few; None of them

   H) A lot; Some; A little; None

   I) Very often; Fairly often; Not very often; Hardly ever; Never

Attitude Toward Boys Being Assertive (ATBASR)

   Scale: C (Very good idea -- Very bad idea)

   Items: (31) How good an idea is it for a boy your age to try to stop a kid your age from picking on a little kid rather than getting the teacher. (33) How good an idea is it for a boy who plays the saxophone very well to try to go to the teacher and prove that he's good enough despite the fact that there are already enough saxophones in the band.

   Formula: Mean of items 31,33

Attitude Toward Boys Taking Risks (ATBRTK)

   Scale: C (Very good idea -- Very bad idea)

   Items: How do you feel about a boy (34a) raising his hand in class when he is not sure of the answer (34b) taking apart a bike to fix it when he is not sure how to do it (34c) trying to bake cookies using a recipe that is much harder than he has used before (34d) trying a new sport when he is not sure he can do it well (34e) climbing onto a high place where he's not sure he can get down.

   Formula: Mean of items 34a-34e

Attitude Toward Boys Being Independent
   (ATBIND4, ATBIND3)

   Scale: C (Very good idea -- Very bad idea)

   Items: Suppose a friend of yours, a boy, likes to take care of his older sister's three-year-old child but is not sure if he should because of what his friends might say. Should he take care of the child even if (29a) his friends want him to do something else with them (29b) his friends think that it is boring (29c) his friends think it is something only girls do (29d) his parents think that it is not something for a boy to do

   Formula: ATBIND4: Mean of items 29a-29d:
             ATBIND3: Mean of items 29a-29c:

Attitude Toward Boys Being Nurturant (ATBNRT)

   Scale: C (Very good idea -- Very bad idea)

   Items: How do you feel about boys (3a) taking care of a younger child at the playground (3b) helping a child with math (3d) helping old people (not living in their home) (3e) helping an adult fix meals for the family

   Formula: Mean of items 3a, 3b, 3d, 3e.

Attitude Toward Boys Being Nurturent
   (ATBNRT 5, ATBNRT 3)

   Scale: C (Very good idea -- Very bad idea)

   Items: How do you feel about boys spending their free time (19a) helping younger students learn to read (19b) helping older people at an old folks home (19c) Jerry is a good basketball player who also likes to help out in an old folks home. He doesn't have time to do both so he thinks he will help out in the old folks home. (19f) Jose' has been helping a grownup fix cars but a little kid needs tutoring in reading. Jose' thinks he will help the kid with reading. (19g) Billy thinks he would like to take care of his sister's child rather than playing with his friends.

   Formula: ATBNRT5: Mean of items 19a, 19b, 19c, 19f, 19g
            ATBNRT3: Mean of items 19c, 19f, 19g

Attitude Toward Boys in Leadership Roles (ATBLDR)

   Scale: C (Very good idea -- Very bad idea)

   Items: How do you feel about boys (16e) being president of your class (16f) being captain of your school's football team (16g) being in charge of your class paper drive and giving orders to the other kids (16h) being editor in charge of the school newspaper.

   Formula: Mean of items 16e-16h

Attitude Toward Boys in The Home (ABBHOM)

   Scale H: (A lot -- None)

   Items: How much time should boys your age spend (13a) helping with making meals and washing dishes (13b) helping keep the house clean (13c) helping take care of younger children.

   Formula: Mean of items 13a-13c

Attitude Toward Boys Showing Independence (ATBIND)

   Scale: C (Very good idea -- Very bad idea)

   Items: How would you feel if a boy your age did something he was interested in doing (22a) when his close friends wanted him to do something else with them (22b) when his close friends thought it was a thing only girls should do (22c) when his parents wished he would do something else.

   Formula: Mean of items 22a-22c

Attitude Toward Girls Being Assertive (ATGASRT)

   Scale: C (Very good idea -- Very bad idea)

   Items: (30) How good an idea is it for a girl your age to try to stop a kid your age from picking on a little kid rather than getting the teacher. (32) How good an idea is it for a girl who plays the saxophone very well to try to go to the teacher and prove that she's good enough despite the fact that there are already enough saxophones in the band.

   Formula: Mean of items 30,32.

Attitude Toward Girls Being Independent
   (ATGIND4, ATGIND3)

   Scale: C (Very good idea -- Very bad idea)

   Items: Suppose a friend of yours, a girl, is interested in fixing cars after school but is not sure if she should because of what her friends might say. Should she work on the cars even if (28a) her friends want her to do something else with them (28b) her friends think that working on cars is boring (28c) her friends think that working on cars is something only boys should do (28d) her parents think it is not good for girls to do this kind of thing.

   Formula: ATBIND4: Mean of items 28a-28d
             ATBIND3: Mean of items 28a-28c

Attitude Toward Girls Being Nurturent (ATGNRT3)

    Scale: C (Very good idea -- Very bad idea)

    Items: How do you feel about girls spending their free time doing these things. (19d) Marsha is a very good basketball player. Last year in her free time she played on the elementary school team. Marsha also likes to help out in an old folks home. She talks to people and plays games with them. This year she doesn't have time to do both things so she thinks she will help out at the old folks home. (19e) Yvonne has been helping a grownup fix cars but a little kid needs tutoring in reading. Yvonne thinks she will help the kid with reading. (19h) Jane thinks she would like to take care of her sister's child rather than playing with her friends.

    Formula: Mean of items 19d, 19e, 19h.

Attitude Towards Girls in Athletics (ATGATH)

    Scale: C (Very good idea -- Very bad idea)

    Items: How do you feel about girls your age (2a) playing football on a team with both boys and girls on the team (2e) playing basketball on a team with boys and girls on the team.

    Formula: Mean of items 2a, 2e.

Attitude Toward Girls in Leadership Roles (ATGLDR)

    Scale: C (Very good idea -- Very bad idea)

    Items: How do you feel about girls (16a) being president of your class (16b) being captain of your school's football team (16c) being in charge of your class paper drive and giving orders to the other kids (16d) being editor in charge of the school newspaper.

    Formula: Mean of items 16a-16d.

Attitude Toward Girls in Mechanical Activities (ATGMC)

    Scale: C (Very good idea -- Very bad idea)

    Items: How do you feel about girls your age (2b) fixing a broken bike (2c) working with an adult on a car motor (2d) building a radio or something else that runs on electricity.

    Formula: Mean of items 2b, 2c, 2d.

Attitude Toward Girls in Them Home (ATGHOM)

    Scale H: (A lot -- None)

    Items: How much time should girls your age spend (13e) helping with making meals and washing dishes (13f) helping keep the house clean (13g) helping take care of younger children.

    Formula: Mean of items 13e-13g.

Attitude Toward Girls Showing Independence (ATGIND)

    Scale: C (Very good idea -- Very bad idea)

    Items: How would you feel if a girl your age did something she was interested in doing (23a) when her close friends wanted her to do something else with them (23b) when her close friends thought it was a thing only boys should do (23c) when her parents wished she would do something else.

    Formula: Mean of items 23a-23c

Attitude Toward Girls Taking Risks (ATGRTK)

    Scale: C (Very good idea -- Very bad idea)

    Items: How do you feel about a girl (35a) raising her hand in class when she is not sure of the answer (35b) taking apart a bike to fix it when she is not sure how to do it (35c) trying to bake cookies using a recipe that is much harder than she has used before (35d) trying a new sport when she is not sure she can do it well (35e) climbing onto a high place where she's not sure she can get down.

    Formula: Mean of items 35a-35e.

Attitude Toward Husbands in The Home
    (ATHHOM4, ATHHOM3)

    Scale: F (All of it -- None of it)

    Items: How much do you think each of these things should be done by husbands (11d) do the grocery shopping, cook the meals, do the dishes, (11e) do the housecleaning (dust, vacuum, scrub the floors, clean the bathroom, (11f) take care of the children (11g) work to earn money to support the family.

    Formula: ATHHOM4: Mean of items 11d-11g
                  ATHHOM3: Mean of items 11d-11f

Attitude Toward Men in Non-Traditional Jobs
(ATMJB3, ATMJB2)

    Scale: C (Very good idea -- Very bad idea)

    Items: How would you feel if more men were (9a) nurses (9b) teachers of children who have problems with seeing or hearing (9c) occupational therapists (help sick or old people learn new skills).

    Formula: ATMJB3: Mean of items 9a-9c
                  ATMJB2: Mean of items 9b, 9c

Attitude Towards Wives in The Home
(ATWHOM3, ATWHOM2)

    Scale: F (All of it -- None of it)

    Items: How much do you think each of these things should be done by wives (11a) take care of things around the house (paint the house, fix leaking faucets) (11b) take care of the car (keep it clean, have the oil changed, and (11c) work to earn money to support the family.

    Formula: ATWHOM3: Mean of items 11a-11c
                  ATWHOM2: Mean of items 11a, 11b

Attitude Toward Women in Non-Traditional Jobs (ATWJB)

    Scale: C (Very good idea -- Very bad idea)

    Items: How would you feel if more women were (8a) car mechanics (8b) truck drivers (8c) machinists (make parts for machines) (8d) owners of hardward stores (8e) geologists (scientists who study rocks and minerals).

    Formula: Mean of items 8a-8e

Beliefs About Boys Being Assertive (BFBASRT)

    Scale: G (All of them -- None of them)

    Items: How many boys your age (27a) stand up for what they think is right (27b) stop somebody from picking on younger kids (27c) tell another kid when they think the other kid is wrong (27d) demand to be treated fairly by grownups (27e) demand to be treated fairly by other kids.

    Formula: Mean of items 27a-27e.

Beliefs About Boys Being Nurturant (BFBNRT1)

   Scale: D (All -- None)

   Items: How many boys are good at (5a) taking care of a younger child at the playground (5b) helping a child with math (5d) helping old people (not living in their home) (5e) helping an adult fix meals for the family.

   Formula: Mean of items 5a, 5b, 5d, 5e.

Belief About Boys Being Nurturant (BFNRT2)

   Scale: G (All of them -- None of them)

   Items: How many boys your age are good at (20a) helping to take care of a younger child (20b) understanding why a child misbehaves (20c) tutoring younger students, that is, helping them to learn things (20d) figuring out what would make someone happy (20e) helping older people with what they need (20f) knowing when to help someone and when not to.

   Formula: Mean of items 20a-20f.

Beliefs About Boys in Leadership Roles (BFBLDR1)

   Scale: G (All of them -- None of them)

   Items: How many boys are good at (18a) organizing things for the group to do (18b) giving each group member a job which they can do well (18d) having good ideas about what the group should do (18e) listening to the ideas of other group members.

   Formula: Mean of items 18a, 18b, 18d, 18e.

Beliefs About Boys in Leadership Roles (BFBLDR2)

   Scale: G (All of them -- None of them)

   Items: How many boys are (18c) too bossy when they lead the group (18f) give all the good jobs to other boys in the group.

   Formula: Mean of items 18c, 18f.

Beliefs About Boys in The Home (BFBHOM)

    Scale H: (A lot -- None)

    Items: How much time do boys your age spend (12a) helping with making meals and washing dishes (12b) helping keep the house clean (12c) helping take care of younger children.

    Formula: Mean of items 12a-12c.

Beliefs About Boys Showing Independence (BFBIND)

    Scale: I (Very often -- Never)

    Items: How often do boys your age actually do something they're interested in (24a) when their friends think only girls do it (24b) when their parents wished they would do something else.

    Formula: Mean of items 24a, 24b.

Beliefs About Boys Taking Risks (BFBRTK)

    Scale: G (All of them -- None of them)

    Items: How many boys your age (27f) don't do things because they might get hurt doing them (27g) don't do things because they might be embarrassed (27h) try it again another way after they fail (27i) pick the easy thing to do instead of the hard thing.

    Formula: Mean of items 27f-27i.

Beliefs About Girls Being Assertive (BFGASRT)

    Scale: G (All of them -- None of them)

    Items: How many girls your age (26a) stand up for what they think is right (26b) stop somebody from picking on younger kids (26c) tell another kid when they think the other kid is wrong (26d) demand to be treated fairly by grownups (26e) demand to be treated fairly by other kids.

    Formula: Mean of items 26a-26e.

Belief About Girls Being Nurturant (BFGNRT2)

　　Scale:　G (All of them -- None of them)

　　Items:　How many girls your age are good at (21a) helping to take care of a younger child (21b) understanding why a child misbehaves (21c) tutoring younger students, that is, helping them to learn things (21d) figuring out what would make someone happy (21e) helping older people with what they need (21f) knowing when to help someone and when not to.

　　Formula:　Mean of items 21a-21f.

Beliefs About Girls in Athletics (BFGATH)

　　Scale:　D (All -- None)

　　Items:　How many girls are good at playing (4a) football, (4e) basketball.

　　Formula:　Mean of items 4a, 4e.

Beliefs About Girls in Leadership Roles (BFGLDR1)

　　Scale:　G (All of them -- None of them)

　　Items:　How many girls are good at (17a) organizing things for the group to do (17b) giving each group member a job which they can do well (17d) having good ideas about what the group should do (17e) listening to the ideas of other group members.

　　Formula:　Mean of items 17a, 17b, 17d, 17e.

Beliefs About Girls in Leadership Roles (BFGLDR2)

　　Scale:　G (All of them -- None of them)

　　Items:　How many girls are (17c) too bossy when they lead the group (17f) give all the good jobs to other girls in the group.

　　Formula:　Mean of items 17c, 17f.

Beliefs About Girls in Mechanical Activities (BFGMC)

　　Scale:　D (All -- None)

　　Items:　How many girls are good at (4b) fixing a broken bike (4c) fixing a car motor (4d) building a radio or something else that runs on electricity.

　　Formula:　Mean of items 4b-4d.

Beliefs About Girls in The Home (BFGHOM)

    Scale H: (A lot -- None)

    Items: How much time do girls your age spend (12e) helping with making meals and washing dishes (12f) helping keep the house clean (12g) helping take care of younger children.

    Formula: Mean of items 12e-12g.

Beliefs About Girls Showing Independence (BFGIND)

    Scale: I (Very often -- Never)

    Items: How often do girls your age actually do something they're interested in (25a) when their friends think only boys do it (25b) when their parents wished they would do something else.

    Formula: Mean of items 25a, 25b.

Beliefs About Girls Taking Risks (BFGRTK)

    Scale: G (All of them -- None of them)

    Items: How many girls your age (26f) don't do things because they might get hurt doing them (26g) don't do things because they might be embarrassed (26h) try it again another way after they fail (26i) pick the easy thing to do instead of the hard thing.

    Formula: Mean of items 26f-26i.

Beliefs About Husbands in The Home
    (BFHHOM4, BFHHOM3)

    Scale: F (All of it -- None of it)

    Items: How much is done by husbands today (10d) grocery shopping, cook the meals, do the dishes (10e) do the house cleaning (dust, vacuum, scrub the floors, clean the bathroom) (10f) take care of the children (10g) work to earn money to support the family.

    Formula: BFHHOM4: Mean of items 10d-10g
                 BFHHOM3: Mean of items 10d-10f

Beliefs About the Sex of People in Jobs Traditionally Held By Men
(SXJBM, SXJBFM)

Scale: E (Almost all are men -- Almost all are women)

Items: How many of the people who do each of these jobs are men and how many are women (7a) car mechanic (7b) truck driver (7e) machinist (makes parts for machines) (7f) pharmacist (gives out medicine in a drugstore) (7g) owner of a hardward store (7h) city council member (someone elected to run a city) (7i) geologist (scientist who studies rocks and minerals) (7j) worker in a factory who puts things together (like a car) 71) sales person in a store who sells cars of TVs or refrigerators.

Formula: SXJBM: Mean of items 7a, 7b, 7e-7j, 71
         SXJBFM: Mean of items 7a, 7e, 7g, 7h, 7i

Beliefs About the Sex of People in Jobs Traditionally Held By Women
(SXJBW, SXJBFW)

Scale: E (Almost all are men -- Almost all are women)

Items: How many of the people who do each of these jobs are men and how many are women. (7c) nurse (7d) secretary (7k) telephone operator (7o) dental assistant (cleans people's teeth or helps dentist fix their teeth (7p) teacher of children who have problems with seeing or hearing (7q) occupational therapist (help sick or old people learn new skills).

Formula: SXJBW: Mean of items 7c, 7d, 7k, 7o-7q
         SXJBFW: Mean of items 7p, 7q

Beliefs About Wives in The Home
(BFWHOM3, BFWHOM2)

Scale: F (All of it -- None of it)

Items: How much is done by wives today (10a) take care of things around the house (paint the house, fix leaky faucets) (10b) take care of the car (keep it clean, have the oil changed) (10c) work to earn money to support the family.

Formula: BFWHOM3: Mean of items 10a-10c
         BFWHOM2: Mean of items 10a, 10b

Interest in Athletics
(INTATH, INTATHF)

Scale: A (Like a lot -- Don't like it at all)

Items: How much would you like to play (1u) football (1v) basketball (1w) dodgeball (1x) soccer (1y) basketball.

Formula: INTATH: Mean of items 1u-1y
INTATHF: Mean of items 1u, 1x

Interest in Mechanical Activities
(INTMC, INTMCF)

Scale: A (Like a lot -- Don't like it at all)

Items: How much would you like to (1a) fix a broken bike (1b) build a model kit (1c) build a radio (1d) fix a leaky faucet (1e) work with an aduly on a car motor.

Formula: INTMC: Mean of items 1a-1e
INTMF: Mean of items 1d, 1e

Interest in Nurturant Activities
(INTNRT, INTNRF)

Scale: A (Like a lot -- Don't like it at all)

Items: How much would you like to (1f) take care of a younger child at the playground (1g) help a younger child with math (1h) teach a younger child how to play a game (1i) sew a button on clothes or sew up a tear (1j) help an adult fix meals for the family (1k) help old people (not living in your home) (1l) help at a recreation center for handicapped people who are deaf, crippled, or blind (1m) take care of sick people (not living in your home) and (1t) run errands for an elderly person.

Formula: INTNRT: Mean of items 1f-1m, 1t
INTNRT: Mean of items 1g, 1h, 1k, 1l

Interest in Occupations, Holland Artistic Category (OCHA2)

Scale: B (Definitely consider -- definitely not consider)

Items: Identify occupations that you would consider or Definitely not consider as a job in the future (6q) reporter (6r) photographer.

Formula: Mean of items 6q, 6r.

Interest in Occupations, Holland Conventional Category (OCHC5)

   Scale: B (Definitely consider -- definitely not consider)

   Items: Identify occupations that you would consider or Definitely not consider as a job in the future (6ff) secretary (6gg) someone who sorts mail in the post office (6hh) bookkeeper (keeps records of money spent and received by a business) (6ii) checkout clerk at a grocery or discount store (6jj) telephone operator.

   Formula: Mean of items 6ff-6jj.

Interest in Occupations, Holland Investigative Category
   (OCHI6, OCHI5)

   Scale: B (Definitely consider -- definitely not consider)

   Items: Identify occupations that you would consider or Definitely not consider as a job in the future (6s) pharmacist (gives out medicine in a drugstore) (6t) geologist (scientist who studies rocks and minerals) (6u) designer of electrical things like TV's, radios, or calculators (6v) scientist who studies how the weather works (6w) scientist who studies how plants and animals grow (6x) designer of airplanes or rockets.

   Formula: OCHI6: Mean of items 6s-6x
            OCHI5: Mean of items 6s, 6u-6x

Interest in Occupations, Holland Enterprising Category
   (OCHE7, OCHE5)

   Scale: B (Definitely consider -- definitely not consider)

   Items: Identify occupations that you would consider or not consider as a job in the future (6y) owner of a hardware store (6z) owner of a business which makes things like shoes or toys or furniture (6aa) manager of a motel or hotel (6bb) owner of a restaurant (6cc) owner of a company which builds houses (6dd) sales person in a store who sells cars or televisions or refrigerators (6ee) city council member (someone elected to help run a city).

   Formula: OCHE7: Mean of items 6y, 6z, 6aa-6ee
            OCHE5: Mean of items 6z, 6aa-6dd

Interest in Occupations, Holland Realistic Category
(OCHR7, OCHR5)

Scale: B (Definitely consider -- definitely not consider)

Items: Identify occupations that you would consider or Definitely not consider as a job in the future (6a) car mechanic (6b) truck driver (6c) electrician (6d) carpenter (6e) worker in a factory who puts things together (like a car or other machine) (6f) machinist (makes parts for machines) (6g) boss in a factory.

Formula: OCHR7: Mean of items 6a-6g
OCHR5: Mean of items 6b-6e, 6g

Interest in Occupations, Holland Social Category
(OCHS9, OCHS5)

Scale: B (Definitely consider -- definitely not consider)

Items: Identify occupations that you would consider or Definitely not consider as a job in the future (6h) nurse (6i) professional athlete (6j) coach (6k) school teacher (6l) librarian (6m) dental assistant (cleans people's teeth or helps dentist fix their teeth) (6n) occupational therapist (helps sick or old people learn new skills) (6o) teacher of children who have problems seeing or hearing (6p) homemaker - a father or mother who stays home and cares for the children, cooks meals and cleans the house.

Formula: OCHS9: Mean of items 6h-6p
OCHS5: Mean of items 6h, 6i, 6k, 6l, 6m

Interest in Science
(INTSCI, INTSCIF)

Scale: A (Like a lot -- Don't like it at all)

Items: How much would you like to (1n) raise goldfish at home (1o) watch the stars and planets and figure out the names of groups of stars (1p) make an insect collection (ants, moths, butterflies, or other insects) (1q) make a collection of different kinds of rocks (1r) read books about rocks, insects, flowers, or stars (1s) do a project for a science fair.

Formula: INTSCI: Mean of items 1n-1s
INTSCIF: Mean of items 1n, 1q, 1r, 1s

Appendix B

FREESTYLE TELEVISION SHOWS: SYNOPSIS AND THEMES

Show 1: PARTNERS

Synopsis:

Penny and Marcus form a partnership providing household repairs. They learn from a quarrel over "who's boss" that cooperation (i.e. dividing the work and combining their various skills) is the best way to get the job done.

Themes:

1) Behavioral skill: cooperation
   Message: Cooperation is necessary to nearly all jobs and activities; it is more than merely "working together." It requires both a combination of skills and a division of labor. These are not always easily achieved and disputes may occur. These disputes, however, can be worked out.

2) Pre-occupational activities: mechanical/technical activities for girls (specifically: home repair work including carpentry, plumbing and electrical repair)
   Message: Girls can be competent in mechanical/technical activities.

3) Adult work/family role: female hardware store owner/operator
   Message: Women can be competent managers.

Show 2: CHEERS!

Synopsis:

Penny is on her way to becoming a cheerleader and Ramon is a member of the soccer team, but they also have a common interest: science. When they discover they must choose between their "traditional" activities and entering the science fair, their friends pressure them to choose the traditional activities. Penny and Ramon resist the peer pressure and go on to do a winning science project.

Themes:

1) Behavioral skill: Independence (specifically: independence from peer pressure)
   Message: Children often do what their friends want them to do. There is, however, satisfaction and perhaps also other rewards for doing what one is interested in doing even if one's friends do not approve.

2) Pre-occupational interests: science for girls and minorities
   Message: Science projects can be interesting activities and girls and minority children can succeed in them.

3) Adult work/family roles: none are featured in this show although a science teacher is a supporting role.

Show 3: FLAG

Synopsis:

Denice proves her ability at flag football, but finds that the coach's wife and some members of the community don't like the idea of a girl on the team. Denice gets the support of her parents and friends and keeps on trying. In the big game she gets her chance and scores the winning touchdown.

Themes:

1) Behavioral skill: None is featured in this show

2) Pre-occupational activities: sports for girls (specifically: flag football)
   Message: Girls can succeed in sports and other sorts of "non-traditional" activities as well.

3) Adult work/family roles: sports-related occupations (e.g., coach)
   Message: Sports-related occupations besides professional athlete do exist.

Show 4: HELPING HAND

Synopsis:

Walter thinks tutoring math will be a cinch until he discovers that his pupil, newcomer, Dolores Cabrillo, can't read the math problems which are written in English. Dolores fearing disgrace swears Walter to secrecy and he and his bi-lingual buddy, Ramon, help Dolores prepare for her math exams. With their helping hands Dolores, of course, passes.

Themes:

1) Behavioral skill: nurturing skills for boys
   Message: Tutoring like other nurturant activities require "helping skills" including empathy and patience.

2) Pre-occupational activities: nurturant activities for boys (specifically: tutoring younger children)
   Message: Nurturant activities such as tutoring can be rewarding activities and boys can be competent in them.

3) Adult work/family roles: teacher and other occupations related to tutoring
   Message: If a child enjoys nurturant activities such as tutoring, there are a variety of occupations he or she may wish to consider.

Shows 5 and 6 (two parts): SCOOP!

Synopsis:

"The changing roles of women and men in society" is the subject Denice and her classmates choose for their newspaper's feature story. Encouraged by their journalism teacher, the members of the newspaper club takes sides in the attempt to show their town is either "fair" or "unfair." Denice as editor gets caught in the middle, but finally the newspaper staff finds that the roles of men and women are changing although there is still plenty of room for further change.

Themes:

1) Behavioral skill: None is featured in this show

2) Pre-occupational activities: school newspaper work
   Message: School newspapers offer a variety of interesting tasks including writing and photography.

3) Adult work/family roles: changes in family roles and a variety of occupational roles are featured.
   Message: Women are entering many occupations which have been sex-typed in the past and men are assuming more extensive family roles. There is still, however, much room for change in these areas. The program provides models of women and men in nontraditional occupations (e.g., male nurse, female doctor, female pharmacist, female bank officer) and non-traditional family roles (working mothers and fathers engaged in child care). The program also provides models of minority men and women in higher prestige occupations (small businessman and woman, construction company owner).

Show 7: HIKE

Synopsis:

Walter persuades his younger sister, Tess, to take a reasonable risk in climbing some steep slopes to find rocks for her collection. Tess breaks away from the group and has to deal with being lost. Later, when Ramon takes an unreasonable risk and gets stuck on a dangerous ledge it's Tess who tells him to "be reasonable," climb no higher and help himself get rescued.

Themes:

1) Behavioral skill: risk-taking
   Message: Reasonable risks can be distinguished from unreasonable risks based on probability of success and degree of risk. Reasonable risks are necessary if one is to learn about and enjoy new things. Unreasonable risks are pointless.

2) Pre-occupational activities: science for girls (specifically: geology)
   Message: Geology (i.e. rock collection and study) can be an interesting activity.

3) Adult work/family roles: female geologist

Message: Women can be competent in scientific occupations such as geology.

Show 8: FREESTYLE VARIETY SPECIAL

Synopsis:

This show is composed of a large variety of animated, filmed and taped segments. These segments are tied together by a troupe of four young entertainers who perform song and dance numbers and by guest host Mike Farrel, star of M*A*S*H. Each of these segments and numbers picks up one of the themes of the curriculum in an entertaining way.

Themes:

1) Behavioral skills: each of the behavioral skills is touched upon briefly
Message: Girls and boys should develop nontraditional skills.

2) Pre-occupational activities: each of the categories of nontraditional activities is touched upon briefly.
Message: There are a variety of nontraditional activities for boys and girls which they may enjoy.

3) Adult work/family roles: Women in nontraditional jobs and fathers more deeply involved in family life are featured throughout.
Message: Traditional sex-roles of men and women are changing.

Show 9: CANDIDATES

Synopsis:

The candidates for 7th grade class president are Denice and big-man-on-campus, Tyler Speer. Denice seeks the advice of her local councilperson Ms. Wilson, and gets some tips on responsible leadership that can help her with her campaign, her adult career and her life.

Themes:

1) Behavioral skill: leadership for girls

Message: Leadership requires a number of skills including the ability to generate one's own ideas, the ability to listen to the ideas of others and the ability to organize the tasks which need to be done.

2) Pre-occupational activities: childhood leadership roles for girls (specifically: class president).
Message: Girls can exercise leadership skills and become competent leaders.

3) Adult work/family roles: politics and other leadership roles for women
Message: Leadership skills are necessary in great variety of occupations including politics. Women can be competent in these occupations.

Show 10: YOUNG AND OLD

Synopsis:

Marcus and Walter volunteer at a center for senior citizens as a part of their social studies assignment. Marcus puts his organizational skills to work and figures he'll have the seniors' recreational program in shape in no time. Marcus and Walter are surprised to find, however, that the seniors have "no time" for Marcus' arbitrary and over-taxing schedule. Marcus and Walter ask the help of the center's occupational therapist and learn about the importance of fully understanding the needs of others when trying to help them.

Themes:

1) Behavioral skill: nurturing skills for boys
Message: Any attempt to help another must be based on an understanding of the needs of that person.

2) Pre-occupational activities: volunteer work for boys (specifically: volunteering in senior citizens center)
Message: Nurturant activities such as volunteer work can be rewarding activities and boys can be competent in them.

3) Adult work/family roles: occupational therapist
Message: Program reviews some of the duties of occupational therapists and emphasizes the importance of helping skills to this occupation.

Show 11: GOOD SIGNS

Synopsis:

A new student who is deaf is "mainstreamed" into the 7th grade class. She is received with a lack of compassion by the students, but it is Penny who takes the initiative to read about deafness, follows through by cultivating the new student's friendship and finally speaks out firmly to the rest of the class on behalf of her new friend.

Themes:

1) Behavioral skill: assertivesness for girls
Message: assertiveness requires that one take the initiative, follow through and stand up for what one wants or feels is right.

2) Pre-occupational activities: none are featured in this show

3) Adult work/family roles: none are featured in this show although a special education teacher for the hearing impaired is a supporting role.

Show 12: HEY, MOM!

Synopsis:

Walter and Tess' Mom, Kathleen, sees the need for another paycheck in the Dinsmore household and finds a job. To pave the way for her return to work she undertakes the task of teaching the family how to take care of themselves and each other by sharing household chores. Mr. Dinsmore is less than enthusiastic, but he eventually notices Kathleen's increased self-esteem from her job and he realizes that his working wife makes for a happier home -- in which more of his participation is needed.

Themes:

1) Behavior skill: none is featured in this show.

2) Pre-occupational activities: household chores for children
Message: When mothers work the whole family has to take more responsibility for running the home.

3) Adult work/family roles: female apprentice machinist, fathers and children assuming increased household responsibilities.
Message: Traditional sex-roles are changing. Women are entering non-traditional occupations and men are participating more fully in family life.

Show 13: GREASE MONKEY

Synopsis:

Chris is very interested in automobiles. She applies for a summer job at a nearby gas station and convinces the crusty old owner to hire her on her merits. While tending the station alone she takes on a job that's too big for her and disaster follows. She summons up her courage to return to work and a mechanic teaches her the fundamentals of auto repair. The next time there's trouble she's prepared to handle it.

Themes:

1) Behavioral skill: risk-taking
   Message: Jobs for which one is not prepared are unreasonable risks. The same jobs may, however, be reasonable risks once one has had some training for them.

2) Pre-occupational activities: mechanical/technical activities for girls (specifically: auto mechanics).
   Message: Girls can learn to be competent in mechanical/technical activities such as auto mechanics.

3) Adult work/family roles: auto mechanic
   Message: Auto mechnics can be an interesting occupation

Appendix C

GOALS AND OBJECTIVES IN
THE FREESTYLE CURRICULUM PLAN

(The following is excerpted from "Curriculum for the Television Career Awareness Project 'Freestyle" -- a Television Series for Grades 4-5-6." Los Angeles: Office of the Los Angeles County Superintendent of Schools. 1978.)

The goal of the Television Career Awareness Project (TV CAP) is to expand, through an interrelated set of broadcast and nonbroadcast experiences, the career awareness of girls and boys aged nine to twelve by increasing their understanding of and influencing their attitudes toward:

--the relationship of current interests and activities to educational progress and career development

--career opportunities; and

--sex-role stereotyping, and ethnicity as it affects sex-role stereotyping (page 6)

Sub-Goal 1. Children will learn to identify their skills and attitudes and relate these to potential career choices without the restrictions of sex-role stereotyping and ethnicity as it affects sex-role stereotyping.

1.1 Children will be able to identify their existing interests, skills, and activities.

1.2 Girls will be able to identify an increased number of nontraditional interests, skills, and activities (e.g., mechanical activities, spatial relationships, athletics, mathematics, science, and household tasks that require physical strength and/or exertion).

1.3 Girls will recognize that there are many non-traditional tasks and activities which they have the ability to perform.

1.4 Girls will be able to identify significant others who can perform non-traditional tasks and activities.

1.5 Boys will be able to identify an increased number of nontraditional activities (e.g., artistic; writing and skill with words; social service; child care; and household tasks such as cooking, dusting, etc.).

1.6 Boys will recognize that there are many nontraditional tasks and activities which they have the ability to perform.

1.7 Boys will be able to identify significant others who can perform nontraditional tasks and activities.

1.8 Children will be able to relate interests, skills, and activities previously considered nontraditional to occupations they know about and to potential career choices.

1.9 Children will recognize that sex-role stereotyping and its interaction with ethnic stereotyping restricts potential career choice.

1.10 Children will recognize that the bilingual ability of many ethnic minorities can create career opportunities which are equally appropriate for both males and females, e.g., international salesperson, translator, teacher, and international telephone operator.

1.11 Children will affirm their acceptance of boys and girls performing nontraditional activities.

1.12 Boys will identify or describe nontraditional activities they see themselves capable of performing.

1.13 Girls will identify or describe nontraditional activities they see themselves capable of performing.

1.14 After participating in the project, children will be able to develop an expanded list of interests and activities. This expanded list will reflect a reduced percentage of traditionally sex-stereotyped choices.

1.15 Children from ethnic minorities will indicate an interest in a greater variety of occupations.

<u>Sub-Goal 2.</u> Children will develop an understanding of the changing roles of men and women as adult workers and family members.

2.1 Children will recognize that girls and boys should prepare for future employment and be able to identify reasons why they should prepare.

2.2 Children will recognize that men and women work out of economic necessity and for personal satisfaction.

2.3 Children will recognize that men and women combine work and family roles for personal fulfillment.

2.4 Children will recognize that men and women who work can obtain positive rewards for themselves and their families from their jobs.

2.5 Children will affirm that it is acceptable for adult males and females to combine work and family roles.

2.6 Children will recognize that changes in work roles for women and men will complement, rather than restrict, changes in work roles for ethnic groups in this country.

2.7 Children, especially those from ethnic minorities, will recognize that in expanding work roles for males and females individuals need not lose their ethnic identity.

2.8 Children will recognize that in families where both partners work it is necessary for household responsibilities and child care to be shared.

2.9 Children will indicate that it is fair for adult males to assume a share of household responsibilities and child care.

2.10 Children will recognize that it is rewarding for all family members when fathers share in family responsibilities, including caring for children.

2.11 Children will affirm that caring for children can provide personal satisfaction.

2.12 Children will recognize that all members of the family benefit when all share in the financial responsibility for the family.

2.13 Children will recognize that the majority of girls will be gainfully employed 25-30 years of their adult life.

2.14 Children will identify a variety of nontraditional occupations as occupations for females.

2.15 Children will describe some of the duties, skills, training, and education necessary for nontraditional occupations for females.

2.16 Children will identify school subjects and/or interests and activities they have or know about which are similar to the skills required for specific nontraditional occupations for females.

2.17 Boys will affirm that it is acceptable for girls to choose nontraditional occupations.

2.18 Girls will be able to identify significant others (parents, teachers, girl friends, etc.) who have given them positive reinforcement for potential nontraditional career choices.

2.19 Given a list of careers for females, an increased number of girls will select nontraditional occupations they would like to explore.

2.20 Given a list of careers for females, individual girls will select an increased number of nontraditional occupations that they would like to explore.

2.21 Given a list of careers for females, boys will select nontraditional occupations they believe girls would like to explore.

Sub-Goal 3. Children, especially boys, will be able to identify helping skills, emotional expressiveness, and empathy for others and recognize how these behaviors relate to work and family roles.

3.1 Children will be able to identify appropriate emotions in a given situation.

3.2 Boys will affirm that it is acceptable to express their emotions openly.

3.3 Children will recognize that within certain ethnic groups the restrictions of sex-role stereotyping inhibit the open expression of emotions.

3.4 Children will accurately describe the feelings of others in given situations.

3.5 Children will be able to compare and contrast the feelings of others with their own.

3.6 Children will affirm that it is good to respect the feelings of others.

3.7 Children will be able to identify ways in which they can help others.

3.8 Children will be able to identify instances when others need help.

3.9 Having identified situations in which others need help, children will recommend ways in which help can be provided.

3.10 Children will identify a variety of nontraditional occupations for males which require helping behavior.

3.11 Children will describe some of the duties, skills, training, and education necessary for nontraditional occupations for males.

3.12 Children will identify school subjects and/or interests and activities they have or know about which are similar to the skills required for nontraditional occupations for males.

3.13 Girls will affirm that it is acceptable for boys to choose nontraditional occupations.

3.14 Boys will be able to identify significant others (parents, teachers, boyfriends, etc.) who have given them positive reinforcement for potential nontraditional career choices.

3.15 Given a list of careers for males, an increased number of boys will select nontraditional occupations they would like to explore.

3.16 Given a list of careers for males, individual boys will select an increased number of nontraditional occupations they would like to explore.

3.17 Given a list of careers for males, girls will select nontraditional occupations they believe boys would like to explore.

<u>Sub-Goal 4.</u> Children will learn about selected behavior strategies, such as independence, initiative, self-direction, assertiveness, and cooperation and how these strategies influence educational progress and occupational preparation. Independence, initiative, and self-direction are especially important for girls.

4.1 Children will identify the ways in which independence can be used as an aid to achievement.

4.2 Children will affirm that independence can be an appropriate strategy to use in achieving a goal.

4.3 Children will identify the ways in which initiative can be used as an aid to achievement.

4.4 Children will affirm that initiative can be an appropriate strategy to use in achieving a goal.

4.5 Children will identify the ways in which self-direction can be used as an aid to achievement.

4.6 Children will affirm that self-direction can be an appropriate strategy to use in achieving a goal.

4.7 Children will identify the ways in which assertiveness can be used as an aid to achievement.

4.8 Children will affirm that assertiveness can be an appropriate strategy to use in achieving a goal.

4.9 Children will identify the ways in which cooperation can be used as an aid to achievement.

4.10 Children will affirm that cooperation can be an appropriate strategy to use in achieving a goal.

Sub-Goal 5. Children, especially girls, will recognize that taking responsibility and providing responsible leadership are essential to educational progress and career development.

5.1 Children will be able to identify some elements of responsibility.

5.2 Children will be able to identify ways in which one can become a responsible person.

5.3 Children will recognize some of the behaviors involved in assuming responsibility.

5.4 Children will recognize that both boys and girls, regardless of ethnic background, are capable of exhibiting responsible behaviors.

5.5 Children will be able to identify instances in which they exhibited responsibility.

5.6 Children will affirm that it is necessary to exhibit responsible behaviors to reach a career goal.

5.7 Girls will be able to perceive themselves in responsible career roles.

5.8 Children will be able to identify some elements of responsible leadership.

5.9 Children will recognize that both boys and girls, regardless of ethnic background, are capable of providing responsible leadership.

5.10 Children will affirm that it is appropriate for girls to assume responsible leadership positions.

5.11 Children will be able to identify careers, or career roles, in which being a responsible leader is a vital factor.

Sub-Goal 6. Children will recognize that taking reasonable risks and learning how to cope with the success and/or failure that results from taking risks are necessary for educational progress and career development.

6.1 Children will be able to identify both reasonable and unreasonable risks.

6.2 Children, especially girls, will recognize that reasonable risks are a necessary part of achievement.

6.3 Children will affirm reasonable risk taking when appropriate to accomplish a goal.

6.4 Children will recognize that it is difficult for boys and girls from certain ethnic or socio-economic groups to take reasonable risks because they fear rejection.

6.5 Girls will recognize that sucess is due primarily to effort, ability, and self-esteem rather than luck.

6.6 Girls will be able to identify or describe personal situations in which their success was due to their ability and effort.

6.7 Girls will affirm that it is acceptable to take pleasure in recognition of their accomplishments by others.

6.8 Children will recognize that failure is caused.

6.9 Children will recognize that failure can be coped with by
 1. analyzing what they might have done differently.
 2. recognizing that they should not have tried the task.
 3. asking for help when they need it, and then
 4. trying again.

6.10 Given a failure situation, after analysis and if appropriate, children will try again using an alternative course of action.

Appendix D

RELIABILITY OF STUDENT OUTCOME MEASURES

In the social sciences, a thorough study of the reliability of measures used in research is considered essential. Since the reliability of a measure informs the researcher about the amount of error inherent in the measurement of a construct, a systematic consideration of reliability is a necessary prerequisite to the analysis phase of any research project.

Psychometricians differentiate among several kinds of reliability. The test-retest method of establishing reliability focuses upon the _stability_ of the obtained score over time. On the other hand, the split-half technique focuses upon the _internal consistency_ or _homogeneity_ of a measure at one point in time. Throughout this study we limit ourselves to an _internal consistency_ or _homogeneity_ definition of reliability. We explore the degree to which individual items belong together in a composite index and the degree to which an index measures one underlying construct.

The reliability of an instrument is not a fixed attribute. More accurately, it is "...a parameter for a particular test in a particular population..." (Nicewander and Price, 1978, p. 408; Samejima, 1977). Therefore a test has many reliabilities. We wanted to investigate the reliabilities of our measures for a total group and for each subgroup which might be separately analyzed. We chose to conduct our analyses at one site where the subgroup sample sizes were uniformly adequate. Of particular concern was the possible differential reliability across grade, sex, or ethnic subgroups. Because there is no reason to believe that data under the home view condition would be significantly more or less reliable than under the school view condition, our choice of site could be made without regard to this factor. On the basis of these considerations, Long Beach appeared to be the best choice for conducting a reliability study.

Methods

The reliability analyses were conducted upon a sample of 1,222 students in Long Beach/Torrance. This analytic sample was the result of including only those respondent with both pre and post-test data. This represents 89 percent of the original sample. A breakdown of number of cases by demographics and treatment type is shown in Table D.1. It should be noted that the grade level and ethnicity totals are not equal to 1,222. This apparent discrepancy is due to an early decision to omit fifth graders (n=306) from the grade level analysis; we believed we could bracket the estimates of reliability adequately at grade 5 with those computed for grades 4 and 6. In addition, we dropped from the ethnicity analysis all students (n=99) who were other than White, Black, or Hispanic.

Table D.1
Long Beach/Torrance Matched Sample
by Sex, Grade Level, Ethnicity and Treatment

Subsample	School Full	School Control	Totals
Sex	871	351	1,222
Male	401	174	575
Female	470	177	647
Grade Level	631	184	815
Grade 4	258	140	398
Grade 6	373	144	517
Ethnicity	805	318	1,123
White	480	253	733
Black	187	6	193
Hispanic	138	59	197

Cronbach's coefficient alpha was chosen as the statistical measure of internal consistency (Cronbach, 1951). Alpha, which can range in value from 0 to 1, represents the proportion of test variance attributable to common factors among the items in a scale. Therefore a high value for alpha is desirable and is evidence that the items in a scale are measuring the same underlying construct. A low value, on the other hand, indicates that the item set may be tapping two or more content domains and should not be used together to form a composite index.

The RELIABILITY subprogram contained in Version 7.2 of the Statistical Package for the Social Sciences (SPSS, Nie et al., 1975) was used to calculate each of the alpha coefficients reported in this study. A listwise deletion option for handling missing data was selected so that each alpha was calculated on the basis of the same number of cases per item within each index.

The reliability analysis was related to and conducted simultaneously with the index construction phase of the evaluation. For this reason the algorithm for the analytic decisions in the reliability analysis is entwined with the algorithm for index construction. In this algorithm a group of $\underline{n}$ potential index items is selected for analysis. (The items which form a potential index were prespecified at the planning phase of the evaluation.) Item means, standard deviations and intercorrelations are computed. Also calculated are: a) alpha for the entire scale; b) alpha for each hypothetical scale if one item were dropped from the scale (jackknife algorithm); c) multiple correlations of each item with the remaining items in the scale.

Then the values of alpha are inspected. When possible, the index is constructed without deleting any items. However, if a much larger value of alpha can be obtained by dropping an item, and the same magnitude of increase will be found in the corresponding attitude or belief scale, the index is constructed without the weakest item. The general rule is: maximize coefficient alpha by dropping items; but do so only if the resulting gain in alpha is large and the integrity of the underlying measurement theory is maintained.

A total of 71 indexes were created, and reliability estimates for each of these indices were computed. For each index the pretest and posttest alphas for the full sample and for the subsamples of sex, grade, treatment and ethnic group were computed. These data are presented in Table D.2 at the end of this appendix. The order of indexes in Table D.2 is approximately the same as the order of the corresponding items in the student questionnaire. For an explanation of the full names of specific indices, the reader should refer to the Glossary in Appendix A.

Adequacy of Indices

In order to evaluate the overall adequacy of the indices from a psychometric perspective, the pretest reliabilities were categorized in two ways. First, the relationship between the number of items in an index and the corresponding reliability was explored. These data are shown in Table D.3.

Table D.3
Summary of Pretest Index Reliabilities
by Number of Items in Index

Number of Items in Index	Number of Indices	Alpha Coefficients		
		Lowest	Highest	Average
2	15	.24	.79	.52
3	16	.44	.80	.67
4	13	.52	.83	.69
5	14	.47	.82	.72
6 and above	14	.55	.94	.79

Two-item indices were, in general, less reliable (average alpha=.52) than were three-item indices (average alpha=.67); but four-item indices tended to be just slightly more reliable (average alpha=.69) than three-item indices. When comparing groups of indices, the general trend was for longer indices to have higher reliabilities.

The indices were also grouped into categories according to reliability ranges. In Table D.4 it is shown that fifty-six percent of the indices had pretest reliability estimates of .70 or greater. Thirty-two percent of the index reliabilities fell in the .50-.69 range. The remaining eleven percent of the indices yielded alphas lower than .50. Although there is little consensus among psychometricians about cut-off points, Nunnally and Durham (1975) note that the standards for reliability should depend upon the intended use of the instrument. According to their judgement, reliabilities of .50 and .60 are "modest." It is almost universally agreed that reliability estimates of .70 or greater are quite respectable and that estimates in the .40's and below are likely to present problems of one sort or another for the analyst.

Table D.4
Summary of Pretest Index Reliabilities
by Alpha Range

Alpha Range	Number of Indices	Percent of Total[1]
.90-.99	1	1.4
.80-.89	12	16.9
.70-.79	27	38.0
.60-.69	11	15.5
.50-.59	12	16.9
.40-.49	5	7.0
.30-.39	1	1.4
.20-.29	2	2.8

[1]Percent of 71 indexes

Differential Reliability

Indices were also grouped according to their measurement content areas. The average alpha for the 8 interest indices was .67. For the 25 attitude indices the average alpha was .66. For the 21 belief indices, alpha averaged .64. As can be seen in these figures, very little variation was observed in the average alpha coefficients by content area.

An inspection of the pretest data in Table 2 shows that there is considerable similarity across the subsamples in the alpha coefficients. For example, when the 14 five-item indices are examined, one is impressed with the fact that the subgroups being compared in the analyses (i.e., boys vs. girls, fourth vs. sixth graders, experimentals vs. controls, and Blacks vs. Whites vs. Hispanics) have very similar alphas. This observation in turn lends credibility to the use of an analytic strategy which does not involve corrections for unreliability since, among other things, it suggests that little, if anything, would be gained from such corrections. Had one or more of the subgroups been consistently and importantly higher or lower in reliability than the other subgroups, the analytic strategy would need to have been modified in order to correct for such differential reliability.

Summary

The pretest reliabilities (Cronbach alphas) for the overall sample in one site, as well as for the subgroups of analytic interest, have been presented and discussed. Most of the coefficients are seen to meet or exceed acceptable levels for social science measurement procedures, with many of the indices attaining very high levels of internal consistency. Not surprisingly, the average coefficients were seen to vary directly as a function of the number of items in the index. Perhaps more importantly for the kind of analytic strategy utilized in this report, little variation in the coefficients was observed as a function of either content area or demographic/experimental subgroup.

Table D.2
Alpha Reliability Coefficients for Long Beach/Torrance Sample

Index Name and Number of Items	Time	Alpha for Full Sample	Alpha for Sample Subgroups							
			Sex		Grade		Treatment		Ethnic Group		
			Male	Female	Four	Six	Exper.	Control	Black	White	Hispan.
INTMC - 5 Interest in mechanical activities	Pre	.76	.69	.59	.75	.75	.76	.76	.73	.76	.80
	Post	.81	.80	.71	.82	.80	.80	.82	.80	.81	.83
INTMCF - 2 Interest in mechanical activities FST	Pre	.50	.48	.40	.43	.53	.50	.50	.50	.50	.60
	Post	.59	.63	.50	.61	.61	.57	.57	.53	.60	.56
INTNRT - 9 Interest in nurturant activities	Pre	.84	.77	.81	.84	.84	.83	.84	.81	.84	.80
	Post	.88	.86	.86	.86	.89	.87	.89	.35	.88	.88
INTNRTF - 4 Interest in nurturant activities FST	Pre	.72	.66	.70	.73	.71	.69	.75	.70	.71	.70
	Post	.80	.78	.78	.78	.83	.78	.81	.70	.81	.79
INTSCI - 6 Interest in scientific activities	Pre	.70	.67	.70	.65	.68	.70	.68	.61	.71	.68
	Post	.77	.72	.81	.72	.78	.77	.76	.74	.77	.77
INTSCIF - 4 Interest in scientific activities FST	Pre	.58	.55	.60	.52	.56	.58	.56	.45	.59	.52
	Post	.69	.62	.75	.61	.68	.69	.67	.71	.68	.72

Note. - FST = subset of items illustrated in the FREESTYLE television shows.

Index Name and Number of Items	Time	Alpha for Full Sample	Alpha for Sample Subgroups							
			Sex		Grade		Treatment		Ethnic Group		
			Male	Female	Four	Six	Exper.	Control	Black	White	Hispan.
INTATH - 5 Interest in athletic activities	Pre	.73	.67	.63	.76	.72	.71	.78	.60	.73	.82
	Post	.75	.75	.65	.76	.73	.72	.79	.70	.74	.76
INTATHF - 2 Interest in athletic activities FST	Pre	.51	.46	.26	.61	.48	.45	.67	.07	.55	.71
	Post	.55	.59	.30	.67	.46	.51	.64	.41	.55	.64
ATGMC - 3 Attitude toward girls in mechanical activ's	Pre	.78	.76	.78	.79	.78	.77	.80	.68	.80	.74
	Post	.86	.83	.87	.86	.84	.84	.87	.77	.88	.82
ATGATH - 2 Attitude toward girls in athletics	Pre	.77	.71	.75	.76	.79	.74	.83	.62	.79	.74
	Post	.84	.77	.84	.85	.83	.82	.85	.78	.87	.78
ATBNRT - 5 Attitude toward boys being nurturant	Pre	.70	.73	.68	.69	.68	.69	.70	.70	.71	.67
	Post	.80	.82	.79	.80	.82	.77	.81	.76	.82	.77
BFGATH - 2 Beliefs about girls in athletics	Pre	.67	.54	.69	.68	.68	.67	.66	.71	.65	.70
	Post	.65	.50	.66	.64	.66	.63	.67	.66	.66	.60

Note. - FST = subset of items illustrated in the FREESTYLE television shows.

Table D.2 (cont.)

Index Name and Number of Items	Time	Alpha for Full Sample	Alpha for Sample Subgroups							
			Sex		Grade		Treatment		Ethnic Group		
			Male	Female	Four	Six	Exper.	Control	Black	White	Hispan.
BFGMC - 3 Beliefs about girls in mechanical activ's	Pre	.74	.68	.77	.79	.69	.75	.73	.72	.74	.72
	Post	.78	.77	.78	.79	.77	.78	.76	.74	.80	.78
BFBNRT1 - 4 Beliefs about boys being nurturant	Pre	.77	.70	.76	.77	.74	.76	.76	.76	.76	.80
	Post	.80	.82	.77	.76	.78	.78	.80	.79	.79	.82
OCHR7 - 7 Interest in Occupations, Hol. Realistic	Pre	.86	.86	.81	.86	.86	.86	.87	.84	.84	.87
	Post	.86	.87	.83	.83	.86	.86	.85	.82	.85	.90
OCHR5 - 5 Interest in Occupations, Hol. Realistic	Pre	.79	.80	.71	.78	.78	.79	.80	.79	.76	.80
	Post	.78	.80	.73	.73	.79	.78	.78	.72	.77	.85
OCHA2 - 2 Interest in Occupations, Hol. Artistic	Pre	.79	.79	.78	.80	.75	.78	.78	.76	.78	.81
	Post	.79	.79	.80	.77	.79	.80	.74	.83	.79	.79
OCHI6 - 6 Interest in occupations, Hol. Investigative	Pre	.84	.83	.86	.85	.81	.84	.83	.84	.83	.86
	Post	.84	.86	.84	.80	.84	.84	.82	.82	.83	.85

Index Name and Number of Items	Time	Alpha for Full Sample	Alpha for Sample Subgroups							
			Sex		Grade		Treatment		Ethnic Group		
			Male	Female	Four	Six	Exper.	Control	Black	White	Hispan.
OCHI5 - 5 Interest in occupations, Hol. Investigative	Pre	.80	.79	.83	.82	.76	.80	.79	.81	.78	.81
	Post	.80	.83	.80	.76	.80	.80	.78	.78	.79	.82
OCHS9 - 9 Interest in occupations, Holland Social	Pre	.78	.77	.79	.76	.78	.80	.74	.75	.77	.79
	Post	.82	.80	.82	.82	.81	.84	.75	.81	.82	.80
OCHS5 - 5 Interest in occupations, Holland Social	Pre	.63	.64	.61	.61	.58	.67	.51	.64	.60	.67
	Post	.71	.71	.70	.71	.68	.74	.61	.75	.70	.71
OCHE7 - 7 Interest in occupations, Hol. Enterprising	Pre	.89	.90	.89	.88	.87	.90	.86	.91	.87	.88
	Post	.88	.89	.88	.87	.87	.88	.86	.89	.86	.88
OCHE5 - 5 Interest in occupations, Hol. Enterprising	Pre	.82	.88	.86	.85	.85	.88	.82	.88	.84	.85
	Post	.85	.87	.85	.85	.84	.86	.82	.87	.84	.83
OCHC5 - 5 Interest in occupations, Hol. Conventional	Pre	.80	.79	.83	.78	.79	.83	.73	.79	.78	.80
	Post	.83	.81	.84	.84	.80	.84	.80	.85	.82	.81

Table D.2 (cont.)

Index Name and Number of Items	Time	Alpha for Full Sample	Sex		Grade		Treatment		Ethnic Group		
			Male	Female	Four	Six	Exper.	Control	Black	White	Hispan.
OCFEM - 11 Interest in female occupations	Pre	.88	.84	.86	.88	.88	.89	.85	.86	.87	.89
	Post	.90	.86	.88	.90	.89	.90	.88	.89	.90	.88
OCMALE - 25 Interest in male occupations	Pre	.94	.94	.94	.94	.93	.94	.94	.94	.93	.95
	Post	.94	.94	.93	.93	.93	.94	.93	.93	.93	.95
OCFST - 9 Interest in occupations	Pre	.79	.79	.83	.80	.75	.80	.77	.78	.75	.81
	Post	.78	.80	.80	.76	.76	.79	.72	.77	.75	.79
SXJBFM - 5 BF Sex of P'pl. in Jobs Trad. Held by Men FST	Pre	.47	.37	.53	.50	.48	.46	.52	.46	.50	.44
	Post	.58	.55	.59	.55	.58	.61	.45	.63	.55	.67
SXJBFW - 2 BF Sex of P'pl. in Jobs Trad. Held by W'n FST	Pre	.45	.36	.51	.53	.34	.44	.49	.17	.49	.55
	Post	.51	.50	.51	.46	.54	.46	.57	.51	.52	.52
SXJBM - 9 BF Sex of P'pl. in Jobs Trad. Held by Men	Pre	.61	.55	.63	.64	.61	.59	.64	.59	.48	.58
	Post	.71	.68	.71	.72	.72	.73	.63	.76	.70	.73

Note. - BF = Belief about; FST = subset of items illustrated in FREESTYLE television shows.

Index Name and Number of Items	Time	Alpha for Full Sample	Sex		Grade		Treatment		Ethnic Group		
			Male	Female	Four	Six	Exper.	Control	Black	White	Hispan.
SXJBW - 6 BF Sex of p'pl. in Jobs Trad. Held by Women	Pre	.55	.52	.58	.43	.57	.56	.54	.54	.48	.62
	Post	.62	.60	.64	.60	.65	.63	.56	.58	.62	.63
ATWJB - 5 AT Women in Non-Traditional Jobs	Pre	.79	.74	.78	.81	.76	.78	.81	.75	.81	.76
	Post	.82	.77	.83	.86	.81	.83	.79	.80	.84	.85
ATMJB3 - 3 AT Men in Non-Traditional Jobs	Pre	.64	.59	.64	.69	.64	.61	.70	.51	.70	.51
	Post	.71	.67	.71	.69	.70	.69	.72	.58	.75	.73
ATMJB2 - 2 AT Men in Non-Traditional Jobs	Pre	.74	.70	.76	.76	.73	.73	.76	.75	.76	.68
	Post	.78	.82	.75	.77	.73	.74	.84	.73	.80	.80
BFWHOM3 - 3 Beliefs about Wives in the Home	Pre	.52	.53	.51	.58	.46	.53	.52	.36	.52	.61
	Post	.62	.60	.62	.65	.52	.59	.68	.55	.58	.76
BFWHOM2 - 2 Beliefs about Wives in the Home	Pre	.51	.51	.50	.48	.46	.54	.44	.41	.50	.59
	Post	.59	.54	.62	.60	.42	.57	.62	.50	.54	.75

Note. - AT = Attitude toward; BF = Belief about

Table D.2 (cont.)

Index Name and Number of Items	Time	Alpha for Full Sample	Alpha for Sample Subgroups								
			Sex		Grade		Treatment		Ethnic Group		
			Male	Female	Four	Six	Exper.	Control	Black	White	Hispan.
BFHHOM4 - 4 Beliefs about Husbands in the Home	Pre	.52	.54	.51	.47	.52	.52	.53	.51	.50	.58
	Post	.75	.76	.74	.77	.70	.72	.77	.72	.74	.80
BFHHOM3 - 3 Beliefs about Husbands in the Home	Pre	.71	.72	.71	.73	.69	.69	.76	.65	.72	.74
	Post	.75	.76	.74	.77	.70	.72	.77	.72	.74	.80
ATWHOM3 - 3 Attitudes toward Wives in the Home	Pre	.65	.62	.68	.73	.64	.66	.62	.56	.68	.62
	Post	.71	.71	.71	.77	.69	.71	.71	.68	.73	.74
ATWHOM2 - 2 Attitudes toward Wives in the Home	Pre	.65	.58	.70	.69	.66	.65	.65	.49	.69	.67
	Post	.74	.73	.75	.77	.69	.76	.70	.70	.76	.77
ATHHOM4 - 4 Attitudes toward Husbands in the Home	Pre	.56	.59	.52	.44	.59	.57	.53	.59	.54	.57
	Post	.61	.59	.61	.61	.57	.58	.61	.43	.64	.60
ATHHOM3 - 3 Attitudes toward Husbands in the Home	Pre	.77	.77	.77	.76	.78	.77	.78	.75	.78	.76
	Post	.81	.80	.82	.84	.77	.81	.81	.76	.81	.84

Index Name and Number of Items	Time	Alpha for Full Sample	Alpha for Sample Subgroups								
			Sex		Grade		Treatment		Ethnic Group		
			Male	Female	Four	Six	Exper.	Control	Black	White	Hispan.
BFBHOM - 3 Beliefs about Boys in the Home	Pre	.68	.65	.66	.68	.71	.67	.68	.72	.69	.64
	Post	.73	.75	.70	.70	.74	.72	.74	.70	.73	.80
BFGHOM - 3 Beliefs about Girls in the Home	Pre	.75	.69	.75	.74	.68	.75	.75	.72	.75	.74
	Post	.79	.74	.79	.77	.75	.77	.83	.78	.77	.86
ATBHOM - 3 Attitude toward Boys in the Home	Pre	.78	.74	.80	.77	.81	.79	.78	.75	.81	.70
	Post	.82	.79	.82	.76	.81	.82	.79	.78	.82	.85
ATGHOM - 3 Attitude toward Girls in the Home	Pre	.79	.82	.78	.80	.77	.79	.81	.81	.79	.77
	Post	.83	.85	.82	.82	.84	.83	.84	.80	.84	.84
ATGLDR - 4 Attitude toward Girls in Leadership Pos'ns	Pre	.83	.67	.78	.83	.81	.83	.81	.83	.82	.83
	Post	.85	.73	.83	.86	.86	.85	.85	.82	.85	.90
ATBLDR - 4 Attitude toward Boys in Leadership Pos'ns	Pre	.79	.77	.68	.78	.75	.79	.78	.84	.77	.79
	Post	.80	.82	.72	.78	.81	.80	.80	.85	.77	.84

Table D.2 (cont.)

| Index Name and Number of Items | Time | Alpha for Full Sample | Alpha for Sample Subgroups ||||||||
| | | | Sex || Grade || Treatment || Ethnic Group |||
			Male	Female	Four	Six	Exper.	Control	Black	White	Hispan.
BFGLDR1 - 4 Beliefs about Girls in Leadership Roles	Pre	.79	.71	.76	.79	.73	.80	.77	.85	.81	.76
	Post	.80	.73	.80	.81	.76	.80	.81	.78	.82	.79
BFGLDR2 - 2 Beliefs about Girls in Leadership Roles	Pre	.44	.24	.50	.36	.50	.43	.44	.37	.44	.40
	Post	.54	.46	.52	.49	.62	.54	.53	.40	.58	.53
BFBLDR1 - 4 Beliefs about Boys in Leadership Roles	Pre	.82	.79	.76	.82	.80	.82	.81	.87	.81	.77
	Post	.83	.78	.81	.84	.79	.83	.82	.86	.83	.81
BFBLDR2 - 2 Beliefs about Boys in Leadership Roles	Pre	.25	.33	.20	.18	.38	.26	.22	.11	.28	.31
	Post	.40	.36	.44	.32	.53	.44	.32	.34	.47	.30
ATGNRT3 - 3 Attitude toward Girls Being Nurturant	Pre	.56	.58	.52	.52	.59	.52	.65	.44	.57	.57
	Post	.71	.71	.69	.72	.71	.66	.81	.67	.61	.75
ATBNRT3 - 3 Attitude toward Boys Being Nurturant	Pre	.65	.59	.65	.63	.69	.64	.67	.48	.69	.67
	Post	.71	.69	.77	.79	.76	.74	.81	.68	.79	.75

| Index Name and Number of Items | Time | Alpha for Full Sample | Alpha for Sample Subgroups ||||||||
| | | | Sex || Grade || Treatment || Ethnic Group |||
			Male	Female	Four	Six	Exper.	Control	Black	White	Hispan.
ATBNRT5 - 5 Attitude toward Boys Being Nurturant	Pre	.72	.72	.70	.69	.75	.71	.74	.65	.74	.69
	Post	.79	.78	.79	.81	.80	.78	.83	.78	.80	.78
BFBNRT2 - 6 Beliefs about Boys Being Nurturant	Pre	.79	.78	.79	.78	.80	.78	.81	.81	.79	.80
	Post	.84	.84	.83	.82	.83	.82	.87	.85	.83	.84
BFGNRT - 6 Beliefs about Girls Being Nurturant	Pre	.87	.87	.86	.88	.86	.86	.90	.87	.88	.87
	Post	.89	.87	.89	.88	.86	.89	.89	.90	.88	.89
ATBIND - 3 Attitude toward Boys Showing Independence	Pre	.44	.48	.41	.39	.43	.44	.44	.48	.43	.52
	Post	.63	.65	.61	.52	.65	.62	.61	.57	.67	.60
ATGIND - 3 Attitude toward Girls Showing Independence	Pre	.53	.51	.55	.48	.48	.54	.51	.49	.53	.64
	Post	.69	.68	.69	.65	.65	.68	.67	.70	.70	.68
BFBIND - 2 Beliefs about Boys Showing Independence	Pre	.45	.43	.47	.51	.30	.47	.40	.53	.43	.44
	Post	.55	.61	.51	.49	.52	.58	.44	.63	.52	.59

Table D.2 (cont.)

| Index Name and Number of Items | Time | Alpha for Full Sample | Alpha for Sample Subgroups ||||||||
| | | | Sex || Grade || Treatment || Ethnic Group |||
			Male	Female	Four	Six	Exper.	Control	Black	White	Hispan.
BFGIND - 2 Beliefs about Girls Showing Independence	Pre	.54	.55	.54	.60	.44	.55	.52	.61	.49	.67
	Post	.63	.64	.62	.63	.56	.62	.63	.63	.62	.70
BFGASRT - 5 Beliefs about Girls Being Assertive	Pre	.71	.69	.71	.67	.71	.70	.74	.71	.71	.73
	Post	.74	.69	.76	.70	.74	.73	.74	.70	.74	.74
BFGRTK - 4 Beliefs about Girls Taking Risks	Pre	.54	.58	.50	.54	.60	.52	.57	.51	.55	.51
	Post	.62	.59	.62	.59	.63	.61	.63	.60	.62	.60
BFBASRT - 5 Beliefs about Boys Being Assertive	Pre	.69	.67	.69	.64	.70	.69	.71	.76	.67	.71
	Post	.74	.70	.74	.72	.72	.72	.73	.78	.71	.75
BFBRTK - 4 Beliefs about Boys Taking Risks	Pre	.60	.54	.64	.65	.60	.60	.59	.56	.61	.65
	Post	.64	.60	.67	.69	.58	.64	.65	.59	.65	.61
ATGAST4 - 4 Attitude toward Girls Being Assertive	Pre	.72	.73	.70	.65	.72	.71	.74	.66	.72	.78
	Post	.79	.80	.78	.78	.81	.80	.71	.72	.80	.81

| Index Name and Number of Items | Time | Alpha for Full Sample | Alpha for Sample Subgroups ||||||||
| | | | Sex || Grade || Treatment || Ethnic Group |||
			Male	Female	Four	Six	Exper.	Control	Black	White	Hispan.
ATGAST3 - 3 Attitude toward Girls being Assertive	Pre	.80	.77	.80	.81	.78	.79	.79	.82	.80	.79
	Post	.86	.85	.86	.87	.86	.86	.84	.76	.88	.86
ATGASRT - 2 Attitude toward Girls Being Assertive	Pre	.24	.37	.13	.23	.19	.24	.24	.31	.15	.34
	Post	.38	.42	.35	.42	.27	.38	.33	.45	.30	.49
ATBASRT - 2 Attitude toward Boys Being Assertive	Pre	.35	.39	.29	.40	.31	.32	.41	.34	.35	.30
	Post	.41	.38	.42	.43	.34	.40	.40	.49	.34	.48
ATBRTK - 5 Attitude toward Boys Taking Risks	Pre	.66	.67	.66	.71	.57	.67	.66	.67	.66	.71
	Post	.73	.71	.74	.81	.63	.73	.74	.69	.73	.77
ATGRTK - 5 Attitude toward Girls Taking Risks	Pre	.71	.70	.72	.79	.63	.72	.68	.71	.70	.75
	Post	.73	.70	.75	.78	.62	.72	.75	.72	.72	.77

Appendix E

DESCRIPTIONS OF THE SEVEN TEST SITES
IN THE FREESTYLE EVALUATION[1]

PART I. SCHOOL FULL VS. CONTROL SITES:
LONG BEACH/TORRANCE, MILWAUKEE, AND ANN ARBOR

Long Beach/Torrance, California.

Both Long Beach and Torrance are part of the greater Los Angeles area which covers a region of 450 square miles. Los Angeles became an American city in 1850, but it was not until the 1920's that it began developing the features by which it is characterized today. This was when the wholesale migration of young people began, attracted by the Southern California climate and "easy living". It was the automobile that was largely responsible for the expansive growth: building height restrictions were enforced until the 1950's because of fear of earthquakes. Thus, the city spread outward to become a city of suburbs connected by freeways. Eventually the suburbs themselves expanded and Long Beach and Torrance are two of these suburbs that lie south of the "central city". With a population of 358,700, Long Beach is nearly three times larger than Torrance which has 134,500 residents. Like the rest of Los Angeles county, these cities were originally created from Spanish land-grant "ranchos" of the 18th century and the styles of many of the homes show Spanish influence. The people in these communities work in many diverse occupations in Long Beach, Torrance, and the general Los Angeles area. Many are employed with the Port of Long Beach and the Long Beach Naval Shipyard, in oil production or in the aircraft industry. Income levels range from low to high, with most in the middle income range.

---

[1] This appendix was written by Christine Lux.

Between the two cities the population is 65% White and 15% Black. Mexican-Americans began settling in the area between 1910-1930, working in the fields, orange groves or on the railroads. The Hispanic population now represents 14% of the residents.[2] Participating schools/classrooms have higher numbers of minority groups so that our sample was 59.6% White, 16.7% Black and 15.7% Hispanic (predominantly Mexican-American). 33 classrooms (in 14 schools) in Long Beach and 12 classrooms (in 6 schools) in Torrance participated in the FREESTYLE study.

Long Beach began a modest staff development program in career education in 1973. There were some initial problems with understanding the concepts and many teachers confused career education with vocational education. However, a well-structured, nine-week staff development course was developed in 1974 and over the following three years, 75 elementary teachers participated. Other career education programs were also presented which attracted hundreds of elementary and secondary teachers. By 1978 50-60 elementary teachers were using the career education guide and teaching career-oriented classrooms. However, the passage of Proposition 13 in that year resulted in a cut in funds that severely hampered the career education program. There was no longer a coordinator to work with the schools and operate the resource center that was developed for elementary grades. There is still considerable emphasis at the senior level and a skeleton program remains at the grade school level. Interest on the part of elementary teachers has continued, despite the loss of funds which cut back the program.

Career education programs began in the early 1970's in Torrance also. Stress was put on the fact that career education can and should be infused into the general curriculum, rather than be separate unit and this was the answer given to teachers who asked "What am I _not_ going to teach in order to teach this?" There is now a School Improvement Plan (SIP) which requires that

---

[2]Where possible, school district racial composition is reported; however, in cases where these records are not kept metropolitan data is presented based on the 1970 census. In the case of Long Beach and Torrance, the figures are for the combined school districts (1977-1978) however, some interpolation was necessary because of unavailable district data from the smaller of the two districts, Torrance.

some career education be built into the plans at each site and career education coordinators are working on this. It is estimated that about 30 percent of the Torrance teachers have a thorough understanding of career education and infuse it into lessons, while the other 70 percent are at least aware of the issue and have instructional materials available to them in their schools.

Both districts are very much aware of the need to combat sex-role stereotyping. Committees exist to comply with Title IX and they formulated district plans about three years ago. The teaching staff is fairly young and sympathetic to these ideas. They are probably more sensitive to the situation than the general community is. Whereas most people are likely to think of this area as supportive to FREESTYLE goals, it was in this site that youngsters of the Mormon faith were removed from classrooms during FREESTYLE lessons at the request of parents who felt these ideas did not fit with their beliefs. Still, on the face of it these communities are probably as supportive of FREESTYLE goals as any of the seven sites in the evaluation.

Milwaukee, Wisconsin.

The city of Milwaukee lies on the western shore of Lake Michigan, about 90 miles north of Chicago. With a population of 700,000 it is the largest city in Wisconsin and a major industrial center. Well-known as the nation's beer producer, it is also a leading manufacturer of automobile parts and electrical equipment and is an important Great Lakes port.

Today about 51% of the population is white.[3] Germans, Irish, and Scandinavians were the earliest residents and during the last century approximately half the population was of German stock. The famous breweries of today began as family businesses in these years. People of German ancestry still comprise 15% of the population and the German influence is still very apparent in the architecture, restaurant fare and many other ways.

Later influxes of people brought Italians, Poles, Czechs, Yugoslavs, and Greeks. Most notable has been the increase in the Black population: whereas

---

[3] This represents enrollment in Milwaukee Public Schools in 1978.

they represented well under 1% of the population at the beginning of the century, they now account for 42% of the population. Following World War II, many Hispanics came to Milwaukee as migrant workers and stayed. They presently comprise 5% of the population.

There is a wide range of income levels and the lowest income families live closest to the downtown area. This includes most of the Blacks and Hispanics.

A total of 61 elementary classrooms (20 schools) in Milwaukee participated in the FREESTYLE study. This included 11 classrooms where the Hispanic population was between 50-100% and two classrooms where it was at least 25%. These were predominantly of Mexican origin. The Black population was 25-50% in many of the schools and in some classrooms it was as high as 70%. This resulted in a sample that was 31% Black, 16% Hispanic, and 50% White. These large numbers make possible an in-depth study of how well the series meets the needs of these racial/ethnic groups. The teachers in these schools were mainly Milwaukee people themselves, although a large percentage live in suburban areas.

Since 1971 Wisconsin has had extensive guidelines for the integration of career education with the local curriculum which have served as a model for many other states. The "Wisconsin State Plan for Career Development" has recently been developed in conjunction with a number of educational institutions to provide a coordinated plan for the delivery of career education from pre-school through college level -- including home and community activities. Initial reaction to career education at the elementary level was positive. However, lately teachers have felt hard pressed with so many other concerns demanding attention (ranging from reading and math projects to desegregation) that emphasis on career education has been shifted to other areas.

About 48 elementary teachers outside the FREESTYLE research project have participated in career education workshops. Presently, emphasis in career education is at the Senior and Junior High level where educators have found it easiest to fit it in, in conjunction with other ongoing projects.

A strong women's movement in Wisconsin has influenced action regarding sex-role stereotyping and this has probably received more attention in Milwaukee than career education. Most recently, the school board delayed adoption of textbooks because they felt there were still instances of sex-role stereotyping and also religious and ethnic stereotyping. In the recent edition of the career guides stereotypic illustrations were replaced and the narrative was edited to eliminate stereotypic language.

Ann Arbor, Michigan.

A small city of 140,000, Ann Arbor is located 45 miles west of Detroit. The city has grown up around the University of Michigan which has largely shaped its character. It is a liberal community and well-educated: 40,00 of the residents are students; of the remainder, 46% of those over 25 years old have had four years of college or more.

The University is by far the single largest employer in the area and is a major resource for the other businesses and industries located here. These include many industrial research firms and government laboratories. Computer technology and other newer technologies are much in evidence and high precision goods (such as hospital/laboratory equipment and scientific instruments) are manufactured. A number of residents commute to Detroit, Flint and other nearby cities where many are employed with the auto industry.

The University is also largely responsible for the diversity of people which make up the Ann Arbor population: nearly 20% of the population is either foreign-born or of foreign-born parentage and people from 100 different countries are represented. 76.9% of the population is White, 15.8% is Black, 1.6% is Hispanic.[4]

Although there is a large degree of transience due to the University, there is also a definite core community, consisting of those who have made Ann Arbor their permanent home and those who have lived here all their lives. Income levels include low, medium, and high, with most in the medium range.

---

[4]These figures come from statistical data completed by the Ann Arbor school for 1978.

A special site, only nine Ann Arbor elementary schools and 26 teachers participated in the research project. The racial/ethnic mixture in these classrooms was 68.2% White, 26.5% Black and 1.2% Hispanic; all income levels were represented. This location -- home to the Institute for Social Research -- was decided on so that personal interviews could be conducted with the children by ISR staff and University student volunteers.

Career education in Ann Arbor elementary schools was first introduced in 1974. It had reasonable support from the central administration, less from classroom teachers and building principals. "It was just a fad, it was adding something extra to the curriculum, it was too early for students to be zeroing in on careers," said the opposition, particularly in the beginning. However, since that time much has been done to create awareness of the career education movement on the part of the public and teaching staff. The district has been involved in Project Cediss to identify materials which can be used in career education programs at the elementary level and during the past two years about 300 elementary teachers (out of nearly 350) have taken part in some type of in-service program devoted to this subject. Consequently, attitudes have changed favorably and teachers now see career education as appropriate and desirable for the elementary school student.

The Ann Arbor schools have probably had a more enlightened attitude toward sex-role stereotyping than the average American community. There have been more females in non-traditional roles in the Ann Arbor community than in many other communities of this type. Over the past several years, provincial attitudes -- where they existed on the part of staff and parents -- have changed to the point where there is now a high degree of awareness of sex-role stereotyping. A major problem educators presently face is the amount of sexist literature that still exists in schools. A Title IX committee reviews school district materials. While it has made a lot of progress it has not yet eliminated the problem.

PART II. SCHOOL FULL VS. SCHOOL VIEW ONLY SITES: WORCESTER AND NORTH KANSAS CITY

Worcester, Massachusetts.

Worcester is a city of 175,000 people located 40 miles west of Boston. It is an old city dating to the 17th century. Its biggest growth occurred during the Industrial Revolution when many factories were set up to manufacture textiles, metals, and machinery. The old factory buildings are still much in evidence and manufacturing still dominates the city's economy. The majority of Worcester people work and live in the city or nearby environs; it is not a commuter community.

The city is 97 percent White. Irish and Italian ethnic groups were responsible for much of the city's growth in the last century and these groups are still quite apparent. There are also some distinctively Greek sections, although their appearance in Worcester is more recent. Blacks comprise about two percent of the population and Hispanics (largely Puerto Rican) another one percent. The population is dominated by long-time residents. In the last quarter-century there have not been any big influxes of new people.

Worcester has a wide range of personal income. Like most older cities the lowest income families are located closest to the city's center while the wealthiest neighborhoods are on the outskirts.

Schools that participated in the FREESTYLE evaluation research project were chosen so that all income levels and racial/ethnic backgrounds would be represented among the students. Of the 13 schools participating in the project, two were chosen for their high levels of Black and Hispanic populations: St. Nicholas Schools was 28% Hispanic, 11% Black; Chandler was 33% Hispanic and 33% Black. Other schools had mainly all-White populations. Different income brackets were represented by two schools where the family income level was low, three where it was low-to-middle, with the rest falling in the middle-income range.

Many of the teachers have been life-long residents of the city and easily identify with particular ethnic sections. A large proportion have graduated from local or state colleges, including Worcester State College (where the emphasis is on the teaching profession). Thus, the teachers hold values which closely parallel those held by other long-time residents.

In introducing a career education program into the public schools it was found that the traditional view of occupational development expressed by many teachers was "whatever will be, will be." Career education programs have now been in existence for the past five years. Every teacher has attended at least one session of "awareness" and some have spent over 100 hours on course work. Elementary teachers have responded most favorably to career education programs.

Sex role stereotyping has also become an important issue. Worcester participated in a program with Boston University during the 1977-78 school year to reduce sex-role barriers in the schools. Each school prepared a year-long plan -- although no actual monitoring occurred and many schools did not follow through. Each school sent representatives to in-service workshops dealing with the issue and administrators were urged to consider it a year-long priority. However, some elementary schools still have "boys" and "girls" lines and/or entrances. Many faculty members, especially older members, consider the whole issue rather ridiculous and irritating. This is more evident in small neighborhood schools as opposed to larger "community" schools (both are represented in the study). Likewise, schools with high Hispanic populations have tended to exhibit more rigid expectations (generated from home) regarding "proper" behavior of students, especially girls (i.e. sports and social activities after school).

North Kansas City, Missouri.

North Kansas City and the twelve other municipalities which make up the North Kansas City School District are part of a suburban area north of Kansas City, Missouri. Composed of residential, industrial and rural sections, it covers an area of 94 square miles with 100,000 residents. The people here commute to jobs with a variety of national companies which have their home offices located in the area. This includes a large number of insurance and paint companies as well as Hallmark Cards and TWA.

The northern suburbs are separated from Kansas City proper by the Missouri River. It is largely a middle income area and residents work at professional, skilled and semi-skilled jobs. The poorest families live close to the downtown area -- south of the river in Kansas City itself. This is where most of the minority groups live. North of the river the people are nearly 100% White and the schools in the study reflect this.[5] Even with a higher than average percentage of minority groups for the area, our sample was still 96.9% White. Blacks represented 1.4% of the sample and Hispanics comprised 0.9%. Apart from a fair amount of people of Italian background, no other ethnic groups are apparent in any number.

The schools have been involved in various programs (special education, in particular) but career education has not been prominent. When it is stressed, the "infusion model" is used, relating the regular curriculum to career possibilities. Teachers interested in career education have been able to take graduate classes or attend workshops organized by a privately funded Teacher Center that is not far away. Their interest in career education was shown in their many requests for more resource materials related to this subject.

As elsewhere, Title IX has resulted in changes at both the secondary and elementary level in North Kansas City schools. All classes are open to both sexes, and textbook adoption is preceded by a screening for both sex-role and racial stereotyping. There are a number of women in the administration and there is a real effort made by members of the staff to implement Title IX. Among the general community, sex-role stereotyping is not an issue and school involvement in this does not arouse particular negative or positive response. More of a community concern is that schools cover the "basic skills," but this concern falls short of applying pressure on the schools to revise school programs.

PART III. HOME VIEW VS. CONTROL SITES: SAGINAW AND COVINA

Saginaw, Michigan.

Saginaw is located in the east-central portion of Michigan with a population of 84,200. Chartered in the 1850's it began as twin villages separated by the Saginaw River, remaining so until the 1880's. The east and

---

[5]Evident from the 1970 census conducted by North Kansas City Schools.

west sides have now been one city for a century, but there is still an evident division in that the wealthier families all live on the west side, while the lower income families live on the east side (average selling price for a home on the east side is less than half that of a home on the west side). The population of the city itself has been decreasing in this decade as people move to the suburban areas.

Saginaw gained prominence in the latter part of the 1800's as a center for eastern Michigan's wealthy lumber barons. The lavish mansions begun in that era are now used as public and professional complexes. The saw mills have been replaced by the auto industry with General Motors the number one employer. Manufacturing and subsidiary industries surround the city.

The population of Saginaw is 38.8% White. There is a large number of residents of German ancestry and also a fair number of French descent. Greeks, Italians, and other ethnic groups are more recent introductions and are small in number. The beet crops which are harvested around Saginaw attract migrant workers, mostly Hispanic. Many stay and live in Saginaw and the Hispanic population is 11%. Many Blacks moved to Saginaw when General Motors located here and they presently comprise 48.4% of the population.[6]

The schools involved in the study had lower numbers of minority groups: 74% White, 5.4% Hispanic and 19.2% Black.

Saginaw served as a site to test the home use of FREESTYLE. This was not the only program in which parents have been asked to participate in home-based activities by Saginaw Schools. Recently parents participated in the School and Family Education (S.A.F.E.) program where they were asked to devote one hour each day at home to reading and study with full family involvement.

Both teachers and administrators are interested in furthering the career education program. They have developed career education teaching materials and organized career "fairs" and other activities. Up to now, emphasis has been at the senior high level. The school system has a career center that is

---

[6]This information was gathered by the Saginaw School District in 1978.

one of the most extensive in the country in the variety of courses if offers to secondary students.

Sex-role stereotyping is a concern of educators who are conscientious about meeting the requirements of Title IX, but the general population is still conservative. There is not a very strong women's movement here. Still, there are always women holding elected office: the president of the Chamber of Commerce is a woman, as are several members of the city council.

Covina, California.

Like Long Beach and Torrance, the city of Covina is part of the greater Los Angeles suburban area and is characterized by the same style of living and the same beginnings. It became an incorporated city at the beginning of this century and the growth rate at this time is slow. Presently there are 34,000 residents, spread out over six square miles. Chief employment is found with the manufacturing plants -- producing electronics equipment, pharmaceutical products and plastics, or in mechanical assembly.

The majority of Covina residents are in the middle of upper-middle income range, but there are some at a lower-income level. Also in the Covina Valley School District is part of the adjoining community of Irvindale, which is predominantly lower to lower-middle income families. The eight schools (sixteen classrooms) in the study represent all income levels.

The mixture of peoples is somewhat different from Long Beach and Torrance: Covina is 82% White, 14% Hispanic (mainly Mexican-Americans) and 1% Black.[7] Irvindale is predominantly Mexican-American. Again, there were higher numbers of minority groups in participating schools, so that our sample was 74.2% White, 22.2% Hispanic and 1.6% Black.

Covina Valley Schools became involved in career education in 1972 when it was chosen as one of the modelling sites for the California Career Education Project. This project featured integration of career relevant activities at all grade levels (K-14). Preliminary efforts were concentrated

---

[7]These figures come from statistical data gathered by Covina Valley Unified Schools in 1978.

at the secondary level and grades K-6 were added the following year. Four elementary schools participated, involving one quarter of all 57 elementary classrooms in the district. Emphasis at the elementary level was placed on self-awareness. TEachers constructed performance objectives, developed career education projects, evaluated career education materials, developed resources. This particular project was concluded after thirty months, but since that time further efforts have exposed many more elementary teachers and principals to career education. Real involvement, however, has depended on teachers themselves and while many have expressed a lot of enthusiasm there are still some that have not taken an interest.

Title IX has generated a lot of changes in the area of sex-role stereotyping and there has been a real effort in the schools to make sure both sexes have access to all course offerings. At the senior level, physical education classes have become coed. At the elementary level, textbooks are examined for sex-role stereotyping and lists of approved texts are provided to schools. Most educators are sympathetic to these goals. One educator noted that the big problem has been to involve students at the secondary level in the new areas that have been opened up to them. Peer pressure to conform to stereotyped ideas is still very evident.

Appendix F

A COMMUNITY OUTREACH EXPERIMENT
TO INCREASE NON-SCHOOL VIEWING,
James Kossler

(The following pages are excerpted from "Community Outreach Final Report," June, 1979)

PART III. OBSERVATIONS AND RECOMMENDATIONS
OF THE COMMUNITY OUTREACH TEAM

As this first phase of the _Freestyle_ project comes to a close - including the participation of the Community Outreach effort - it may be helpful to summarize some general observations regarding outreach and make some recommendations which might serve as guides for others responsible for designing and implementing similar efforts.

1) OBSERVATION: Representatives of the Outreach effort attended all meetings of the Management Council, Core Committee, and Advisory Board.

RECOMMENDATION: While the consortium concept is a good one and some participation by all program components in the development stages of the project is advisable, we recommend that the Community Outreach team be only minimally involved in the early stages of the project, because in reality, the Outreach effort cannot begin until the project products are finalized. The budget for Outreach - which was less than the cost of one television show - did not allow for biweekly meetings through two years of development, if anything was going to be saved for actual Outreach implementation.

2) OBSERVATION: The Outreach team was required to revise the list of potential participating groups as the focus of the project changed.

RECOMMENDATION: The problem experienced by the Freestyle Outreach group are probably not unique. As the project came more into focus during the first two years, it became increasingly obvious that the potential audience for such a program would be considerably different from that originally envisioned. Groups that might be interested in diminishing ethnic prejudice are not necessarily interested in a project that deals with sex-role stereotyping. Community groups, typically, have "pet" interests and activities which may or may not be compatible with the goals of such a special project. Once the actual products of the project have been produced it is then possible to determine with greater clarity which groups might be interested in participating. From a scheduling point-of-view, this probably suggests that Outreach activities for a project involving a television series or printed materials be conducted during a second series of broadcasts. Another reason for waiting until a "product" is in hand is the natural reluctance of community groups to make even a tentative commitment to something that is not yet finalized. Written project goals and even detailed show treatments of scripts don't really adequately describe how the shows will look. If potential groups can view some of the actual shows during the negotiation for participation, it would be much easier to obtain a commitment.

3) OBSERVATION: The longer the series ran, the lower the weekly attendance was at the various community sites.

RECOMMENDATION: In spite of pep talks, leader feed-back sessions, etc. the attendance at the community sites gradually decreased as the series went into its final weeks. There were a number of reasons for this which might be of help to those planning similar types of activities.

   a. Television follow-up activities are not a natural occurance on the home level. Most families watch several hours of television a night with little or no discussion of what was viewed. In the home, watching television is a very passive activity. Follow-up discussion can be carried out on a one-time or occasional basis but it simply cannot be sustained over a thirteen week period.

In a classroom, follow-up activities are natural and can be easily sustained by incorporating such activities into a formal curriculum. In fact, some of the Outreach groups which were adult instruction classes maintained a fairly steady attendance. Community members however, soon grew weary of such discussions.

b. The repetitive nature of the shows led to a feeling among community group leaders that they had already discussed a given subject. It should be noted that this is not a reflexion on the quality of the shows themselves - most members indicated a greater enjoyment of some of the later shows - but the feeling persisted that the themes had already been discussed. The repetition/reinforcement of course, was intentionally built into the series for classroom purposes. However, for use with community members, it would be better to condense the series into one or two shows which can be followed-up with enthusiasm.

c. Very careful attention needs to be paid to the broadcast schedule for such a series. If an impact is desired on the adult population, then the program(s) needs to be broadcast during "prime" viewing hours. Sunday morning or during dinner time may be convenient for the broadcaster but these are surely not convenient viewing times for working adults with children.

Also, serious problems in attendance occured once the series got into the Thanksgiving-New Year's period. People are just too busy during that time to watch a television series. Community groups have all kinds of activities during the holiday season (plays, food drives, Christmas parties, etc.) which are more important than the series. Also, parents are not as involved in normal community meetings when the children are out of school. Finally, the level of family activity (especially Christmas shopping) increases during this time. Our recommendation: limit the series for adults to one or two shows and broadcast them during prime time in October or after January.

4) OBSERVATION: Many community participants felt that the series was too "high society" to be relevant to their life styles.

RECOMMENDATION: Again, this observation is not a reflexion on the quality of the shows, which were uniformly professional. It is also not a criticism of the program designers or script writers. Upon reflection, we feel it points up a problem which could be characteristic of all such similar projects.

Essentially the problem is that the project received conflicting input from the Advisory Board and the viewing public. The Advisory Board was very carefully composed of representatives of different professions and different geographic regions. Unfortunately, the Board was not composed of folks from different economic strata. As a result, when the project attempted to portray barrio or ghetto life-styles (admittedly with some technical flaws) the Advisory Board reacted strongly that the project should not show ethnic groups as poor or lower middle class. After all, the Board members were all successful professionals and that was not the way they lived.

The project then elevated the economic status of the performers - putting them in sprawling ranch-style houses in suburban communities. When community members who live in the barrio and in the ghetto saw these scenes they reacted by saying 'hey, that's not the way we live!'

It may be that there really is no complete solution to this problem. However, it is possible that a lot of this kind of conflict can be discussed and worked out by the Advisory Board if the Board itself includes some blue collar, non-professional representatives.

5) OBSERVATION: The community Outreach effort benefitted - in terms of credibility as the television project - from its association with KCET.

RECOMMENDATION: While the East Los Angeles College Foundation enjoys a fine reputation in the community as a service organization, it has not previously been involved in a television project. The association with KCET in this project was a warm and cooperative one and the opportunity to hold information and training meetings for community leaders at KCET added a degree of credibility - in terms of television expertise - to the community Outreach coordinators.

However, it might be suggested for future such project that the commjnity Outreach effort be coordinated by and through the producing television station. The station might use the services of a community group to assist in the effort but the leadership for the activity should come from the station. This would accomplish a couple of worth-while results:

a. Community groups which are considering participation in such a project would have a clear understanding that they will be cooperating with a recognized media group in a given metropolitan area.

Community groups rarely have an opportunity to work closely with a group like KCET and they are impressed by such a relationship. County Schools, USC or ELAC do not have the same "glamor" appeal as does a television station.

    b. If the Outreach effort - with its regular contact with community members - was coordinated by the station, the executive producer and other creative members of the project could use those contacts to review and refine, on a regular basis, the presentation of ethnic minorities in the series.

    c. The television station would also have more of a sense of "ownership" of the Outreach effort and would probably be more inclined to make adjustments in its broadcast schedule to accomodate the series. Also, the production team might wish to add at the end of the shows slides which encourage participation in the Outreach activities and which indicate how additional materials might be ordered. Finally, promotional advertising for the series might also include Outreach activities. For example, a recent series on Parenthood, which was produced by another station, included several pages of Outreach materials in all the local television magazines (TV Guide, TV Times, etc.) and on the television pages of the local newspapers.

While the cooperative effort between KCET and East Los Angeles College Foundation has worked very well, it is our suggestion that, in the future, such projects might be strengthened if the coordination is maintained by the producing television station.

6) OBSERVATION: Community group leaders are critical factors in the level of cooperation that is provided by each group.

RECOMMENDATION: One of the interesting phenomenon encountered by the East Los Angeles College Foundation's field coordinator when he attempted to obtain commitments to participate from various community groups was what might be called the "quid-pro-quo" mentality. It was the general feeling throughout the project that community groups would "jump" at the opportunity to participate in the series once they were informed about the timeliness of the topic. In fact, very few community groups were initially excited about participating in a project which is dealing with breaking down sex-role stereotypes. It might be argued - and perhaps rightly so - that this very attitude on the part of the groups makes them prime candidate for such a project. If this is the case, some one in the community group has to be given a reason for acting as an advocate of the program.

Community groups, in general, and leaders, in particular, feel that they have been "used" by outside projects with little tangible benefit coming to the group or leader. In essence, what they are saying is that the production team is paid, the curriculum unit is paid, but the groups who have to commit their time, use of their facilities, etc. are asked to do their part voluntarily.

In future such efforts it might be very wise to request additional funds in the budget to pay at least the community group leaders. This would seriously restrict the possibility of replicating the Outreach model on a wide scale but it just may be that such replication is neither possible nor desirable. At least those who participated in the pilot activities would not feel that they were in an entirely "giving" mode and never in a "receiving" mode. The privilige of participating in the program, in itself is not viewed by community groups as benefit they have received.

On a final note, KCET voluntarily designed and printed special awards for participation in the Freestyle program. This was a very fine idea that was received very well by those leaders who worked hard in the project. KCET should be commended for the thoughtfulness.

Appendix B: Participating Groups

Belvedere Foster Parents Association (1 group)

International Institute (1 group)

Service for Asian American Youths (1 group)

East Los Angeles Foster Parents (1 group)

Adult Basic Education (6 groups)

Delta Head Start (4 groups)

Right-to Read (2 groups)

Tribal American (1 group)

Asian American Drug Abuse Program (1 group)

Siquoria Schools (1 group)

East Los Angeles Leonas (1 group)

Sunset Juniors (1 group)

Pacific Oaks College (1 group)

Cal-State University/LA Women's Center (1 group)

Foster Parents (1 group)

Appendix C: Sample Leader Preparation Sheet

PROGRAM #2   "CHEERS"

  I. STORY SYNOPSIS:

  Please see Highlights (pp 12-13) of the Freestyle Guide

  II. PROGRAM GOAL:

  Viewers will learn the meaning of independent behavior; will see the behavior portrayed in a positive manner; and, will be encouraged to practice independence as an expression of self-realization.

  III. KEY CONCEPT:

  Independence: doing what one feels one ought to do without being influenced by what others think one should do (pp 45-46, Freestyle Guide).

  IV. RELATED CONCEPTS:

  Cooperation

  Assertiveness

  Reasonable risk taking

Appendix G

FREESTYLE TEACHER TRAINING

[The following description of the teacher training program was prepared by its designers at the Office of the L. A. County Superintendent of Schools. Further information can be gotten from Ms. Pat Seeley 213/922-6111. The program described here was used to train "School Full" teachers in the evaluation study.]

FREESTYLE Project

FREESTYLE is an innovative curriculum project on career awareness for children ages nine through twelve, their parents and teachers. Through a series of thirteen television programs, use of supplementary printed materials and related classroom activities, the FREESTYLE project seeks to expand children's awareness by influencing those attitudes, behaviors, abilities, and interests that affect educational progress and future career choices. A major thrust of this curriculum is the reduction of sex role and ethnic stereotyping as it affects both the educational and career aspirations of young people

Overview of Staff Development Program

A mediated inservice program for teachers and administrators has been developed by the Office of the Los Angeles County Superintendent of Schools. The program presents the rationale and need for FREESTYLE as well as the goals and objectives. Activities involve the teachers in viewing and discussing selected television programs from the series and in participating in demonstrations of effective ways to use television as a teaching tool.

Objectives of Staff Development Program

As a result of the inservice workshop experience, participants will acquire:

-a knowledge of the goals, rationale and objectives of the television series.

-an increased awareness of the changing roles of men and women including new career opportunities.

-an increased awareness of the ways in which sex role stereotypes limit the development of the human potential of boys and girls.

-an understanding of techniques for using the television series for expanding student awareness of career opportunities for girls and boys.

-an increased understanding of a wider range of appropriate behaviors for both males and females including cooperativeness and assertiveness.

-an understanding of ways in which the objectives of the series can be related to elementary school subjects (e.g., language arts, social sciences, mathematics, art, etc.)

-an understanding of techniques for using the television series to help children expand their career potential and learn new behavior skills.

Staff Development Workshop Program

A description of the content and activities for each module of the Staff Development Program follows:

I. Introduction

   Description of FREESTYLE: The Rationale, Need, and Goals.

II. "Partners": An Approach to Teaching Students About Cooperation.

   Participants

   -take part in a brainstorming activity to introduce the concept of cooperation and to prepare for viewing the television program "Partners."

   -discuss how the telecast handled the concept of cooperation.

   -explore appropriate classroom follow-up activities.

-discuss teacher's role in preparing students to view telecast, in monitoring viewing and in providing follow-up activities to expand and deepen concepts.

-examine related suggestions in the FREESTYLE GUIDE.

III. "Grease Monkey": An Approach to Developing an Understanding of Non-Traditional Skills and Interests.

Participants

-engage in role playing to demonstrate how sex typing of activities determines activities children select and influences their attitudes and behavior.

-view and discuss "Grease Monkey" -- the television program that shows a young girl involved in a non-traditional activity (mechanic).

-discuss productive behavior strategies and role play examples of assertiveness.

-examine FREESTYLE GUIDE to identify possible classroom follow-up activity.

IV. "Teaching With FREESTYLE"

Participants view a video cassette in which four teachers demonstrate effective ways to use one of the FREESTYLE television programs.

V. "Scoop": Using the Content of FREESTYLE to Supplement Other Areas of the Curriculum.

Participants

-take part in a pre-viewing activity focused on changing roles of men and women in the world of work and the effects of sex role stereotyping on careers.

-view "Scoop" -- a television program that shows a school newspaper club collecting information about the jobs of men and women in their community.

-discuss implementation of FREESTYLE goals and objectives in the telecast "Scoop."

-brainstorm ways to use the content of the television program to provide practice in language arts, social studies, mathematics and fine arts.

-examine and discuss suggestions in the FREESTYLE GUIDE.

VI. Resource Materials for Teacher and Student Use

Participants

-review FREESTYLE GUIDE and CURRICULUM FOR THE TELEVISION CAREER AWARENESS PROJECT.

-discuss effective ways to use these materials.

-examine TEACHER RESOURCE PACKET and discuss ways to use the information to modify curriculum and curriculum materials; as background for discussions with colleagues and parents; and as an aid in planning instruction.

-examine INDIVIDUALIZED STAFF DEVELOPMENT MINI-MODULES and discuss use for staff development.

-follow through the instructions for one of the mini-modules which involves
    taking the pre-test
    listening to audio tape
    checking answers to pre-test
    completing follow-up activities

VII. Evaluation

Appendix H

TEACHER POST SERIES QUESTIONNAIRE

PART I: RESPONSES TO SELECTED QUESTIONS
FROM THE TEACHER POST SERIES QUESTIONNAIRE

B2. FREESTYLE consists of 13 1/2-hour TV shows, available in 1/4-hour segments for classroom use. If this series were available in a form which allowed you to choose how often you showed it, what would your preference be?

Response	percent
1 two 1/4-hours per week lasting one semester	61
2 one 1/4-hour per week lasting one school year	4
3 one 1/2-hour per week lasting one semester	26
4 one 1/2-hour, every other week lasting one year	9
Total	100

B3. Currently there are 13 half hours of television available, packaged as either half-hours or quarter-hours. If you were using the series again, would you like to have:

Response	Percent
1 fewer TV shows	10
2 about the same number of TV shows	51
3 more TV shows	39
Total	100

B5. Ignoring the number of shows currently available, over what span of time would you like to use FREESTYLE in your curriculum?

Response	Percent
1 about 1 month total	2
2 about 2 months	7
3 one semester -- the length of the current experiment	46
4 1-2 months longer	9
5 a full school year	36
Total	100

D8. How much do you think the magazine contributed to student understanding of:

Item	not at all	a little	quite a bit	a great deal
a the relationship between childhood interests and occupations?	2	57	37	4
b how pervasive sex-role stereotypes are?	3	48	43	5
c the range of activities and interests 9-12 year olds can pursue right now?	3	46	43	9
d what people do in various adult occupations?	2	36	49	14

NOTE: N=118. Teachers who did not use the Magzaine with their students did not complete these ratings.

E5. Think about FREESTYLE (TV series and related materials). How important would it be to the curriculum of each of these grades?

| Grade | Importance | | | |
	not at all	not very	some-what	very
a third or below	32	33	31	4
b fourth	1	16	43	41
c fifth	..	5	27	68
d sixth	..	2	16	82
e seventh or above	..	2	25	73

B. **Fit with district priorities** (asked of SF teachers only)

E6. Your district has certain priorities for what is taught at the grade level you are now teaching. How does spending time on FREESTYLE fit with these priorities? To meet the priorities:

Response	Percent
1 I would have to leave FREESTYLE out of the curriculum entirely	2
2 I would have to spend less time . .	27
3 I could spend about the same amount of time	65
4 I could spend more time on FREESTYLE	7
Total	100

F1. How would you recommend FREESTYLE to other teachers at your grade level in your district?

Response	Percent
1 I would not recommend it at all	*
2 I'd recommend it with serious reservations	4
3 I'd recommend it with some reservations .	24
4 I'd recommend it strongly	28
5 I'd recommend it very strongly	43
Total	100

PART II: TEACHER POST SERIES QUESTIONNAIRE FORM

There were four versions of this questionnaire, distributed to teachers according to the role they played in the evaluation. The content varied in each questionnaire. The most extensive version is the one for School Full teachers reproduced here. For the most part, the others had subsets of questions from this form. A notable exception is the version for control teachers which had a section in which they queried their students about viewing of the FREESTYLE series.

Institute for Social Research
The University of Michigan
Ann Arbor, Mich. 48106
Proj. No. 471611

Form Approved
O.M.B. No. 51-S-78019
Expiration Date 4-30-79

Evaluation of FREESTYLE Television Series

Teacher
Post Questionnaire

Teacher Label

*** PLEASE NOTE ***

This questionnaire has been "teacher-tested." We feel confident that the questions asked are relevant and to the point. We hope you do too!

****

In the FREESTYLE experiment classrooms had varying assignments, ranging from extensive classroom use of the series to no use at all. Questions in this booklet vary according to your assignment. Don't be surprised if some sections or pages appear to be missing. This is intentional.

This report is authorized by law (20 U.S.C. 1221(e).
While you are not required to respond, your cooperation is needed to make the results of this evaluation comprehensive, accurate and timely.

Form SF

A. FREESTYLE MESSAGES FROM OTHER SOURCES

As you learned in the FREESTYLE training last fall, the television series has the following major goals for children:

--increase the acceptance of adults in non-traditional work and family roles

--encourage boys and girls to explore interests which in the past have been stereotyped according to sex. These include mechanical, scientific, and athletic interests for girls and helping activities for boys

--develop "behavioral skills" which are thought to be important for attaining good jobs, especially
  .for girls: leadership, independence, and assertiveness
  .for boys: helping skills
  .for both boys and girls: cooperation and reasonable risk-taking

1. Since last September, have the children in your class been exposed to units of instruction that cover some of these same topics? A unit of instruction could be anything from two weeks to four months. Think about units of your own making as well as commercial products such as the "Bread and Butterflies" movie series. If your classroom was designated to use FREESTYLE, do not include activities directly related to the conduct of the FREESTYLE series.

   ☐ (1) No, there were no other units of instruction
   ☐ (2) Yes, there were some other units of instruction   1:5

2. Describe these units briefly: _____
   _____   1:6-7
   _____   1:8-9
   _____
   _____

-1-

B. TELEVISION SHOWS

1. Here's your chance to fill out a report card on the FREESTYLE series. First, consider the television shows themselves (apart from the other materials.) Use the following letter grades:

   A = superior
   B = above average
   C = average
   D = below average
   E = failing

   How good are the television shows in conveying the messages of FREESTYLE:
                                                              GRADE
   a. in a way that is clear to children?.......... _____   1:10-11
   b. in a way that is believable to children?..... _____   1:12-13
   c. in a way that holds the attention of
      children during viewing?..................... _____   1:14-15
   d. in a way that stimulates class
      discussions?................................. _____   1:16-17

2. FREESTYLE consists of 13 1/2-hour TV shows, available in 1/4-hour segments for classroom use. If this series were available in a form which allowed you to choose how often you showed it, what would your preference be? (CHOOSE ONE)   1:18

   frequency   duration

   ☐ (1) two 1/4-hours per week.........approximately one semester
         (this option is the   or term
         current arrangement)

   ☐ (2) one 1/4-hour per week..........approximately one school year
         (part "a" one week,
         part "b" the next week)

   ☐ (3) one 1/2-hour per week..........approximately one semester
         (parts "a" and "b" shown   or term
         back to back)

   ☐ (4) one 1/2-hour, every...........approximately one school year
         other week

-2-

PART B (cont.)

3. Currently there are 13 half-hours of television available, packaged as either half-hours or quarter-hours. If you were using the series again, would you like to have:

- [ ] (1) fewer TV shows
- [ ] (2) about the same number of TV shows   1:19
- [ ] (3) more TV shows

4. The three topic areas covered in the series are described below. Imagine that you were using the series again, but could rearrange the emphasis given to these three areas. However, in order to give more emphasis to one area, it would be necessary to give less emphasis to one or both of the other areas. With this in mind, indicate how much emphasis you would like to see given to each of the three topic areas below compared to the emphasis given to them in the present series. REMEMBER: IF YOU INDICATE THAT MORE EMPHASIS SHOULD BE GIVEN TO ONE OF THESE AREAS, YOU MUST ALSO INDICATE WHICH OTHER AREA(S) SHOULD GET LESS EMPHASIS.

The amount of emphasis given should be:

FREESTYLE Topic Areas	Much less	Some-what less	About the same	Some-what more	Much more	
a. accepting adults who are involved in non-traditional jobs and family roles..................	☐	☐	☐	☐	☐	1:20
b. encouraging boys and girls to explore childhood interests which are stereotypically in the domain of the opposite sex............	☐	☐	☐	☐	☐	1:21
c. developing "behavioral skills" such as leadership, independence, assertiveness, helping skills, cooperation, and reasonable risk-taking..................	☐	☐	☐	☐	☐	1:22

5. Ignoring the number of shows currently available, over what span of time would you like to use FREESTYLE in your curriculum?

- [ ] (1) about 1 month total
- [ ] (2) about 2 months
- [ ] (3) one semester -- the length of time in the current experiment   1:23
- [ ] (4) 1-2 months longer than now
- [ ] (5) a full school year

-3-

C. TEACHER'S GUIDE ("FREESTYLE GUIDE")

1. Overall, what grade would you give to the "FREESTYLE GUIDE" as an aid for teachers? Again use one of five letter grades from "A" to "E".

    Grade for the Teacher's Guide: _____   1:24-25

2-5. These next questions ask about parts of the teacher guide. For each part there are two questions: the first question in each pair asks how much you actually used the guide for the purpose listed; the second question asks how helpful you found the guide for that purpose when you did use it.

	(a) How often did you actually use it?					(b) When you did make use of it, how helpful did you find it?					
	No shows	A few shows	Some shows	Most shows	Every show	Not at all helpful	Not very helpful	Moderately helpful	Quite helpful	Very helpful	
	(1)	(2)	(3)	(4)	(5)	(1)	(2)	(3)	(4)	(5)	
2. "Highlights"	☐	☐	☐	☐	☐	☐	☐	☐	☐	☐	:26-27
3. "Preview Activity"	☐	☐	☐	☐	☐	☐	☐	☐	☐	☐	:28-29
4. "Talk Topics"	☐	☐	☐	☐	☐	☐	☐	☐	☐	☐	:30-31
5. "More to Come" Activities	☐	☐	☐	☐	☐	☐	☐	☐	☐	☐	:32-33

6. The "More to Come" activities are designed to be "infused" into other curricular areas (language arts, math, etc.). To achieve the goals of FREESTYLE, how important is it to use these activities in addition to viewing and discussing the TV shows?

___ (1) not at all important ___ (2) a little important ___ (3) somewhat important ___ (4) very important   1:34

-4-

D. FREESTYLE MAGAZINE

1. How would you grade the magazine for students at your grade level in terms of:

   GRADE
   a. clarity of language.................. _____ 1:35-36
   b. appeal of the art................... _____   :37-38
   c. intrinsic interest of the stories
      and activities...................... _____   :39-40

2. How important would you say using the magazine is for achieving the goals of FREESTYLE?   :41

   ___(1) not at all   ___(2) not very   ___(3) somewhat   ___(4) very
           important   important   important   important

3. How important would you say the magazine is for <u>building interest</u> in FREESTYLE?   :42

   ___(1) not at all   ___(2) not very   ___(3) somewhat   ___(4) very
           important   important   important   important

4. How much class time did you spend having students work on activities in the magazine? (If you didn't use the magazine at all, use zero here. Use "1" for time between zero and one hours. Beyond one hour, round the the nearest whole hour).

   _____ hours (to the nearest whole hour)   :43-44

5. How much class time did you use for discussion of magazine activities?

   _____ hours (to the nearest whole hour)   :45-46

6. How often, if ever, did you assign reading or activities in the magazine as homework?   :47

   ___(1) never   ___(2) once   ___(3) two-three   ___(4) four or
                                          times   more times

7. During the semester about how much of the magazine did the students complete?   1:48

   ___(1) none   ___(2) less   ___(3) about   ___(4) more   ___(5) all of it
                          than half   one half   than half

-5-

PART D (cont.)

8. (If you did not use the magazine, skip this page.) How much do you think the magazine contributed to student understanding of:

	not at all	a little	quite a bit	a great deal
a. the relationship between child-hood interests and adult occupations?..	☐	☐	☐	☐
b. how pervasive sex-role stereotypes are?...	☐	☐	☐	☐
c. the range of activities and interests 9-12 year-olds can pursue right now?...	☐	☐	☐	☐
d. what people do in various adult occupations?................	☐	☐	☐	☐

   1:49

   1:52

-6-

E. FREESTYLE'S FIT WITH THE CURRICULUM

1. Think of a typical week in which you used FREESTYLE. How much time did you spend on FREESTYLE-related activity to the nearest half-hour?

   a. preparation time........................ _____ hours   1:53-55
   b. class viewing time (include viewing time plus set-up time)............................... _____ hours   :56-58
   c. class discussion time (include discussion of shows, and other activities directly related to the series)........................... _____ hours   :59-61

2. If you were not participating in this experiment, but were trying to incorporate FREESTYLE into your curriculum, how much time would you spend on FREESTYLE compared to the time you actually spent?

   a. preparation time:
      ___(1) less time   ___(2) about the same   ___(3) more time   :62
   b. class viewing time
      ___(1) less time   ___(2) about the same   ___(3) more time   :63
   c. class discussion time
      ___(1) less time   ___(2) about the same   ___(3) more time   :64

3. Think of the overall curriculum for your grade level and the time you usually spend in each area or subject. Think also about FREE-STYLE -- the TV shows, the activities, etc. How much does it fit into each of the curricular areas you teach?

   ------FREESTYLE fits-------

	not at all	a lit-tle bit	pretty well	very well	I don't teach this subject
a. reading....................	☐	☐	☐	☐	☐
b. other language arts........ (spelling, writing, etc.)	☐	☐	☐	☐	☐
c. social studies.............	☐	☐	☐	☐	☐
d. mathematics................	☐	☐	☐	☐	☐
e. science....................	☐	☐	☐	☐	☐
f. career education...........	☐	☐	☐	☐	☐
g. physical education.........	☐	☐	☐	☐	☐
h. science....................	☐	☐	☐	☐	☐

   :65

   1:72

PART E (cont.)

4. For this experiment FREESTYLE may have fit perfectly into some parts of your curriculum. On the other hand you might have found yourself having to "steal time" from some curricular area because it did not fit perfectly. How much did you have to "steal time"?

   ___(1) not at all   ___(2) a little   ___(3) some   ___(4) a lot   2:5

   4a. Which curricular areas did you "steal" from?

   _____   :6-7
   _____   :8-9
   _____   :10-11

5. Think about FREESTYLE -- the TV series and related materials as they are currently designed. How important an addition would FREESTYLE be to the curriculum of each of these grades?

	not at all	not very	somewhat	very important
a. third grade or below.......	☐	☐	☐	☐
b. fourth.....................	☐	☐	☐	☐
c. fifth......................	☐	☐	☐	☐
d. sixth......................	☐	☐	☐	☐
e. seventh or above...........	☐	☐	☐	☐
f. other (specify level below).	☐	☐	☐	☐

   :12

   :17

   2:18-19

PART E (cont.)

6. Your district has certain priorities for what is taught at the grade level you are now teaching. How does spending time on FREESTYLE fit with these priorities?

   6a. THE WAY IT IS NOW IN MY DISTRICT:

   To meet the priorities of the district (choose one)

   ☐ (1) I would have to leave FREESTYLE out of the curriculum entirely
   ☐ (2) I would have to spend less time
   ☐ (3) I could spend about the same amount of time
   ☐ (4) I could spend more time on FREESTYLE

   2:20

   6b. THE WAY I THINK IT SHOULD BE IN THIS DISTRICT: (choose one)

   ☐ (1) Teachers should not spend any time on FREESTYLE
   ☐ (2) Teachers should spend some time on FREESTYLE, but not as much time as I did
   ☐ (3) Teachers at my grade level should spend about the same amount of time on FREESTYLE as I did this last semester
   ☐ (4) Teachers at my grade level should spend even more time than I spent on FREESTYLE this last semester

   2:21

-9-

F. RECOMMENDATIONS REGARDING FREESTYLE

1. Overall, which statement best represents your feelings about recommending FREESTYLE (the series and related materials) to <u>other teachers at your grade level in your district</u>?

   ☐ (1) I would not recommend it at all
   ☐ (2) I'd recommend it with serious reservations
   ☐ (3) I'd recommend it with some reservations
   ☐ (4) I'd recommend it strongly
   ☐ (5) I'd recommend it very strongly
   ☐ (8) I can't say; I didn't see enough of the series

   2:22

   1a. Explain briefly the reason(s) for your recommendation.

   _____ 2:23-24
   _____ 2:25-26

-10-

PART F (cont.)

2-6. There are a variety of ways that FREESTYLE could be used, ranging from extensive use of the TV shows in the classroom to no classroom use at all -- only viewing at home. While extensive use in the classroom might be desirable, the demands of teaching other subjects might make this impossible. Below, indicate how willing you would be to use FREESTYLE in each of the ways described

	not at all	maybe	probably	definitely
2. Students view the shows in school (35 minutes per week) and there is class discussion and related activities associated with each show					2:27
3. Students view the shows in school (35 minutes per week including viewing and set-up time), but there is NO classroom discussion				
4. Students view the shows in school (35 minutes per week including viewing and set-up time), and there is minimal classroom discussion if the students initiate it				
5. Students view the show at home once a week during non-school hours. You as a teacher build a weekly unit around the TV show (1/2-hour of discussion per week minimum)				
6. Students view the show at home once a week during non-school hours. Parents are encouraged to watch and discuss it with their child, but there is no classroom time set aside for discussion or activities					2:31

(0 in 2:32-61)

-11-

I. SCHOOL SYSTEM SUPPORT FOR FREESTYLE

Two goals of FREESTYLE are to:

-- increase the acceptance of adults in non-traditional work and family roles
-- encourage boys and girls to explore interests which in the past have been stereotyped according to sex, including mechanical, scientific, and athletic interests for girls and helping activities for boys

1. How supportive do you think each of the following individuals or groups are of the two goals of the FREESTYLE series as given above?

	Not at all supportive (1)	Not very supportive (2)	Moderately supportive (3)	Very supportive (4)
a. other teachers in the building	☐	☐	☐	☐
b. the principal of the building	☐	☐	☐	☐	2:62
c. the central administration of the district	☐	☐	☐	☐
d. the school board	☐	☐	☐	☐
e. parents of school-aged children in the community	☐	☐	☐	☐	2:66

(0 in 2:67-71)

-12-

K. EQUIPMENT

1. When your class viewed FREESTYLE, was it in color or black-and-white?

- [ ] (1) always color
- [ ] (2) usually color
- [ ] (3) 1/2 the time color; 1/2 black and white
- [ ] (4) usually black and white
- [ ] (5) always black and white

2:72

L. COMMENTS

Are there any other things you would like to say about FREESTYLE?

_____
_____
_____
_____
_____
_____
_____

When you complete this questionnaire, put it in the stamped self-addressed envelope addressed to ISR, enclose anything else requested, and drop it in the mailbox.

Thank you so much! Your time will benefit teachers and school districts around the country! We hope to have a report back to you before the school year is over.

Appendix I

STUDENT QUESTIONNAIRE: "MY INTERESTS AND ACTIVITIES"

TEACHER: READ TO CLASS

This questionnaire asks about such things as the activities you like to do and the jobs you think might interest you when you grow up. This is not a test and there are no right or wrong answers.

I will read each question. Don't mark your answer until I have finished reading the question. In marking your answers, use a no. 2 (or softer) black lead pencil. Do NOT use a ball-point pen, felt-tip pen or a pencil with hard lead. Make each of your marks heavy and completely fill in the oval. Erase completely any answer you wish to change. Do NOT write or make any other marks in this booklet.

You are not required to answer these questions, but your answers will help us develop a good career education program for children like you.

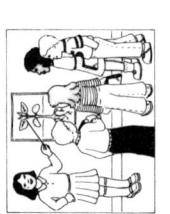

MY INTERESTS AND ACTIVITIES

Name _____
       (First)   (Last)

School _____

PART 1
(APPROXIMATELY TWENTY MINUTES)

To begin with, we want to find out the things you would like to do if you had the chance. On the next page are some things that people your age do. For each one darken the oval which tells how much you would like to do it. If you don't know what the activity is, darken the last oval. Try these examples.

	Like it a lot	Like it pretty much	Like it a little	Don't like it at all	Don't know what that is
a. eat ice cream cones	O	O	O	O	
b. clean up your room	O	O	O	O	
c. play the game of SNOOZLE	O	O	O	O	O

You probably like to eat ice cream cones so you should have darkened one of the first two ovals.

How about cleaning your room?

How about playing SNOOZLE?

That's not really a game so you should have darkened the last oval which says you don't know what that is.

Does everyone understand?

On the next pages you should fill in the answers as I read each question. Don't get ahead of me.

Are you a
- O boy?
- O girl?

Are you in the
- O 4th grade?
- O 5th grade?
- O 6th grade?

---

1. How much would you like to do each of these things if you had the chance?

	Like it a lot	Like it pretty much	Like it a little	Don't like it at all	Don't know what that is
a. fix a broken bike	O	O	O	O	O
b. build a model kit (car, plane, boat, and so forth)	O	O	O	O	O
c. build a radio or something else that runs on electricity	O	O	O	O	O
d. fix a leaky faucet	O	O	O	O	O
e. work with an adult on a car motor	O	O	O	O	O
f. take care of a younger child at the playground	O	O	O	O	O
g. help a younger child with math	O	O	O	O	O
h. teach a younger child how to play a game	O	O	O	O	O
i. sew a button on clothes or sew up a tear	O	O	O	O	O
j. help an adult fix meals for the family	O	O	O	O	O
k. help old people (not living in your home)	O	O	O	O	O
l. help at a recreation center for handicapped people who are deaf, crippled, or blind	O	O	O	O	O
m. take care of sick people (not living in your home)	O	O	O	O	O
n. raise goldfish at home	O	O	O	O	O
o. watch the stars and planets and figure out the names of groups of stars	O	O	O	O	O
p. make an insect collection (ants, moths, butterflies, or other insects)	O	O	O	O	O
q. make a collection of different kinds of rocks	O	O	O	O	O
r. read books about rocks, insects, flowers, or stars	O	O	O	O	O
s. do a project for a science fair	O	O	O	O	O
t. run errands for an elderly person	O	O	O	O	O
u. play football	O	O	O	O	O
v. play basketball	O	O	O	O	O
w. play dodge ball	O	O	O	O	O
x. play soccer	O	O	O	O	O
y. play baseball	O	O	O	O	O

A number of times in this questionnaire we will ask whether you think some idea is a good idea or a bad idea. You can give us your answer by darkening the oval that says how you feel. The choices will be these:

—A very good idea
—A good idea
—A bad idea
—A very bad idea

For example: Darken the oval which tells best how you feel.

	Very good idea	Good idea	Bad idea	Very bad idea
How do you feel about school children having vacations?	O	O	O	O

STOP UNTIL YOUR TEACHER TELLS YOU TO GO AHEAD

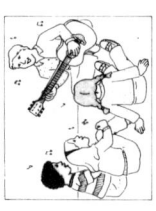

-5-

2. How do you feel about GIRLS your age doing these things if they want to:

	Very good idea	Good idea	Bad idea	Very bad idea
a. playing football on a team with both boys and girls on the team	O	O	O	O
b. fixing a broken bike	O	O	O	O
c. working with an adult on a car motor	O	O	O	O
d. building a radio or something else that runs on electricity	O	O	O	O
e. playing basketball on a team with both boys and girls on the team	O	O	O	O

3. Now think about BOYS your age. How do you feel about BOYS doing these things if they want to:

	Very good idea	Good idea	Bad idea	Very bad idea
a. taking care of a younger child at the playground	O	O	O	O
b. helping a child with math	O	O	O	O
c. playing football on a team with both boys and girls on the team	O	O	O	O
d. helping old people (not living in their home)	O	O	O	O
e. helping an adult fix meals for the family	O	O	O	O

Here are a few of the same activities again. How many girls and boys your age are good at doing them? The answers you can give are these:

—All
—Most
—Some
—A few
—None

4. How many GIRLS are good at:

	All	Most	Some	A few	None
a. playing football	O	O	O	O	O
b. fixing a broken bike	O	O	O	O	O
c. fixing a car motor	O	O	O	O	O
d. building a radio or something else that runs on electricity	O	O	O	O	O
e. playing basketball	O	O	O	O	O

-6-

5. How many BOYS are good at:

	All	Most	Some	A few	None
a. taking care of a younger child at the playground	O	O	O	O	O
b. helping a child with math	O	O	O	O	O
c. playing football	O	O	O	O	O
d. helping old people (not living in their home)	O	O	O	O	O
e. helping an adult fix meals for the family	O	O	O	O	O

6. It will be a long time before you choose an adult job. However, you probably know now that there are some jobs you would not consider doing and others that you would consider doing. What do you think about each of these jobs for yourself? For each one darken the first oval if you **definitely** would consider doing it; darken the second oval if you probably would consider it; darken the third oval if you probably would **not** consider it; darken the fourth oval if you **definitely** would **not** consider it. You may not know some of the jobs on the list. If you don't know one of them, darken the last oval labeled "I don't know what that job is."

	Definitely consider	Probably consider	Probably NOT consider	Definitely NOT consider	I don't know what that job is
a. car mechanic	O	O	O	O	O
b. truck driver	O	O	O	O	O
c. electrician	O	O	O	O	O
d. carpenter	O	O	O	O	O
e. worker in a factory who puts things together (like a car or other machine)	O	O	O	O	O
f. machinist (makes parts for machines)	O	O	O	O	O
g. boss in a factory	O	O	O	O	O
h. nurse	O	O	O	O	O
i. professional athlete	O	O	O	O	O
j. coach	O	O	O	O	O
k. school teacher	O	O	O	O	O
l. librarian	O	O	O	O	O
m. dental assistant (clean people's teeth or help dentist fix their teeth)	O	O	O	O	O
n. occupational therapist (help sick or old people learn new skills)	O	O	O	O	O
o. teacher of children who have problems with seeing or hearing	O	O	O	O	O
p. homemaker — a father or mother who stays home and cares for the children, cooks meals, and cleans the house	O	O	O	O	O
q. reporter (write stories for a newspaper)	O	O	O	O	O
r. photographer (take pictures for a newspaper)	O	O	O	O	O
s. pharmacist (give out medicine in a drug store)	O	O	O	O	O
t. geologist (scientist who studies rocks and minerals)	O	O	O	O	O
u. designer of electrical things like TVs, radios, or calculators	O	O	O	O	O
v. scientist who studies how the weather works	O	O	O	O	O
w. scientist who studies how plants and animals grow	O	O	O	O	O
x. designer of airplanes or rockets	O	O	O	O	O
y. owner of a hardware store	O	O	O	O	O
z. owner of a business which makes things like shoes or toys or furniture	O	O	O	O	O
aa. manager of a motel or hotel	O	O	O	O	O
bb. owner of a restaurant	O	O	O	O	O
cc. owner of a company which builds houses	O	O	O	O	O
dd. sales person in a store who sells cars or televisions or refrigerators	O	O	O	O	O
ee. city council member (someone elected to help run a city)	O	O	O	O	O
ff. secretary	O	O	O	O	O
gg. someone who sorts mail in the post office	O	O	O	O	O
hh. bookkeeper (keep records of money spent and received by a business)	O	O	O	O	O
ii. check-out clerk at a grocery or discount store	O	O	O	O	O
jj. telephone operator	O	O	O	O	O

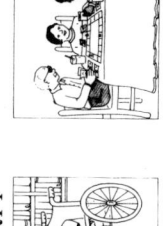

END OF PART 1

PART 2
(APPROXIMATELY TWENTY MINUTES)

WHAT DO YOU THINK?

On this page are the names of some jobs which people have. Think about the kind of people who do the jobs, whether they are usually men or usually women. If you think almost all of the people who do the jobs are **men**, darken the first oval. If you think that more than half are **men**, darken the second oval. If you think about half of them are men and half women, darken the third oval. If you think more than half are **women**, darken the fourth oval. If you think almost all are **women**, darken the last oval.

7. What do you think is true today? How many of the people who do each of these jobs are men and how many are women?

	Almost all are MEN	More than half are MEN	About half are men, half are women	More than half are WOMEN	Almost all are WOMEN
a. car mechanic	O	O	O	O	O
b. truck driver	O	O	O	O	O
c. nurse	O	O	O	O	O
d. secretary	O	O	O	O	O
e. machinist (makes parts for machines)	O	O	O	O	O
f. pharmacist (gives out medicine in a drug store)	O	O	O	O	O
g. owner of a hardware store	O	O	O	O	O
h. city council member (someone elected to help run a city)	O	O	O	O	O
i. geologist (scientist who studies rocks and minerals)	O	O	O	O	O
j. worker in a factory who puts things together (like a car)	O	O	O	O	O
k. telephone operator	O	O	O	O	O
l. sales person in a store who sells cars or TVs or refrigerators	O	O	O	O	O
m. owner of a restaurant	O	O	O	O	O
n. designer of electrical things like TVs, radios, or calculators	O	O	O	O	O
o. dental assistant (cleans people's teeth or helps dentist fix their teeth)	O	O	O	O	O
p. teacher of children who have problems with seeing or hearing	O	O	O	O	O
q. occupational therapist (help sick or old people learn new skills)	O	O	O	O	O

-9-

8. What do you think it would be like if things were different than they are today? How would you feel if more WOMEN were:

	Very good idea	Good idea	Bad idea	Very bad idea
a. car mechanics	O	O	O	O
b. truck drivers	O	O	O	O
c. machinists (make parts for machines)	O	O	O	O
d. owners of hardware stores	O	O	O	O
e. geologists (scientists who study rocks and minerals)	O	O	O	O

9. How would you feel if more MEN were:

	Very good idea	Good idea	Bad idea	Very bad idea
a. nurses	O	O	O	O
b. teachers of children with problems with seeing or hearing	O	O	O	O
c. occupational therapists (help sick or old people learn new skills)	O	O	O	O

10. When people get married, they must do things such as earn money, take care of children, and take care of things around the house. The husband and wife must decide who is going to do these things. Think about families you know where there are both a husband and wife. How do husbands and wives divide things up in these families? (Don't think just about your family.)

First, how much is each of these things done by WIVES today?

	All of it	Most	Some	A little	None of it
a. take care of things around the house (paint the house, fix leaky faucets, and so forth)	O	O	O	O	O
b. take care of the car (keep it clean, have the oil changed, and so forth)	O	O	O	O	O
c. work to earn money to support the family	O	O	O	O	O

Now think about HUSBANDS, how much is done by HUSBANDS today?

	All of it	Most	Some	A little	None of it
d. do the grocery shopping, cook the meals, do the dishes, and so forth	O	O	O	O	O
e. do the housecleaning (dust, vacuum, scrub the floors, clean the bathroom, and so forth)	O	O	O	O	O
f. take care of the children	O	O	O	O	O
g. work to earn money to support the family	O	O	O	O	O

-10-

11. How do you think things **should be**?

First, how much do you think each of these things **should be done** by WIVES?

	All of it	Most	Some	A little	None of it
a. take care of things around the house (paint the house, fix leaky faucets, and so forth)	O	O	O	O	O
b. take care of the car (keep it clean, have the oil changed, and so forth)	O	O	O	O	O
c. work to earn money to support the family	O	O	O	O	O

Now think about HUSBANDS, how much do you think each of these things should be done by HUSBANDS?

	All of it	Most	Some	A little	None of it
d. do the grocery shopping, cook the meals, do the dishes, and so forth	O	O	O	O	O
e. do the housecleaning (dust, vacuum, scrub the floors, clean the bathroom, and so forth)	O	O	O	O	O
f. take care of the children	O	O	O	O	O
g. work to earn money to support the family	O	O	O	O	O

12. Now think about children your age.

How much time do BOYS your age spend doing each of these things?

	A lot	Some	A little	None
a. help with making meals and washing dishes	O	O	O	O
b. help keep the house clean	O	O	O	O
c. help take care of younger children	O	O	O	O

How much time do GIRLS your age spend doing each of these things?

	A lot	Some	A little	None
e. help with making meals and washing dishes	O	O	O	O
f. help keep the house clean	O	O	O	O
g. help take care of younger children	O	O	O	O

-11-

13. How do you think things **should be**?

How much time **should** BOYS your age spend doing each of these things?

	A lot	Some	A little	None
a. help with making meals and washing dishes	O	O	O	O
b. help keep the house clean	O	O	O	O
c. help take care of younger children	O	O	O	O

How much time **should** GIRLS your age spend doing each of these things?

	A lot	Some	A little	None
e. help with making meals and washing dishes	O	O	O	O
f. help keep the house clean	O	O	O	O
g. help take care of younger children	O	O	O	O

14. When you grow up, do you expect that you will have a job outside the home?

O Yes, I definitely will
O Yes, I probably will
O No, I probably will not
O No, I definitely will not

15. If you get married, would you want the person you marry to have a job outside the home?

O Yes, definitely
O Yes, probably
O No, probably not
O No, definitely not

END OF PART 2

-12-

PART 3
(APPROXIMATELY TWENTY MINUTES)

16. First, how do you feel about a girl being the leader of a group of boys and girls is your age? Think about groups like your school classes, clubs, or sports teams, **with both boys and girls in them**. If you think it's a very good idea to have a girl as a leader, darken the first oval. If you think it's a good idea, darken the second oval. If you think it's a bad idea, darken the third oval. If you think it's a very bad idea, darken the last oval.

How do you feel about GIRLS doing these things?

	Very good idea	Good idea	Bad idea	Very bad idea
a. being president of your class	O	O	O	O
b. being captain of your school's football team	O	O	O	O
c. being in charge of your class' paper drive and giving orders to the other kids	O	O	O	O
d. being editor in charge of the school newspaper	O	O	O	O

Now, how about BOYS?

	Very good idea	Good idea	Bad idea	Very bad idea
e. being president of your class	O	O	O	O
f. being captain of your school's football team	O	O	O	O
g. being in charge of your class' paper drive and giving orders to the other kids	O	O	O	O
h. being editor in charge of the school newspaper	O	O	O	O

17. Next, think about girls as leaders of groups that have both boys and girls in them. Darken the oval which tells how you feel.

How many GIRLS:

	All of them	Most	Some	A few	None of them
a. are good at organizing things for the group to do	O	O	O	O	O
b. are good at giving each group member a job which they can do well	O	O	O	O	O
c. are too bossy when they lead the group	O	O	O	O	O
d. have good ideas about what the group should do	O	O	O	O	O
e. listen to the ideas of other group members	O	O	O	O	O
f. give all the good jobs to other girls in the group	O	O	O	O	O

-13-

18. Next, think about BOYS as the leaders of these groups.

How many BOYS:

	All of them	Most	Some	A few	None of them
a. are good at organizing things for the group to do	O	O	O	O	O
b. are good at giving each group member a job which they can do well	O	O	O	O	O
c. are too bossy when they lead the group	O	O	O	O	O
d. have good ideas about what the group should do	O	O	O	O	O
e. listen to the ideas of other group members	O	O	O	O	O
f. give all the good jobs to other boys in the group	O	O	O	O	O

19. There is some time every day when you must do certain things. You have to sleep, eat meals, and go to school. There is other time that is your own **free time**; you can play or do what you want then. How do you feel about boys and girls doing some of the things below in their **free time**? Darken the oval to show whether you think it is a very good idea, a good idea, a bad idea, or a very bad idea.

	Very good idea	Good idea	Bad idea	Very bad idea
a. Some younger students in your school need help learning how to read. How would you feel if some **boys** in your class spent their free time helping them learn to read?	O	O	O	O
b. How would you feel if some **boys** in your class spent some of their free time in old folks' homes helping older people with their projects and activities?	O	O	O	O
c. Jerry is a very good basketball player. Last year in his free time he played on the elementary school team. Jerry also likes to help out in an old folks home. He talks to the people and plays games with them. This year he doesn't have time to do both things so he thinks he will help out at the old folks home instead of playing basketball. How good an idea do you think this is?	O	O	O	O
d. Marsha is a very good basketball player. Last year in her free time she played on the elementary school team. Marsha also likes to help out in an old folks home. She talks to people and plays games with them. This year she doesn't have time to do both things so she thinks she will help out at the old folks home instead of playing basketball. How good an idea do you think this is?	O	O	O	O
e. Yvonne is interested in cars and in her free time after school has been helping a grown up fix cars. A little kid at school is having trouble with his reading and needs help after school. Yvonne likes to help younger children with their school work but doesn't have time to do both. She thinks she should help the kid with reading instead of working on cars. How good an idea do you think this is?	O	O	O	O

-14-

f. José is interested in cars and in his free time after school has been helping a grown up fix cars. A little kid at school is having trouble with his reading and needs help after school. José likes to help younger children with their school work but doesn't have time to do both. He thinks he should help the kid with reading instead of working on cars. How good an idea do you think this is? ....

	Very good idea	Good idea	Bad idea	Very bad idea
f.	○	○	○	○
g.	○	○	○	○
h.	○	○	○	○

g. Billy and Jane both like to take care of little children. Their older sister has a three-year old child. The older sister would like some help after school taking care of the child. She asks Billy and Jane if they would like to take the child to the playground once or twice a week. First, think just about Billy; he'd have to give up playing with his friends. How good an idea is it for Billy to take care of the child instead of playing with his friends? ....

h. How about Jane? She would also have to give up playing with her friends. How good an idea is it for Jane to take care of the child instead of playing with her friends? ....

Now think about how many boys and girls your age are good at helping others do the kinds of things we've just been talking about. First think about boys.

20. How many BOYS your age are good at:

	All of them	Most	Some	A few	None of them
a. helping to take care of a younger child	○	○	○	○	○
b. understanding why a child misbehaves	○	○	○	○	○
c. tutoring younger students, that is, helping them to learn things	○	○	○	○	○
d. figuring out what would make someone happy	○	○	○	○	○
e. helping older people with what they need	○	○	○	○	○
f. knowing when to help someone and when not to	○	○	○	○	○

21. How about girls; how many GIRLS your age are good at:

	All of them	Most	Some	A few	None of them
a. helping to take care of a younger child	○	○	○	○	○
b. understanding why a child misbehaves	○	○	○	○	○
c. tutoring younger students, that is, helping them to learn things	○	○	○	○	○
d. figuring out what would make someone happy	○	○	○	○	○
e. helping older people with what they need	○	○	○	○	○
f. knowing when to help someone and when not to	○	○	○	○	○

-15-

Think about kids your age doing things they're interested in doing (such as sports, hobbies, or school activities) when others may not think it's such a good idea. The first questions are about boys.

22. How would you feel if a BOY your age did something he was interested in doing:

	Very good idea	Good idea	Bad idea	Very bad idea
a. when his close friends wanted him to do something else with them	○	○	○	○
b. when his close friends thought it was a thing only girls should do	○	○	○	○
c. when his parents wished he would do something else	○	○	○	○

23. How would you feel if a GIRL your age did something she was interested in doing:

	Very good idea	Good idea	Bad idea	Very bad idea
a. when her close friends wanted her to do something else with them	○	○	○	○
b. when her close friends thought it was a thing only boys should do	○	○	○	○
c. when her parents wished she would do something else	○	○	○	○

24. How often do you think BOYS your age actually do something they're really interested in:

	Very often	Fairly often	Not very often	Hardly ever	Never
a. when their friends think only girls do it	○	○	○	○	○
b. when their parents wished they would do something else	○	○	○	○	○

25. How often do you think GIRLS your age actually do something they're really interested in:

	Very often	Fairly often	Not very often	Hardly ever	Never
a. when their friends think only boys do it	○	○	○	○	○
b. when their parents wished they would do something else	○	○	○	○	○

END OF PART 3

-16-

PART 4
(APPROXIMATELY TWENTY MINUTES)

26. Think about how kids your age act in different situations. First, I'd like to ask you about GIRLS. If you think almost all girls act this way, darken the first oval. If you think most act this way, darken the second oval. If you think some act this way, darken the third oval. If you think a few act this way, darken the fourth oval. If you think none act this way, darken the last oval.

		All of them	Most	Some	A few	None of them
a.	How many girls your age stand up for what they think is right?	O	O	O	O	O
b.	How many girls your age stop somebody from picking on younger kids?	O	O	O	O	O
c.	How many girls your age tell another kid when they think the other kid is wrong?	O	O	O	O	O
d.	How many girls your age demand to be treated fairly by grownups?	O	O	O	O	O
e.	How many girls your age demand to be treated fairly by other kids?	O	O	O	O	O
f.	How many girls your age don't do things because they might get hurt doing them?	O	O	O	O	O
g.	How many girls your age don't do things because they might be embarrassed?	O	O	O	O	O
h.	When girls try to do something and they fail, how many of them give up rather than trying it again another way?	O	O	O	O	O
i.	When girls have a choice, how many of them pick the easy thing to do instead of the hard thing?	O	O	O	O	O

27. Now think about BOYS.

		All of them	Most	Some	A few	None of them
a.	How many boys your age stand up for what they think is right?	O	O	O	O	O
b.	How many boys your age stop somebody from picking on younger kids?	O	O	O	O	O
c.	How many boys your age tell another kid when they think the other kid is wrong?	O	O	O	O	O
d.	How many boys your age demand to be treated fairly by grownups?	O	O	O	O	O
e.	How many boys your age demand to be treated fairly by other kids?	O	O	O	O	O
f.	How many boys your age don't do things because they might get hurt doing them?	O	O	O	O	O
g.	How many boys your age don't do things because they might be embarrassed?	O	O	O	O	O
h.	When boys try to do something and they fail, how many of them give up rather than trying it again another way?	O	O	O	O	O
i.	When boys have a choice, how many of them pick the easy thing to do instead of the hard thing?	O	O	O	O	O

28. There are a lot of different things you like to do in your free time; things like sports, hobbies, and playing with friends. Suppose a friend of yours, a girl, is very interested in fixing cars. After school she often helps a grown up friend work on an old car. Some days, though, she's not sure if she should do this because of what her friends say to her. What do you think?

		Very good idea	Good idea	Bad idea	Very bad idea
a.	Should she work on the cars even if her friends want her to do something else with them?	O	O	O	O
b.	Should she work on the cars even if her friends think that working on cars is boring?	O	O	O	O
c.	Should she work on the cars even if her friends think that working on cars is something only boys should do?	O	O	O	O
d.	Should she work on cars even if her parents think it is not good for girls to do this kind of thing?	O	O	O	O

29. Suppose a friend of yours, a boy, likes very much to take care of kids. After school, he often helps his older sister take care of her three-year-old child. Some days, though, he's not sure he should do this because of what his friends say to him. What do you think?

		Very good idea	Good idea	Bad idea	Very bad idea
a.	Should he take care of the child even if his friends want him to do something else with them?	O	O	O	O
b.	Should he take care of the child even if his friends think that it is boring?	O	O	O	O
c.	Should he take care of the child even if his friends think that it is something only girls do?	O	O	O	O
d.	Should he take care of the child even if his parents think that it is not something for a boy to do?	O	O	O	O

30. You're on the playground and a little kid in second grade is being picked on by some kids in your grade. A girl you know thinks it's very unfair and wants to make the big kids stop. Someone else thinks she ought to go get the teacher instead. The girl says no, she will do it herself. How good an idea is it for her to try by herself to get the big kids to stop?

31. You're on the playground and a little kid in second grade is being picked on by some kids in your grade. A boy you know thinks it's very unfair and wants to make the big kids stop. Someone else thinks he ought to get the teacher instead. The boy says no, he will do it himself. How good an idea is it for him to try by himself to get the big kids to stop?

32. Your school has a band. A girl you know plays the saxophone very well, but didn't get chosen to play because there were already enough saxophones in the band. She thinks this is unfair and thinks she should go to the teacher and prove that she's good enough to play. A friend says no, that she should just wait this year and try again next year. How good an idea is it for her to go see the teacher right now?

33. A boy you know plays the saxophone very well, but didn't get chosen to play because there were already enough saxophones in the band. He thinks this is unfair and thinks he should go to the teacher and prove that he's good enough to play. A friend says no, that he should just wait this year and try again next year. How good an idea is it for him to go see the teacher right now?

When you try something new you often "take a chance" that you might fail. Sometimes you take a chance you might get hurt, other times you take a chance you might be embarrassed in front of your friends. When you play a sport you've never played before you take a chance that you might not do it well and someone will make fun of you. Some chances are better to take than others.

34. Here are some things where BOYS might take a chance of failing. How do you feel about a boy taking these chances?

   a. raise his hand in class when he is not sure of the answer
   b. take apart a bike to fix it when he is not sure how to do it
   c. try to bake cookies using a recipe that is much harder than he has used before
   d. try a new sport when he is not sure he can do it well
   e. climb onto a high place where he's not sure he can get down

35. Now, how do you feel about GIRLS taking these chances?

   a. raise her hand in class when she is not sure of the answer
   b. take apart a bike to fix it when she is not sure how to do it
   c. try to bake cookies using a recipe that is much harder than she has used before
   d. try a new sport when she is not sure she can do it well
   e. climb onto a high place where she's not sure she can get down

END OF PART 4

PART 5
(APPROXIMATELY FIVE MINUTES)

TO THE TEACHER:

Ask these questions only in the January-February time period.

If your class did **not** watch FREESTYLE in school or at home during the last few months, skip to item 41.

36. Since October you have been watching a TV show called "Freestyle." The show has had stories about Denice, Marcus, Walter and other kids. The kids did many different kinds of things. They had part-time jobs, did projects for school and played in sports. Darken the oval which says how much you learned about each of these things from watching "Freestyle."

	I learned a lot	I learned a little	I didn't learn anything
a. what girls do for fun	○	○	○
b. what boys do for fun	○	○	○
c. how girls behave	○	○	○
d. how boys behave	○	○	○
e. the kinds of things girls are good at doing	○	○	○
f. the kinds of things boys are good at doing	○	○	○
g. what it is like to be a leader	○	○	○
h. what it is like to help other people	○	○	○
i. the kinds of jobs adult women have	○	○	○
j. the kinds of jobs adult men have	○	○	○
k. what it is like to work at grown up jobs	○	○	○
l. what husbands and wives do around the home to help the family	○	○	○
m. what boys and girls do around the home to help the family	○	○	○

37. Overall, how much have you liked watching the "Freestyle" television shows? I liked them:
    - ○ A lot
    - ○ Pretty much
    - ○ A little
    - ○ Not at all

TO THE TEACHER:

If your class did **not** watch "FREESTYLE" at school, skip to item 41.

38. Compared to other shows you watch on TV at home, how much fun was it to watch "Freestyle" was:
    - ○ A lot more fun
    - ○ A little more fun
    - ○ A little less fun
    - ○ A lot less fun

39. Compared to most other things you do in class at school, how much fun was it to watch the "Freestyle" television shows?
    - ○ A lot more fun
    - ○ A little more fun
    - ○ A little less fun
    - ○ A lot less fun

40. Compared to most other things you talk about in class, how interesting were the discussions you had about things in the "Freestyle" shows?
    - ○ A lot more interesting
    - ○ A little more interesting
    - ○ A little less interesting
    - ○ A lot less interesting

41. This is the end of the questionnaire. Thank you very much for helping us out. Your answers will help make better things for use in schools in the coming years.

Appendix J

RAW DATA ON PERSISTENCE

Table J.1
Mean Scores Across Time for 14 FREESTYLE Indexes,
Long Beach and Ann Arbor Experimentals

		Long Beach T1-T2 Sample		Ann Arbor T1-T2-T3 Sample		
		T1	T2	T1	T2	T3
1. Attitude toward girls in mechanics (ATGMECH)	Boys	2.38/.88	2.84/.82	2.64/.80	3.01/.73	2.90/.70
	Girls	2.73/.80	3.14/.70	2.94/.74	3.30/.61	3.31/.57
	Total	2.54/.86	2.98/.78	2.78/.78	3.14/.69	3.09/.68
2. Beliefs about girls and mechanics (BFGMECH)	Boys	2.07/.84	2.44/.80	2.03/.71	2.48/.71	2.30/.66
	Girls	2.43/.81	2.67/.73	2.53/.78	2.75/.69	2.61/.68
	Total	2.23/.84	2.55/.78	2.26/.78	2.60/.71	2.44/.68
3. Attitudes toward girls in athletics (ATGATH)	Boys	2.47/.97	2.93/.87	2.65/.91	3.09/.71	2.99/.67
	Girls	3.08/.80	3.47/.65	3.43/.59	3.61/.46	3.55/.48
	Total	2.75/.95	3.18/.82	3.01/.87	3.33/.66	3.24/.65
4. Belief about girls in athletics (BFGATH)	Boys	2.55/.95	2.84/.79	2.57/.79	3.05/.75	2.85/.67
	Girls	3.15/.80	3.31/.64	3.20/.71	3.35/.56	3.30/.60
	Total	2.83/.93	3.06/.76	2.86/.81	3.19/.68	3.06/.68
5. Attitudes toward boys in helping activities (ATBNRT)	Boys	3.03/.68	3.22/.62	3.26/.60	3.54/.42	3.29/.58
	Girls	2.95/.69	3.33/.63	3.25/.62	3.51/.55	3.43/.54
	Total	3.00/.69	3.27/.62	3.25/.61	3.52/.48	3.36/.56
6. Beliefs about boys in helping activities (BFBNRT1)	Boys	3.39/.84	3.31/.73	3.36/.72	3.37/.69	3.31/.63
	Girls	2.70/.70	3.06/.78	2.81/.77	3.29/.65	2.88/.60
	Total	3.07/.86	3.20/.76	3.10/.79	3.33/.67	3.11/.65
7. Attitudes toward girls as leaders (ATGLDR)	Boys	2.25/.72	2.58/.70	2.20/.69	2.68/.74	2.51/.62
	Girls	3.17/.55	3.33/.53	3.21/.54	3.41/.48	3.36/.47
	Total	2.67/.79	2.92/.73	2.67/.80	3.02/.73	2.90/.70
8. Beliefs about girls as leaders (BFGLD1@)	Boys	2.90/.85	3.05/.75	3.03/.84	3.32/.74	3.03/.85
	Girls	3.72/.67	3.57/.61	3.83/.59	3.80/.52	3.69/.53
	Total	3.27/.87	3.28/.74	3.40/.84	3.55/.69	3.33/.79
9. Attitudes toward boys as leaders (ATBLDR)	Boys	3.51/.46	3.42/.50	3.44/.43	3.42/.44	3.41/.43
	Girls	2.96/.67	3.20/.61	2.84/.80	3.26/.60	3.18/.60
	Total	3.27/.63	3.32/.56	3.16/.70	3.34/.52	3.30/.53

Note: Samples are comprised of respondents with complete data who were in classrooms where FREESTYLE was implemented at levels 5-6. Long Beach T1-T2 sample: Girls=435, Boys=513, Total=948. Ann Arbor T1-T2-T3 sample: Girls=126, Boys=150, Total=276.

Cell entries are the mean and standard deviation

Table J.1 (Cont.)
Mean Scores Across Time for 14 FREESTYLE Indexes,
Long Beach and Ann Arbor Experimentals

		Long Beach T1-T2 Sample		Ann Arbor T1-T2-T3 Sample		
		T1	T2	T1	T2	T3
10. Beliefs about boys as leaders (BFBLD1@)	Boys	3.78/.75	3.61/.74	3.71/.78	3.69/.74	3.61/.71
	Girls	3.05/.76	3.11/.72	3.14/.79	3.39/.72	3.12/.69
	Total	3.44/.84	3.38/.77	3.45/.83	3.55/.75	3.38/.74
11. Beliefs about the sex of those in female jobs (SXJBW)	Boys	3.81/.54	3.62/.54	3.75/.51	3.63/.57	3.64/.44
	Girls	3.81/.54	3.64/.44	3.81/.44	3.60/.38	3.62/.31
	Total	3.81/.52	3.63/.50	3.78/.48	3.62/.49	3.63/.39
12. Attitude toward more men in female jobs (ATMJB3)	Boys	2.46/.70	2.87/.66	2.76/.58	3.12/.64	2.94/.64
	Girls	2.77/.64	3.17/.56	2.80/.65	3.33/.64	3.12/.53
	Total	2.60/.69	3.01/.63	2.78/.61	3.21/.65	3.02/.60
13. Beliefs about the sex of those in Male jobs (SXJBM)	Boys	2.15/.40	2.30/.45	2.17/.38	2.34/.44	2.39/.37
	Girls	2.31/.34	2.46/.35	2.34/.36	2.46/.36	2.53/.35
	Total	2.22/.38	2.37/.41	2.24/.38	2.40/.41	2.46/.37
14. Attitude toward more women in male jobs (ATWJB)	Boys	2.40/.65	2.76/.66	2.53/.68	2.99/.62	2.82/.55
	Girls	2.87/.58	3.08/.50	3.10/.52	3.33/.55	3.22/.49
	Total	2.62/.66	2.91/.62	2.79/.68	3.15/.61	3.00/.56

BIBLIOGRAPHY

Andrews, F. M., Morgan, J. N., Sonquist, J. A., & Klem, L. Multiple Classification Analysis (Revised 1973). Ann Arbor: Institute for Social Research, The University of Michigan, 1967.

Clarke, P. & Kline, F. G. Media effects reconsidered: Some new strategies for communication research. Communication Research, 1974, 1, 224-240.

Cohen, J. Statistical Power Analysis and the Behavioral Sciences (Rev. Ed.). New York: Academic Press, 1977.

Cronbach, L. J. Coefficient alpha and the internal structure of tests. Psychometrika, 1951, 16, 297-334.

Cronbach, L. J. Research on Classrooms and Schools: Formulation of Questions, Design, and Analysis. Palo Alto, CA: Occasional Papers of the Stanford Evaluation Consortium, 1976.

Cronbach, L. J., Ambron, S. J., Dornbusch, S., Hess, R., Hornik, R., Phillips, D. C., Walker, D., & Weiner, S. S. Acts, Numbers, and Lamentations: Toward a Reform in Program Evaluation. (In press)

Ettema, J. S. Working Together: A Study of Cooperation Among Producers, Educators, and Researchers to Create Educational Television. Ann Arbor: Institute for Social Research, 1980.

Fishbein, M. and Ajzen, I. Belief, Attitude, Intention and Behavior: An Introduction to Theory and Research. Reading, Mass.: Addison-Wesley, 1975.

Gump, J. P., & Rivers, L. W. A consideration of race in efforts to end sex bias. In E. Diamond (Ed.) Issues of Sex Bias and Sex Fairness in Career Interest Measurement. Washington, D.C.: National Institute of Education, 1975.

Guttentag, M., & Bray, H. Undoing Sex Stereotypes. New York: McGraw Hill, 1976.

Horst, D. P., & Tallmadge, G. K. A Practical Guide to Measuring Project Impact on Student Achievement. Washington: U.S. Office of Education, 1976. (USGPO #017-080-01460-2)

Johnston, J., & Wise, R. Using evaluation results in planning: Alternative views of the decision-maker and the researcher. Paper presented at the

Annual Meeting of the American Educational Research Association, Toronto, 1978.

Kob, J. *Begleituntersuchung zur Ferneshserie Sesamstrasse*. Hamburg: Hans Bredow Institute, 1975.

McClure, R. D. and Patterson, T. E. Television news and political advertising: The impact of exposure on voter beliefs. *Communication Research*, 1974, 1, 3-31.

McGuire, W. J. Attitude change: The information processing. In C. G. McClintock (Ed.) *Experimental Social Psychology*. New York: H & H, Rinehart and Winston, 1972.

Morgan, J. N., & Duncan, G. *Five Thousand American Families -- Patterns of Economic Progress. Vol. IV: Analyses of the First Seven Years*. Ann Arbor: Institute for Social Research, 1976.

Nicewander, W. A., & Price, J. M. Dependent variable reliability and the power of significance tests. *Psychological Bulletin*, 1978, 85, 2, 405-409.

Nie, N.H., Hull, C. H., Jenkins, J. G., Steinbrenner, K., & Bent, D. *Statistical package for the social sciences* (2nd edition). New York: McGraw-Hill, 1975.

Nunnally, J. C. & Durham, R. L. Validity, reliability and special problems of measurement in evaluation research. In E. L. Struening and M. Guttentag (Eds.), *Handbook of Evaluation Research*, (Vol. 1). Beverly Hills: Sage, 1975.

Prediger, D. J., Roth, J. D., & Noeth, R. J. *A Nationwide Study of Student Career Development; A Summary of Results*. Iowa City: American College Testing Program, 1973.

Ray, M. L. Marketing communication and the hierarchy-of-effects. In P. Clarke (Ed.) *New Models for Mass Communication Research*. Beverly Hills: Sage Publications, 1973.

Rogers, E. M. & Shoemaker, .F. *Communication of Innovation: A Cross-Cultural Approach*. New York: Free Press, 1971.

Rothschild, M. L. & Ray, M. L. Involvement and political advertising effect. *Communication Research*, 1974, 1, 264-285.

Samejima, F. A use of the information function in tailored testing. *Applied Psychological Measurement*, 1977, 1, 233-247.

Tallmadge, G. K. *Joint Dissemination Review Panel, Ideabook*. Washington: National Institute of Education, 1977.

Tomlinson, T., & Ten Houten, D. System awareness, exploitive potential and ascribed status of elites. Paper presented at American Psychological Association Annual Meeting, Montreal, 1973.

Triandis, H. C. Attitude and Attitude Change. New York: John Wiley & Sons, 1971.

Wise, R., Charner, I., & Randour, M. L. A conceptual framework for career awareness in career decision making. The Counseling Psychologist, 1976, 6(3), 47-53.